TIMING IS EVERYTHING

The Politics and Processes of New Zealand
Defence Acquisition Decision Making

TIMING IS EVERYTHING

The Politics and Processes of New Zealand
Defence Acquisition Decision Making

PETER GREENER

E PRESS

Published by ANU E Press
The Australian National University
Canberra ACT 0200, Australia
Email: anuepress@anu.edu.au
This title is also available online at: http://epress.anu.edu.au/timing_citation.html

---

National Library of Australia
Cataloguing-in-Publication entry

Author:	Greener, Peter.
Title:	Timing is everything : the politics and processes of New Zealand defence acquisition decision making / Peter Greener.
ISBN:	9781921536649 (pbk.) 9781921536656 (pdf.)
Notes:	Includes index. Bibliography.
Subjects:	New Zealand. Ministry of Defence--Procurement. New Zealand. Defence Force--Procurement. Defense contracts--New Zealand. Military supplies. Government purchasing--New Zealand. New Zealand--Armed Forces--Procurement.
Dewey Number:	355.62120993

All rights reserved. No part of this publication may be reproduced, stored in a retrieval system or transmitted in any form or by any means, electronic, mechanical, photocopying or otherwise, without the prior permission of the publisher.

The *Canberra Papers on Strategy and Defence* series is a collection of publications arising principally from research undertaken at the SDSC. Canberra Papers have been peer reviewed since 2006. All Canberra Papers are available for sale: visit the SDSC website at <http://rspas.anu.edu.au/sdsc/canberra_papers.php> for abstracts and prices. Electronic copies (in pdf format) of most SDSC Working Papers published since 2002 may be downloaded for free from the SDSC website at <http://rspas.anu.edu.au/sdsc/working_papers.php>. The entire Working Papers series is also available on a 'print on demand' basis.

Strategic and Defence Studies Centre Publications Program Advisory Review Panel: Emeritus Professor Paul Dibb; Professor Desmond Ball; Professor David Horner; Professor Hugh White; Professor William Tow; Professor Anthony Milner; Professor Virginia Hooker; Dr Coral Bell; Dr Pauline Kerr

Strategic and Defence Studies Centre Publications Program Editorial Board: Professor Hugh White; Dr Brendan Taylor; Dr Christian Enemark; Miss Meredith Thatcher (series editor)

Cover design by ANU E Press

This edition © 2009 ANU E Press

Contents

Abstract	vii
About the Author	ix
Acknowledgements	xi
Acronyms and Abbreviations	xiii
List of Figures and Tables	xvii
Foreword by Gerald Hensley	xix
1. Introduction—The Policy Background and the Policy Framework	1
2. The ANZACS, Part 1—The Frigate that wasn't a Frigate	23
3. Oranges and Lemons—HMNZS *Charles Upham*	53
4. 'No, Minister….'—The ANZAC Frigates, Part II	77
5. 'The Deal of the Century'—The F-16s	89
6. 'I see no submarines'—Upgrading the *Orions*	109
7. Plotting and Sedition, or Necessary Acquisition? The LAV IIIs	127
8. Politics and Processes: Reflections on the Characteristics of the Decision-Making Process	151
Appendix 1: Sole, Prime and Shared Responsibilities	157
Appendix 2: ANZAC Ship Baseline Characteristics	159
Appendix 3: User Requirement	161
Appendix 4: Recommendations of the Final Report of the Air Combat Capability Study—October 1998	163
Bibliography	165
Index	185

Abstract

The spectre of block obsolescence of major weapons platforms loomed throughout the 1980s, facing successive governments with significant challenges as they worked to make sustainable decisions on replacement or upgraded equipment for the New Zealand Defence Force.

This book identifies the critical factors that shaped and influenced defence acquisition decision-making processes from the election of the Fourth Labour Government in 1984 and the subsequent ANZUS crisis, through to the 11 September 2001 terrorist attacks on the United States and the following 'war on terror'. It explores and analyses decision-making processes in relation to six acquisition decisions which have been made over a 20-year period. These are the decisions on the ANZAC frigates; the military sealift ship HMNZS *Charles Upham*; the second and third decisions on the ANZACs; the lease of the F-16 strike aircraft; the upgrading of the P-3C *Orion* maritime patrol aircraft; and the purchase of light armoured vehicles for the Army—the LAV IIIs.

Whilst many factors are brought to bear, this book outlines how it is that New Zealand's own view of the world, external relationships, politics and political influence, and the timing of decisions are amongst the most significant elements that impact on the decision-making process, whilst individual actors play a significant part in shaping the process. Although there has been a great deal of publicity in recent years about rivalry between the Services and the place of bureaucratic politics, this book argues that nonetheless officials continued to work with rigour over time to provide the best judgement and advice possible to Ministers. Three out of six of the case studies which have been analysed—the ANZAC frigates, the upgrade of the P-3 *Orions* and the LAV III—have been implemented or are in the process of successful implementation. In each case, officials worked to ensure that they provided the Government of the day with the most appropriate advice upon which to base decisions, although that advice has not always been popular. Each case study demonstrates key aspects of the decision-making process, providing specific insights into the way defence decisions are made.

About the Author

Peter Greener is Senior Fellow at the Command and Staff College, New Zealand Defence Force, Trentham, Wellington. Professionally qualified as a psychotherapist, he has a Master of Public Policy from Victoria University of Wellington, and a PhD in Politics from the University of Auckland. Dr Greener joined the New Zealand Defence Force in 2008, having previously been Head of School, School of Public Health & Psychosocial Studies at the Auckland University of Technology where he had been a senior staff member since 1997. Prior to joining AUT he had been Director of the Auckland Family Counselling and Psychotherapy Centre for some 12 years. Dr Greener has been a Visiting Fellow at the University of Bradford, and Fellow of the Asia Pacific College of Security Studies, Honolulu. From 1995–99 he was Chair of the Auckland Branch of the New Zealand Institute of International Affairs.

Dr Greener's research interests include the aetiology, management and resolution of conflict; post conflict development; and the politics of defence decision-making. He brings to these interests the perspective of his many years experience as a psychoanalytic psychotherapist. Dr Greener has edited and contributed to a number of books including *Turning the tide—A New Approach to Conflict Resolution* (2001); *Push for Peace* (2005); *Legacy of Armistice—why Afghanistan?* (2006); *The Balkan Question—is there an answer in sight?* (2007); and *"very, very, very good friends"? New Zealand United States Relationships* (2008). He was also a contributing author to *The No-Nonsense Guide to Conflict and Peace* (2005 and 2006).

Acknowledgements

My grateful thanks go to my PhD supervisor, Associate Professor Steve Hoadley, for his unwavering patience, unstinting support and insightful challenge over the time it took to complete the thesis on which this book is based.

During the course of my research I interviewed a large number of officials and Service personnel both active and retired, academics and non-governmental organisation representatives. Their reflections, recollections and considered comment have been of immense value, contributing significantly to my understanding of the politics and processes involved in defence decision making. I would like to thank particularly Gerald Hensley, former Secretary of Defence, who not only gave of his time and expertise in answering my questions, but also kindly agreed to write the Foreword to this publication; and Graham Fortune, Andrew Wierzbicki, Hamish Bunn and Esther Mendoza at the Ministry of Defence, who together ensured that I was furnished with all of the official information that I requested, and spent a considerable amount of time answering my queries. The staff of the Defence Library was also unfailingly helpful, as was Andrew South, librarian at AUT University's North Shore campus, who provided significant support and advice as I searched for research material.

I want to thank Captain Helen Marks of the Royal Australian Navy, who put me in touch with Admiral Michael Hudson and Rear Admiral David Campbell, each of whom had a great deal of involvement with the ANZAC frigate project. Kate Dewes at the Christchurch office of the Foundation for Peace Studies Aotearoa-New Zealand provided access to extensive archive material regarding the ANZAC frigate debate. I also want to thank the Gleisner family who always welcomed me and provided hospitality on my many trips to Wellington to undertake research.

Finally my love and thanks to my wife and family, whose tolerance and patience has known no bounds over the years.

Acronyms and Abbreviations

ABCA	America, Britain, Canada, Australia
ADF	Australian Defence Force
ANZAM	Anglo-New Zealand-Australia-Malaya
ANZUK	Australia, New Zealand and the United Kingdom
ANZUS	Australia, New Zealand and United States Treaty
APC	Armoured Personnel Carrier
APEC	Asia-Pacific Economic Cooperation
ASLAV	Australian Light Armoured Vehicle
ASW	Anti-Submarine Warfare
CA	Chief of Army
CAB	Cabinet
CAF	Chief of Air Force
CDF	Chief of Defence Force
CDR	Closer Defence Relations
CGS	Chief of General Staff
CNS	Chief of Naval Staff
CVR (T)	Combat Vehicle Reconnaissance (Tracked)
DCARR	*Defence Capability and Resourcing Review*
DCNS	Deputy Chief of Naval Staff
DCRP	Defence Consolidated Resource Plan
DLOC	Directed Level of Capability
DMF	Data Management Function
DPMC	Department of the Prime Minister and Cabinet
DPS	Defence Planning System
EEZ	Exclusive Economic Zone
ESMZ	Electronic Surveillance Measures
FAC	Forward Air Control
FPDA	Five Power Defence Arrangements
FSV	Fire Support Vehicle
GDP	Gross Domestic Product
GST	Goods and Services Tax
HVR	HVR Consulting Services

IED	Improvised Explosive Device
IFVL	Infantry Fighting Vehicle Light
IMV	Infantry Mobility Vehicle
LAV	Light Armoured Vehicle
LAV III	Light Armoured Vehicle (Third Generation)
LSS	Logistic Support Ship
LTDP	*Long-Term Development Plan*
L-3	L-3 IS Communications Integrated Systems
MAD	Magnetic Anomaly Detector
MLU	Mid-Life Upgrade
MMP	Mixed Member Proportional
MoD	Ministry of Defence
MSS	Military Sealift Ship
MTVL	Mobile Tactical Vehicle Light
NATO	North Atlantic Treaty Organization
NZDF	New Zealand Defence Force
NZLAV	New Zealand Light Armoured Vehicle
OPV	Offshore Patrol Vessel
QAMR	Queen Alexandra's Mounted Rifles
RAAF	Royal Australian Air Force
RAF	Royal Air Force
RAN	Royal Australian Navy
RCAF	Royal Canadian Air Force
RFA	Royal Fleet Auxiliary
RFT	Request for Tender
RN	Royal Navy
RNZAF	Royal New Zealand Air Force
RNZIR	Royal New Zealand Infantry Regiment
RNZN	Royal New Zealand Navy
RPG	Rocket Propelled Grenade
RSA	Royal New Zealand Returned and Services' Association
SAR	Search and Rescue
SAS	Special Air Service
SEATO	South East Asia Treaty Organisation

SONZD 1997   *The Shape of New Zealand's Defence: A White Paper*, 1997
STR   Cabinet Strategy Committee

UNSC   United Nations Security Council

List of Figures and Tables

Figure 1.1: Organisational Structure of the Ministry of Defence 17
Table 4.1: Comparison of Annual Costs for Mixed and ANZAC Fleets 80
Table 4.2: Force Structure Options 81

Foreword

In February 1942, facing a Japanese invasion, the New Zealand Prime Minister pleaded with Washington for arms. New Zealand, he pointed out, was virtually unarmed: "This, we feel, is not our fault." It is hard to see who else's it was; it is a mark of independent countries to take care of their own security.

The risk of invasion has since become very remote, but for almost two decades the effectiveness of the country's Defence Force has been plagued by obsolescent equipment and seemingly interminable arguments over its replacement. Some of this is endemic in democracies unthreatened and at peace. In New Zealand's case the problem was exacerbated by 'block obsolescence'—the remarkably successful burst of procurement in the late 1960s meant that ships, aircraft and army transport all came up for replacement in the 1990s.

Overcoming this was not helped by a defence budget which fell steadily after 1989. From a post-war average of 1.8 per cent of GDP, spending on defence fell by almost half—to under 1 per cent of GDP. This sharpened the need to make choices, and it also sharpened the inter-Service and political lobbying for what was left.

This is the background against which the author analyses six acquisition decisions made since 1984. Importantly he studies the *politics* as well as the *processes* involved in the selection of these major acquisitions. On the whole the processes have worked well, with no evidence of corruption (always a risk given the huge sums at stake). Cost overruns, that other universal curse of defence procurement, have also been limited by the philosophy of wherever possible buying only established technology. Where this had to be stretched, as in integrating the separate systems in the Anzac frigate build, I can confess that at least one Secretary of Defence was gripped by some anxious moments.

New Zealand's main difficulties, Dr Greener demonstrates, came in the politics of procurement. Buying ships, aircraft or armoured personnel carriers brings out in every democracy the armchair strategists and lobbyists for particular equipment and even brands. In this country the size of the sums involved brought political divisions. It was not that large items like frigates or combat aircraft cost more for New Zealand than for other countries—in many cases they cost less—but that in the recent international climate many New Zealanders could not see the *need* to buy them at all.

In this climate a broad bipartisanship in Parliament over defence policy broke down. In the course of the past three decades defence and its equipment became intensely politicised, reflecting the deeper divisions over New Zealand's foreign policy and position in the world. Our inability as a nation to make up our minds on what we want the Defence Force to do has, as this analysis gently points out, in some cases been costly, in some cases damaging to effectiveness, and in most confusing to those serving in the forces.

Deployments of aircraft and ships to the Middle East (and the equipment needed to support them) have been decried, withdrawn and reinstated. Lessons about the value of interoperable maritime patrol aircraft and the need for military sealift have been forgotten and expensively relearned. Political fashions come and go, but they are not the most desirable way of choosing major equipment which will be used by the Defence Force for thirty or more years.

An unsettled defence strategy has also intensified inter-Service rivalry. A healthy rivalry is a fact of life among the three Services, and the occasional effort, such as Canada's, to merge them into one organisation and uniform has only made matters worse. The competition for access to a falling budget, though, tempted some to go beyond the acceptable limits. It led to the rise of factions within the army with, as Dr Greener makes clear, some constitutionally improper behaviour—leaks and private briefings by some which an official enquiry identified as 'designed to advance the interests of the Army'.

This study is not a jeremiad. It accepts the thought and honest effort which went into time-consuming argument and sometimes compromised outcomes. Given the difficulties it may seem surprising that the Defence Force managed the important re-equipment that it did. Over the period a blue-water navy was maintained and repeatedly deployed in distant waters; the *Orion* were re-winged to give them a further twenty years of life; naval helicopters were bought; and much better armoured personnel carriers acquired for the two regular battalions.

Nonetheless, the analysis makes it clear that we could do better. Political fashions can be deterred or at least weakened by a better understanding of the long-term needs of defence; inter-Service rivalries can be contained by a more durable defence planning system. This well-researched and accurate look at the lessons of the past two decades does not suggest the answers—there are no easy ones—but it shines a clear light on the difficulties of defence procurement, a hitherto rather shadowy subject which is of major importance to both the finances and the standing of our country.

Gerald Hensley
January 2009

Chapter 1

Introduction — The Policy Background and the Policy Framework

Defence decision-making, whilst from time to time making newspaper headlines, is rarely the subject of prolonged debate in New Zealand. Notable exceptions to this would be the controversy over access for nuclear-capable US warships, or the purchase of ANZAC frigates, during the 1980s. It was clear from this time that much of the equipment of New Zealand's defence forces was going to require replacement or significant upgrading. How decisions on defence acquisitions have been made since that time constitutes the research topic under investigation in this volume.

The Historical Background

Before moving on to investigate recent acquisition case studies, it is important to set the historical background against which more recent policy decisions have been made, and describe the foreign and defence policy framework within which decisions for defence acquisitions are developed and implemented.

Prior to the Second World War, New Zealand defence planning revolved essentially around the expectation that the Royal Navy (RN) and the British fleet would ensure New Zealand's protection. At the Imperial Conference of 1937 New Zealand Prime Minister Michael Savage was firm in his desire to have Britain promise to send a fleet to the Far East. He received a qualified promise from Sir Samuel Hoare, First Lord of the Admiralty, who indicated that it would be possible in the current circumstances to send the fleet, while still retaining sufficient ships to fulfil European requirements. New Zealand defence planning continued on this understanding.

On 1 September 1939 Germany entered Poland, and two days later Britain declared war, followed almost immediately by New Zealand. On 5 September 1939 Savage broadcast from his sick-bed what was to become an immortal speech:

> Both with gratitude for the past and with confidence in the future we range ourselves without fear beside Britain. Where she goes we go. Where she stands we stand.[1]

These sentiments were given substance only a week later, when the New Zealand Government offered an army division for service in Europe, and put over 500 personnel at the disposal of the Royal Air Force (RAF). The Naval Division had already come under RN command. By June 1940 the second echelon of the New Zealand Expeditionary Force was in the south of England, training to repel the expected German invasion. That same month Britain told New Zealand that she might not after all be able to send the fleet to Singapore if Japan entered the war.

This was devastating news for New Zealand, and it became clear that the only nation who could assist in the region was the United States. Peter Fraser, by now Prime Minister, told the British that he wished to establish diplomatic relations with Washington, and in January 1942 Walter Nash arrived there as New Zealand Minister. US support for New Zealand was quick to follow, with two divisions landing in New Zealand in June 1942.[2]

The US presence in New Zealand, coupled with public sentiment and pressure from Britain resulted in the decision to keep the 2nd Division in the Middle East, where it had been in action since the previous November.[3] This decision received a less than favourable response from the Australians, who had already moved two of their divisions from the Middle East. Relationships with Australia became even cooler the following year when, in May 1943, New Zealand once more decided to leave the 2nd Division in the Middle East.[4] The development of the 3rd Division in the Pacific, with postings first to Fiji, then New Caledonia and the Solomon Islands, did not seem to ameliorate the concern.[5]

Despite the forging of the ANZAC spirit in the First World War, the Second World War saw each country, for the most part, operating in separate theatres. However, as is so often the case between rivalrous cousins, both countries saw advantages in banding together to ensure that a post-war world would take account of them. Each country particularly had concerns about US intentions in the Pacific following the end of the war.

In order to explore closer trans-Tasman relations, in January 1944 Peter Fraser met with the Australian Prime Minister John Curtin, and his Minister for External Affairs, Dr Herbert Vere Evatt. The outcome of a series of meetings that took place during the Canberra conference was the Australia–New Zealand Agreement, which established both a formal treaty between the two countries, and the continuous Australia–New Zealand Secretariat. The document declared: 'It would be proper for Australia and New Zealand to assume full responsibility for policing or sharing in policing such areas in the Southwest and South Pacific as may from time to time be agreed upon.'[6]

The Agreement also stressed that the construction of wartime bases gave no basis for territorial claims, and insisted that no change in the sovereignty of any Pacific island territory occur without their agreement. Both the Americans and the British were concerned about the tenor of the Canberra Pact, and Sir Alister McIntosh noted: 'Care was taken henceforth to exclude New Zealand forces from any very effective role in the fighting against Japan.' Whilst McIntosh went on to comment that, 'so far as New Zealand was concerned, it was a diversion',[7] John C. Beaglehole thought that in the Canberra Pact New Zealand:

> most clearly announced its independence of mind, its intention of pursuing a policy in the Pacific, intelligible in terms not of subordination to British hesitations and abstraction, but of the strategic needs, enlightened self-interest and duty to Polynesian peoples of a quite independent power.[8]

That independent stance was to be to the fore once more during the development phase of the United Nations.

Developing Nationhood: The inception of the United Nations, and the adoption of the Statute of Westminster

New Zealand had not originally been a strong supporter of the League of Nations, but this situation had changed by the mid-1930s. Bill Jordan, Labour's High Commissioner in London, spoke passionately to the League Council in September 1937:

> My nation is a small one; you may say, if you please, that it is insignificant in size and perhaps in strength; but it will stand by the Covenant and the policy of collective security in order to maintain peace, or to restore it when it is broken, and to give safety to the people of our generation.[9]

By 1938 however it was becoming clear that the League did not have the authority to intervene meaningfully in the deteriorating international situation, and that its mandate could not be fulfilled. Whilst the League, springing out from the aftermath of the First World War, had failed, New Zealand was determined to help ensure that its successor, the United Nations, developed in the closing stages of the Second World War, would not.

In February 1943, UK Prime Minister Winston Churchill sent his thoughts on post-war security to US President Franklin Delano Roosevelt, proposing the creation of a world organisation for the preservation of peace. The following month in a broadcast Churchill declared that he favoured the establishment after the war of a world institution representing the United Nations (the wartime coalition), and eventually to include all nations of the world.[10]

By August of that year the Americans had developed a set of proposals that they wished to discuss amongst the Big Four—the United States, the Soviet Union, Great Britain and China. On 21 August 1943 a conference was held at Dumbarton Oaks outside Washington, DC, and the form of a United Nations Organisation was established.[11] It was over a year later when the draft proposal was made more widely available, and it was considered by the Australia–New Zealand meeting in November 1944. A number of resolutions were drawn up, which were approved by both Cabinets. New Zealand's Prime Minister Peter Fraser was concerned to ensure that small states could play an effective part in the new organisation. At the San Francisco conference held in April 1945, at which the final version of the United Nations Charter was drawn up, 'the New Zealand Delegation played a useful role quite disproportionate to the country's size'.[12] This was to become the hallmark of New Zealand in the international arena in subsequent years. As Sir Alister McIntosh observed:

> New Zealand had become an active member of the middle and smaller powers arraigned against the great, while staunchly advocating the United Nations as the best means of securing universal peace and justice and placing the fullest insistence on its organs for the solutions of international problems. New Zealand's chief concern, always, was the peace-keeping role of the United Nations; hence its stubborn adherence to the concept of collective security.[13]

Whilst New Zealand was a charter member of the United Nations, paradoxically it was not yet a sovereign nation. Whilst Britain had enacted the Statute of Westminster in 1931 in order to give complete independence to the dominions of the British Empire, it was not to apply to the Dominions of Australia, New Zealand or Newfoundland until adopted by their respective parliaments. New Zealand had considered adopting the Statute during the Second World War, as the Australians had done, but were concerned that it might send the wrong message to the Germans. The Statute was finally adopted in 1947. Even then, Frederick Widdowson Doidge of the National Party spoke out against adoption, '"on grounds of sentiment"', noting that "loyalty to the Motherland is an instinct as deep as religion"'.[14]

Developing Alliances: The ANZUS Pact, ANZAM and the South East Asia Treaty Organisation

In 1949 the National Party was returned to power in New Zealand, and loyalty to Britain and the Commonwealth remained paramount. It was with Britain and Australia that defence planning was developed. New Zealand's defence forces held traditions that were inherently British, and new equipment for the armed forces continued to be procured from Britain until the mid-1960s. The Royal New Zealand Navy (RNZN) had only been formed in 1941[15] and a British admiral remained in charge of the fleet in the 1950s. Up until 1960, at least one of the three Chiefs of Staff was a British officer on secondment.[16]

ANZUS

However, the outbreak of war on the Korean peninsula on 25 June 1950 was to see a rapid development in New Zealand/US relations. New Zealand's response to a call from the United Nations for assistance in the conflict was to commit two frigates.[17] As the situation continued to deteriorate, New Zealand decided to commit ground troops despite there being apparent reluctance on the part of Australia and Britain to do so. Nevertheless, Britain did announce on 25 July 1950 that it would send ground forces, and New Zealand made its offer that same day.[18] New Zealand forces were to remain in Korea well beyond the armistice of July 1954, with a final withdrawal of troops in 1957.

At the time of outbreak of hostilities, there was still no official peace treaty with Japan. The United States now saw this as an urgent issue to be resolved, as it moved to halt the spread of communism in Asia.[19] This wish provided Australia and New Zealand with some negotiating power in their desire for a formal defence alliance with the United States, and the Pacific Security (ANZUS) Treaty was formally signed on 1 September 1951.[20] A month before the war in Korea began, Frederick Doidge, who was by now Minister of External Affairs, opined, 'I regard an American guarantee of our security as the richest prize of New Zealand diplomacy', though he added cautiously that, 'in embarking on any formal step in this direction we must be certain that we are not appearing to be turning away from Britain'.[21] This dual relationship with Britain and the United States, tempered by New Zealand's commitment to the United Nations, continued to be central to New Zealand's foreign and defence policy for the following 33 years.

ANZAM

Notwithstanding fighting alongside the United States in Korea, the New Zealand forces along with their Australian counterparts were part of a British Commonwealth division. Traditional ties with Britain would continue throughout the 1950s.

After the Second World War, the Australians had developed a Commonwealth defence contingency plan known as ANZAM—The Anglo-New Zealand-Australia-Malaya area. In 1955 New Zealand was to respond to its responsibilities under ANZAM, when the British asked for support during the Malayan Emergency. New Zealand promised to commit two frigates, a fighter bomber squadron, half a transport squadron and a Special Air Service (SAS) squadron. In announcing New Zealand's support, Prime Minister Sidney Holland commented that New Zealand needed to pull its weight 'in the British boat ... That, is a British thing to do.'[22] No. 14 Squadron RNZAF was withdrawn from Cyprus in April 1955 to be based in Singapore, and they were re-equipped with de Havilland *Venoms* leased from the British. The Squadron's first offensive action took place on 1 May when five of the Squadron's original *Vampires* attacked terrorist positions.[23] The Squadron continued to fly until 1958, when it was replaced by 75 Squadron which was equipped with English Electric

Canberra bombers. These aircraft flew alongside no. 45 Squadron RAF until the Emergency in Malaya ended in July 1960.[24]

The SAS squadron of 133 personnel was attached to the British 22nd SAS Regiment early in 1956, and was replaced by the 1st Battalion, the New Zealand Regiment consisting of 740 personnel. This in turn was replaced by the 2nd Battalion in 1959.[25]

South East Asia Treaty Organisation

Whilst communist forces were becoming an increasing problem for the British in Malaya, the United States in 1954 was concerned, especially after the events of the Korean War, about the possibility of French defeat in Indochina, and a communist regime being established. Emergency meetings of ANZUS were called and the United States called for united action to support the French. Fortunately a settlement was reached before the Americans could bring more pressure to bear, but it highlighted the importance of collective defence for the region.[26] New Zealand remained concerned that any collective treaty should include Britain, and in the event it did. New Zealand became a signatory to the Manila Treaty (the South East Asia Collective Defence Treaty) along with Britain, the United States, Australia, France, the Philippines, Pakistan and Thailand, on 8 September 1954. New Zealand was pleased that the South East Asia Treaty Organisation (SEATO) would reinforce New Zealand's connections with Britain and the United States, along with the United Nations. Clifton Webb, the Minister of External Affairs, commented: 'The Treaty gives great emphasis to the prime import of the United Nations as the principal body charged with maintaining peace and security.'[27] The connections with Britain and the United States, which had taken New Zealand into action in Korea and Malaya in the 1950s, would lead New Zealand into action again during the 1960s. Involvement on active duty first came in 1962, when Bristol Freighters of no. 41 Squadron supported SEATO's response to communist insurgence on Thailand's border. Engagement with the region was about to expand considerably.

Collective Security in Action: Confrontation, and the Vietnam War

The 1961 *Review of Defence Policy* spelt out clearly the importance of collective security to New Zealand:

> If our policy is one of collective security we must retain the confidence and support of the countries on whose assistance we rely: these are principally the United Kingdom, the United States, and Australia. To do this we must join them in defending what they regard as *their* [sic] vital interests as well as our own, and make the best contribution we can. … New Zealand's 'area of primary strategic interest' thus includes, as well

as our more immediate neighbourhood the South Pacific Region, the SEATO treaty area in South-East Asia.[28]

It was to be no time at all before that commitment was to be called upon. Southeast Asia continued to be the focus of Government concern, and in the White Paper the Government confirmed its plans for a greatly enhanced Army. Presaging the *Defence Policy Framework* of June 2000, it said:

> The Government has continued to place emphasis on 'forces in being,' but has decided to place greater emphasis on ground forces with adequate provision for reinforcement, believing that this is the most appropriate and useful contribution it can make in South-East Asia. *It has therefore given priority to the maintenance of fully trained regular ground forces and the means of transporting them to possible theatres of operations.* [29]

When the period of 'Confrontation' between the newly formed State of Malaysia and Indonesia reached crisis point in 1964, the New Zealand Army was early on the scene. The 1st Battalion, Royal New Zealand Infantry Regiment became part of the 28th Commonwealth Infantry Brigade Group from August 1964 until August 1966. In 1965 and 1966 New Zealand SAS detachments served once more with the British 22nd SAS Regiment. The Royal New Zealand Air Force (RNZAF) deployed six *Canberra* bombers in September 1964, and the RNZN crewed two British mine sweepers, which were commissioned into the RNZN for 16 months from April 1965.[30]

Whilst New Zealand had readily committed forces in Malaysia, a request from the United States to send forces to the growing conflict in Vietnam was met less enthusiastically. As early as 1961 the observation had been made in Wellington that 'the vital issue for Australia and New Zealand was not to restore stability in South Vietnam, but to preserve our position with the United States as our major ally'.[31]

Cabinet eventually agreed in May 1963 to send a non-combatant field engineer team, although it was a year later before they went. US President Lyndon Johnson again asked New Zealand to commit further troops in December 1964, arguing that he could not ask the American people to make sacrifices if its closest allies in the area would not support them. Cabinet once more decided that it would not contribute combat troops, and that its first priority was Malaysia.[32] However, by May 1965 Cabinet had approved the commitment of 161 Battery, Royal New Zealand Artillery. Initially under American command, the Battery joined the 1st Australian Task Force in June 1966. In May 1967 a small rifle company from the 1st Battalion was added, complemented by a second in December 1967, both companies forming part of an ANZAC battalion.[33]

The commitment of the New Zealand Army to Vietnam was New Zealand's first expedition without British involvement, and spoke to the importance of the ANZUS alliance at the time. New Zealand troops remained involved in a combat role until December 1971, and the first and second Army Training Teams were withdrawn after the election of the Labour Government, in December 1972.

The New Zealand Army was supported throughout its time in Vietnam by the RNZAF, with no. 40 Squadron deploying the first troops in July 1965. From 1968 until 1971 no. 40 Squadron ran weekly flights into South Vietnam, eventually evacuating New Zealand Embassy staff during the fall of Saigon in April 1975.[34]

Growing Independence: 1971–84

During the 1970s New Zealand's international relationships underwent significant change. Britain had already indicated that it would be withdrawing forces from east of Suez, although the new conservative government of 1970 indicated that Britain would retain a small presence. In anticipation of the British withdrawal, the five nations involved in the AMDA (the Anglo-Malaysian Defence Agreement)—Australia, New Zealand, Britain, Malaysia and Singapore—entered into the Five Power Defence Arrangements (FPDA) on 1 November 1971.[35] At the same time Britain was in the final stages of negotiation for entry into the European Economic Community (EEC).

The following year a new White Paper was released which spoke of the need to take account of 'the changes apparent in the last few years in the policies and attitudes of New Zealand's major allies, the United States, Britain, and Australia'.[36] It went on to add:

> The keystone of New Zealand's security since 1952 has been ANZUS ... the ANZUS Treaty is basic to New Zealand's defence policy. In the changing international situation, it is more than ever desirable that the signatory states work, individually and collectively to enhance the reciprocal benefits deriving from the treaty.[37]

Within weeks, the Third Labour Government came to power, intent on establishing a new sense of New Zealand independence. It did not initiate a new defence review, but acting on its election manifesto withdrew the final troops from Vietnam, and ended National Service.[38] In proclaiming the Government's new position, Prime Minister Norman Kirk said:

> New Zealand for its part intends to follow a more independent foreign policy. It has emerged from the phase in its national development where it allowed its policies to be determined by the views and interests of its most influential ally: at one time Britain, more recently the United States. From now on when we have to deal with a new situation, we shall not say, what do the British think about it, what would the Americans want us to do? Our starting point will be, what do we think about it?[39]

As if to emphasise this renewed independent spirit, the Labour Government established diplomatic relations with the People's Republic of China and the Democratic Republic of Vietnam.[40]

At the same time there was determined opposition to French nuclear testing in the Pacific. The French had begun atmospheric tests in French Polynesia in 1966, and the Labour Party indicated that it would 'run up the New Zealand flag' on a frigate and take it to Mururoa Atoll to protest.[41] In 1973 Prime Minister Norman Kirk said: 'What we want to do is publicise what is happening in this remote part of the world so as to stimulate world opinion still further and attract wider support for the rights of small nations.'[42]

New Zealand and Australia had both protested to the International Court of Justice, and they joined together to protest in the Pacific, with HMNZS *Otago* and the Australian tanker *Supply* sailing together to Mururoa. HMNZS *Otago* stayed on station for three weeks, relieved by HMNZS *Canterbury* which stayed for another two.

To reinforce its opposition to nuclear weapons, the Government in 1975 promoted a resolution at the United Nations which called for the development of a nuclear-free zone in the South Pacific.[43] This was to be achieved a decade later when eight South Pacific countries signed the South Pacific Nuclear-Free Zone Treaty on 6 August 1985.[44]

However, by this time explosions of a different kind had occurred, as changes in New Zealand's foreign and defence policy changed significantly the nature of longstanding relationships with its major ally the United States. Whilst the South Pacific Nuclear-Free Zone Treaty allowed for the transit of nuclear weapons and port visits in the area, the policy of the Labour Government, elected in 1984, did not.

1984: ANZUS and Beyond

Walter Nash had spelt out a vision in 1958, during the term of the Second Labour Government, which was to be pursued a quarter of a century later, by the Fourth Labour Government: 'We stand for the suspension of nuclear tests, a complete ban on further production of nuclear weapons and the destruction of existing stocks with facilities for inspection in all fields by agreement by the powers concerned.'[45]

Bill Rowling speaking at the Labour Party annual conference in May 1982 said that 'nuclear weapons will not be allowed into New Zealand ports under a Labour Government, and that's the message'.[46] In June 1984 Labour MP Richard Prebble introduced a private member's bill into Parliament calling for the prohibition of nuclear weapons. On 13 June 1984 Marilyn Waring, a National MP, crossed the floor to support the bill. Although the bill was defeated, Prime

Minister Robert Muldoon claimed he could no longer command a majority and called a snap election.[47]

At the time of the election, 58 per cent of the population opposed visits by nuclear-powered ships and Labour had promised to ban both nuclear-propelled and nuclear-armed vessels.[48] David Lange had argued for a review of the Party's wish to ban nuclear-powered vessels, fearful of the impact on the relationship with the United States if both nuclear-powered and nuclear-armed vessels were banned. He commented:

> Shutting out their nuclear-powered ships for the same reasons we shut out their nuclear weapons seemed to be offering an unnecessary affront to the Americans. If we continued to lock propulsion and weapons together and did not distinguish them, I was not sure how I could persuade the United States of the essential rationality of our policy.[49]

The argument, however, was not to be won. Nonetheless, David Lange was keen to ensure that the essence of the ANZUS Treaty should remain, convinced that Labour could not fight the election successfully if the future of ANZUS was to be called into question. Bill Rowling, now foreign affairs spokesman, offered a solution to the controversy surrounding ANZUS: 'The Labour Party should fight the election on an undertaking to seek a review of the ANZUS alliance. ... [seeking] to broaden the scope of the ANZUS Treaty.'[50] This was seen as an option that would be easily accepted by those within the party who saw the importance of ANZUS to the electorate. Labour fought the election with a promise to ensure a nuclear-free New Zealand and to renegotiate the terms of association with Australia and the United States. Labour won, though the new Prime Minister, David Lange, acknowledged that the nuclear-free policy was not decisive.

In January 1985 the United States requested that the USS *Buchanan* be allowed to visit New Zealand. As the vessel was capable of carrying nuclear weapons the request was declined, and New Zealand asked that the United States substitute a *Perry*-class frigate. Lange was later to comment: 'It was our policy to make the attempt to reconcile what proved to be irreconcilable, but when a choice had to be made between ANZUS and the nuclear-free policy I advised my cabinet colleagues to give the nuclear-free policy precedence.'[51] The United States would not agree to the substitution and the visit did not proceed. Whilst Lange was to say in the same month as the USS *Buchanan* crisis that 'our commitment to ANZUS and the broader Western community remains firm',[52] the United States was to subsequently withdraw from most of its military and intelligence cooperation with New Zealand.

Although the Australian response was initially cool, the Australian Government indicated that it did not wish to see the trans-Tasman relationship affected by the dispute. The 1987 *Defence Review* highlighted very clearly the continued and growing importance of the trans-Tasman relationship.[53] It is against this background of strained and changing relationships that the first case study, the ANZAC ship project, is set.

The Fourth Labour Government was to lose the 1990 election, but by this time, although the electorate had firmly turned against Labour, it had nonetheless embraced New Zealand's nuclear-free policy: 'In 1989, when it was getting hard to find anyone who'd admit to being a Labour voter, over eighty percent of the population declared themselves to be in favour of the nuclear-free policy. ... There wasn't any going backwards.'[54]

Through the 1990s and into the Twenty-First Century

In the 1991 Defence White Paper, *The Defence of New Zealand*, the new National Government sought to move New Zealand towards a defence strategy of 'Self-Reliance in Partnership':

> Before the election we signalled that New Zealand's defence policies were too isolationist in their thrust and that we would bring New Zealand back to its correct place in the international community. This statement of defence policy sets out my Government's commitment to an internationalist approach to New Zealand's foreign and defence policies rather than a purely regional outlook.[55]

Jim Bolger, now Prime Minister, was determined to see New Zealand's relationship with the United States improve, and took that sentiment with him when he went to New York in September 1991 to address the United Nations General Assembly. Afterwards he was to have a private meeting with US President George H.W. Bush, at which the issue of New Zealand's anti-nuclear stance was discussed. At the meeting Bush said that he would 'soon be making an announcement that would help the New Zealand problem'.[56] Four days later the United States announced that it intended to remove all nuclear weapons from surface naval vessels. The next day, the British followed suit, and British naval vessels would once again visit New Zealand waters. This was not, though, to become the case with the United States.

Two years later Bolger was to speak with US President Bill Clinton, this time at the 1993 Asia-Pacific Economic Cooperation (APEC) meeting, held in November in Seattle, Washington. Notwithstanding Bolger's own observation to Clinton that the Somer's Committee on Nuclear Propulsion had concluded that essentially nuclear-powered vessels were safe, he noted that there had been no change in the public's attitude towards nuclear-propelled ships. Public opinion was to ensure that New Zealand's anti-nuclear legislation remained intact. Although Clinton undertook to have officials review the presidential directive on nuclear ships, US policy also remained unchanged.

In 1993 New Zealand was to take its place on the world stage, having been elected to the United Nations Security Council (UNSC) in October 1992. Amongst the reasons cited for New Zealand's success in the election were the nation's consistent support for collective security; its significant contribution to peacekeeping operations; and its independent voice—characteristics which had been developed over more than half a century.[57] The significant contribution to peacekeeping was about to grow during New Zealand's term on the UNSC.

Following the end of the Cold War, there was optimism for a time that the world was entering a new era of peace. That optimism was ill-founded as ethnic conflicts erupted around the globe. Europe saw the greatest conflict since the end of the Second World War, as the former Yugoslavia disintegrated. In March 1994 the United Nations approached New Zealand informally to request that combat troops be sent to Bosnia. There was significant public debate on the issue, and senior defence officials and foreign policy advisors disagreed publicly about whether troops should be sent.[58] However, wishing New Zealand to be seen as a good international citizen re-engaging with the international community, the National Government committed New Zealand peacekeepers to the conflict area. When 250 New Zealand troops arrived in the former Yugoslavia in September 1994, their Commanding Officer, Lieutenant Colonel Graeme Williams described the deployment of Kiwi Company as 'the largest number of troops in one deployment that the Government has committed to active service since the Korean War of the 1950s'.[59]

By May 1995 public support for New Zealand troops to be involved in United Nations peacekeeping operations had increased, with 78 per cent of those polled indicating support.[60] It was also apparent, however that peacekeeping was an increasingly dangerous activity. The 1997 White Paper noted the changing nature of peace support operations. The history of peacekeeping for over 40 years had been one requiring lightly-armed forces, usually deployed at the agreement of both parties to a conflict. During the 1990s this situation changed, and the White Paper acknowledged this:

> Since the end of the Cold War, however, peace missions have increasingly been launched during hostilities. The consent of the warring parties has been neither complete nor continuous. These peace enforcement missions are a higher-order task than peacekeeping as they involve conventional high-intensity operations.[61]

Recognising the dangers involved, the Government committed to equipping the defence forces for their task:

> The Government's first priority will be to rectify the most critical deficiencies in those capabilities where there is more likely to be a need

in the short term, that is re-equipping the Army so that it can undertake the more demanding peace support operations.[62]

The New Zealand Army was to be committed to a significantly demanding peace support operation sooner than might have been anticipated at this time. In September 1999, New Zealand hosted the APEC summit. Events close to home, in East Timor, were to dominate the agenda. Initially it had been thought that East Timor would be a side issue at the meeting, but by the time Clinton arrived the stakes had increased. Clinton had warned that if the violence in East Timor did not end, Indonesia 'must invite—it must invite—the international community to assist in restoring security'.[63] At first New Zealand had considered sending a company of about 120 troops, as part of an international force, but ultimately a battalion group was committed, working alongside the Australians in a highly demanding environment. This was to be a much larger commitment than that made in Bosnia and, with six rotations of a battalion group, almost 3500 Service personnel were committed to the East Timor operation from 1999–2001.[64] Resources and manpower were stretched to the limit, and shortcomings in equipment—the lack of a logistic support ship and poor reliability of the Armoured Personnel Carriers (APCs) among them—highlighted once more the difficulties facing the New Zealand Defence Force (NZDF), and the importance of planning for new acquisitions.

The New Zealand Government changed once more in 1999, with a Labour-led coalition coming to power. The importance of peacekeeping was highlighted by the Labour-led Government when it was elected in 1999, and a new approach to defence was one of the Labour Party's key priorities. In its *Defence Policy Framework*, the Government in June 2000 spelt out the importance of peacekeeping to New Zealand's role in the world:

> The Government considers peace support operations are important for maintaining security and stability. New Zealand will make as full a contribution to such actions as is reasonably possible. We will continue to base our global engagement on active support for, and participation in, United Nations and appropriate multi-national peace support operations.[65]

The new Government's policy was to have a significant impact almost immediately on decisions made about all of the acquisitions under consideration; no further frigates were to be purchased; HMNZS *Charles Upham* was to be sold; the F-16 lease was to be cancelled, as was Project *Sirius*; and the number of light armoured vehicles (LAVs) to be purchased was to be increased. The events surrounding each of these decisions will be explored in detail in the following chapters.

Overview of Chapters

Chapter 1 introduces the book and provides a background context for the case studies. Chapters 2–7 focus on the six case studies chosen for analysis. Chapter 2 explores the process that led to the decision in 1989 to purchase two ANZAC frigates. The choice of the ANZAC frigates was controversial and caused much public discussion and debate. What lay behind the choice of the ANZAC frigates? Why did a Labour Government pursue the purchase of further frigates, when the defence policy of the previous National Government indicated that alternatives to frigates should be explored?[66] What were the alternatives and why were they not pursued? Now that New Zealand has two in service, what are the tangible benefits that can be identified?

Chapter 3 examines the events surrounding the acquisition of HMNZS *Charles Upham*. The agreement in 1994 to purchase the heavy lift ship HMNZS *Charles Upham* was not originally surrounded by public controversy, but was the subject of long delays, and subsequently became headline news. What factors were taken into account in the final decision-making process? Once the vessel had been bought, why were adequate funds for its conversion not made available?

Chapter 4 reviews the second and third ANZAC frigate decision-making processes of 1997 and 1998. Having committed to the purchase of two ANZAC frigates with an option to purchase two more, why, when strong arguments were made that a minimum three frigate force was necessary to fulfil New Zealand's policy requirements, was the subsequent decision made not to purchase even a third vessel?

Chapter 5 explores the events surrounding the controversial decision to pursue the opportunity to lease F-16 strike aircraft from the United States, at a time when no such plans had been signalled in previous defence reviews. The first 14 of the RNZAF's major maritime strike and ground support aircraft, the A-4K *Skyhawks*, were originally purchased in 1968, and entered service in 1970. Notwithstanding the significant sums that were spent to upgrade both the airframe and the avionics of the aircraft, it was clear by the 1990s that the aircraft would need to be replaced by 2007 at the latest. However, the decision to lease the F-16s was made some eight years prior to this deadline. How did the decision to lease the F-16s in 1999 come about—and how was the decision to abandon the lease made?

Chapter 6 explores the P-3 *Orion* upgrades. The P-3 *Orions* have been an essential part of New Zealand's maritime patrol capability for many years now. Why and how have these aircraft continued in service for so long? What has influenced the decisions which have been made about upgrading them to maintain their viability? In particular, what led to the cancellation of Project *Sirius* (the plan to significantly upgrade the anti-submarine warfare (ASW) capability of the aircraft), and how was the decision taken to develop the current new suite of avionics? The chapter recounts the early upgrade under Project *Rigel*, and the re-winging of the aircraft under Project *Kestrel*. It then goes on to analyse the events leading up to the decision taken by a National-led Government to proceed with Project *Sirius*; the subsequent events leading to the Labour decision to cancel the project; and then finally analyses the processes which led to the decision to upgrade the aircraft's sensor and avionics equipment under Project *Guardian*.

Chapter 7 reviews another controversial decision—taken in August 2000 by a Labour-led Government—to buy 105 LAV IIIs. Whilst capital expenditure in the Army has been significantly less than in the other Services, the sums spent remain considerable. Nevertheless, it was apparent from deployments to Bosnia and East Timor, among others, that the Army was facing an equipment crisis. When it came to reviewing armoured equipment needs, what led to the purchase of the LAV III armoured vehicles? What alternatives were considered, and why did the Army have some of their most pressing needs met when, some would argue, the other two Service branches did not?

Chapter 8, the Conclusion, draws together the observations arising from the case study chapters. It answers the following questions:

- What conclusions can be drawn from the case studies examined in detail in this book?
- What can be learned about the way defence decision-making is undertaken in New Zealand?

The Policy Framework

Before moving on to the case studies themselves, it is appropriate to briefly set out the framework within which defence acquisition recommendations are developed and then actioned.

The major actors involved in defence decision-making processes are the Minister of Defence and his Cabinet colleagues, the Secretary of Defence and staff of the Ministry of Defence, and the Chief of Defence Force and appropriate staff from each of the three Services. The Acquisition Division of the Ministry of Defence is responsible for the acquisition of equipment for the three Services of the NZDF. Following receipt of a 'user requirement' developed by the NZDF, the Division takes responsibility for seeking Government approval, develops and prepares the strategy for acquisition, and undertakes the tendering and evaluation process. Once the equipment has been acquired, the Division manages the acquisition through the delivery and warranty period.[67]

Defence policy-making and defence decision-making have in the past been challenged by the relatively rapid pace of change of personnel involved, both politicians and senior bureaucrats. Whilst in the United Kingdom there were 22

Ministers of Defence during the 40 years after the Second World War,[68] New Zealand saw 11 Ministers of Defence in the 20 years after 1972. Over that period there were also six changes to the Chief of Defence Staff/Chief of Defence Force, and five changes of Secretary of Defence.[69] In the past 10 years there have been four Ministers of Defence, three Secretaries, and four Chiefs of Defence Force.

As the actors have changed over time so also have the processes and the framework. The Fourth Labour Government made wide-sweeping changes to the structure and function of many parts of the Public Service during the years after it gained office. Separating policy advice and purchasing from daily management of services was central to its philosophy, and Defence was subject to scrutiny just as were other elements of the public sector.[70] Derek Quigley and the other directors of Strategos Consulting were commissioned at this time to undertake a *Defence Resource Management Review*, which was published on 4 December 1988. In commenting on the *Review*, the Ministers of Finance and Defence noted: '1989 will see the beginning of substantial changes in the Ministry of Defence. ... Resource Management in the Ministry of Defence has to be improved.'[71] The recommendations of the Strategos Report were to abolish the Defence Council; to separate policy from operations; and to have the Ministry of Defence responsible for the former, and the NZDF responsible for the latter. Those recommendations were implemented in 1989. Some 12 years later *Jane's Defence Weekly* was to comment:

> The resulting structure rather than separating operations from policy, as was the intention, has left both institutions without the resources to fully carry out their respective functions, while at the same time providing two conflicting streams to the government.[72]

The 'two conflicting information streams' were to come rudely to public attention during the debates over the acquisition of the LAV III, and these events among others were to lead the Government to call for a review of accountabilities and structural arrangements between the Ministry of Defence, the NZDF and the three Service arms.

When the review, to become known as the Hunn Report, was published in September 2002, it recommended a number of significant changes, not least that the two arms be re-established as a single organisation. The *Review* noted: 'Neither of these organisations has been working effectively. The NZDF has been riven with internal dissention.'[73]

Despite the clear recommendation for a single organisation, the Government decided against it. Minister of Defence Mark Burton indicated that changes had already been made to help achieve a greater degree of 'jointness' between Services and between agencies. He advised that steps would be taken to ensure that duplication would be eliminated; that the three Service Chiefs' roles would be to 'raise, train and maintain' their respective Services; and that the roles and responsibilities of the Secretary of Defence and Chief of Defence Force would be clarified.[74] The roles of the Ministry of Defence remain, therefore, to:

- provide timely, high-quality advice to help the Government make well-informed decisions about the defence of New Zealand and its interests;
- conduct audits and assessments of the NZDF and the acquisition activities of the Ministry of Defence; and
- arrange for the acquisition of significant items of military equipment needed to meet NZDF capability requirements.

In order to carry out these roles, the Ministry remains organised as follows:

Figure 1.1: Organisational structure of the Ministry of Defence

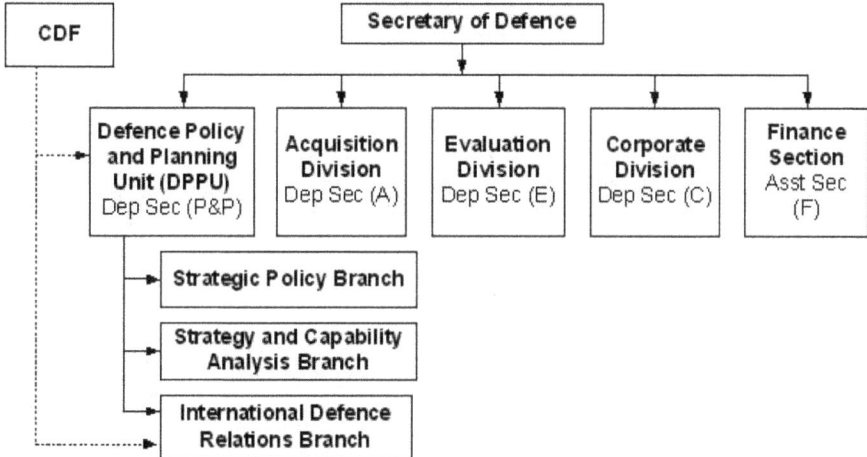

(*Source*: The Ministry of Defence: Organisational Structure of the Ministry, available at <http://www.defence.govt.nz/reports-publications/election-brief-2005/ roles-org-mod.html>, accessed 12 March 2009)

Forward Planning

In order to ensure fiscally responsible forward planning and decision-making, it is common to expect that financial forecasting will form a central part of the decision-making process. However, James Rolfe noted in his 1993 text that no White Paper since 1970 had spelt out the financial requirements for the defence proposals contained within them, and added that this 'seems to be a major omission for a policy document which often makes a point of the long-term nature of defence planning'.[75]

Up until 1989, Defence had maintained an *Indicative Defence Resource Plan* which provided the framework for force development over both the short and long term, but it ceased to function from 1989 because of organisational changes and changes in fiscal guidance. In its place was introduced the Defence Planning

System (DPS). The aim of the DPS was to 'enable [the] CDF [Chief of Defence Force] and Sec Def to provide high quality advice to Government in respect of funding choices for investment in the NZDF'.[76] Rolfe raised the prospect of the DPS providing greater certainty for planners, reducing the need for White Papers being written to try and match funding and policy. In the event, the DPS never functioned comprehensively because it was 'too complex and not use-friendly'.[77] Despite ongoing attempts to revive the DPS, it ultimately failed.

The DPS was replaced by the *Capability Management Framework*, approved on 22 April 2004. It allowed for the development of two new bodies—the Executive Capability Board (comprising the Secretary of Defence and Chief of Defence Force) and the Integrated Capability Management Committee (adding second tier staff).[78] Linked with the Defence *Long-Term Development Plan* (LTDP), first released in 2002 and updated regularly, the *Capability Management Framework*

> is a governance and management system designed to support Defence and Government decision makers in developing effective, long-term investments in defence capabilities. It provides clarity in responsibility, accountability and process for defence policy development, capability definition and acquisition through to the introduction into service and the disposal of capabilities.[79]

The LTDP is described as

> a planning tool to enable decisions on defence acquisitions to be taken in the context of the Government's defence policy, the priority of projects and affordability ... The LTDP has a role in forward focus over 10 years and was constructed as an active document, to be updated regularly.[80]

There have been four updates of the LTDP to date. Of the case studies analysed in this book, the P-3K *Orion* upgrade is the only one to fall within the orbit of the LTDP.

Conclusion

For over more than half a century New Zealand has been developing an increasingly independent voice in foreign and defence policy. This chapter has outlined the development of New Zealand's modern defence and foreign policy history, and has sketched out how the policy process works within a contemporary setting. Having established some fundamental aspects of New Zealand's approach, the following chapters move on to explore the acquisition decision-making process and impinging factors in detail. The implications of changes of government, and changes in policy, public opinion and the international security environment, as well as other external pressures, and the part played by individual actors, among others, will be considered as each case

Introduction—The Policy Background and the Policy Framework

study is analysed and as the book moves towards developing a greater understanding of defence decision-making processes.

Whilst the planning process in Defence has been reviewed and refined in recent years, and the Defence Policy and Planning Unit was reported as having improved coordination in the planning process, this is but one element in the acquisition decision-making process.[81] The following chapters explore in detail the range of elements which impact on those processes.

ENDNOTES

[1] Text of New Zealand Prime Minister Michael Savage's address, broadcast 5 September 1939, *Dominion*, 6 September 1939, cited in Malcolm McKinnon, *Independence and Foreign Policy: New Zealand in the World since 1935*, Auckland University Press, Auckland, 1993, p. 33.

[2] McKinnon, *Independence and Foreign Policy: New Zealand in the World since 1935*, p. 46.

[3] Major G.J. Clayton, *The New Zealand Army: A History from the 1840s to the 1990s*, New Zealand Army, Wellington, 1990, p. 114.

[4] Sir Alister McIntosh, 'The origins of the Department of External Affairs and the formulation of an independent foreign policy', in *New Zealand in World Affairs: Volume I, 1945-1957*, New Zealand Institute of International Affairs, Wellington: 1991, p. 21.

[5] W. David McIntyre, *New Zealand Prepares for War*, University of Canterbury Press, Christchurch, 1998, p. 239.

[6] McIntosh, 'The origins of the Department of External Affairs and the formulation of an independent foreign policy', p. 22.

[7] McIntosh, 'The origins of the Department of External Affairs and the formulation of an independent foreign policy', p. 23.

[8] John C. Beaglehole, 'The Development of New Zealand Nationality', p. 8, cited in McKinnon, *Independence and Foreign Policy: New Zealand in the World since 1935*, p. 55.

[9] William Jordan, speech at the 98th Session of the League Council on 16 September 1937, cited in McIntyre, *New Zealand Prepares for War*, p. 164.

[10] E. Luand, *A History of the United Nations*, St Martins Press, New York, 1982, p. 20.

[11] Martin Gilbert, *A History of the Twentieth Century, Volume Two: 1933-1951*, Harper Collins, London, 1998, p. 605.

[12] McIntosh, 'The origins of the Department of External Affairs and the formulation of an independent foreign policy', p. 25.

[13] McIntosh, 'The origins of the Department of External Affairs and the formulation of an independent foreign policy', p. 26.

[14] Frederick W. Doidge, cited in W.D. MacIntyre, 'Peter Fraser's Commonwealth', in *New Zealand in World Affairs, Volume 1, 1945-1957*, p. 68.

[15] R.J. McDougall, *New Zealand Naval Vessels*, GP Books, Wellington, 1989, p. 4.

[16] I.C. McGibbon, 'The Defence of New Zealand 1945-1957', in *New Zealand in World Affairs, Volume 1, 1945-1957*, pp. 147–48.

[17] Clayton, *The New Zealand Army: A History from the 1840s to the 1990s*, p. 133.

[18] F.L.W. Wood, 'New Zealand Foreign Policy 1945-1951', in *New Zealand in World Affairs, Volume 1, 1945-1957*, p. 105.

[19] Alan Burnett, *The A-NZ-US Triangle*, Strategic Defence Studies Centre, The Australian National University, Canberra, 1988, p. 5.

[20] McGibbon, 'The Defence of New Zealand 1945-1957', p. 159.

[21] Frederick W. Doidge, cited in Burnett, *The A-NZ-US Triangle*, p. 7.

[22] Sidney Holland, cited in McGibbon, 'The Defence of New Zealand 1945-1957', p. 169.

[23] Matthew Wright, *Kiwi Air Power*, Reed Books, Auckland, 1998, p. 134.

[24] Geoffrey Bentley and Maurice Conly, *Portrait of an Air Force*, Grantham House, Wellington, 1987, pp. 140–45.

[25] Clayton, *The New Zealand Army: A History from the 1840s to the 1990s*, pp. 139–40.
[26] McKinnon, *Independence and Foreign Policy: New Zealand in the World since 1935*, p. 125.
[27] T.C. Webb cited in McKinnon, 'From ANZUS to SEATO', in *New Zealand in World Affairs, Volume 1, 1945-1957*, p. 138.
[28] *Review of Defence Policy 1961*, Government Printer, Wellington, 1961, p. 4.
[29] *Review of Defence Policy 1961*, p. 6. My emphasis
[30] Matthew Wright, *Blue Water Kiwis*, Reed Books, Auckland, 2003, p. 185.
[31] Minutes of Chiefs of Staff Committee, COS (61) M.46, 14 December 1961, 478/4/6 cited in Roberto Rabel, 'Vietnam and the Collapse of the Foreign Policy Consensus', in Malcolm McKinnon (ed), *New Zealand in World Affairs Volume II 1957-1972*, New Zealand Institute of International Affairs, Wellington, 1991, p. 44.
[32] McKinnon, *Independence and Foreign Policy: New Zealand in the World since 1935*, p. 156.
[33] McKinnon, *Independence and Foreign Policy: New Zealand in the World since 1935*, p. 156; and Clayton, *The New Zealand Army: A History from the 1840s to the 1990s*, p. 141.
[34] Wright, *Kiwi Air Power*, p. 146.
[35] Ian McGibbon, 'Forward Defence: The Southeast Asian Commitment', in McKinnon (ed), *New Zealand in World Affairs Volume II 1957-1972*, p. 34. Whilst in the years immediately after its inception its future value was to be questioned, the FPDA endures some 37 years later, with significant annual exercises taking place with the military involvement of all five nations. See James Rolfe, *Anachronistic Past or Positive Future: New Zealand and the Five Power Defence Arrangements*, CSS Working Paper no. 4/45, Centre for Strategic Studies, Victoria University, Wellington; 'Flying Fish 2003', *Air Force News*, no. 40, August 2003, pp. 24–25; 'Five Power Defence Partners operating together', *Navy Today* 93, October 2004, pp. 4–5; and 'HMNZS TE KAHA', *Navy Today* 137, October 2008, pp. 26–27.
[36] *Review of Defence Policy 1972*, p. 3.
[37] *Review of Defence Policy 1972*, p. 16.
[38] James Rolfe, *Defending New Zealand: A Study of Structures, Processes and Relationships*, Institute of Policy Studies, Wellington, 1993, pp. 58–59.
[39] *New Zealand Foreign Affairs Review*, June 1973, p. 7; cited in McKinnon, *Independence and Foreign Policy: New Zealand in the World since 1935*, p. 185.
[40] Steve Hoadley, *The New Zealand Foreign Affairs Handbook*, Second Edition, Oxford University Press, Auckland, 1992, p. 19.
[41] Kate Dewes and Robert Green, *Aotearoa/New Zealand at the World Court*, The Raven Press, Christchurch, 1991, p. 11.
[42] Norman Kirk cited in Dewes and Green, *Aotearoa/New Zealand at the World Court*, p. 7.
[43] Helen Clark, 'New Zealand's Non-Nuclear Initiative', in Ranginui Walker and William Sutherland (eds), *The Pacific: Peace, Security & the Nuclear Issue*, United Nations University, Tokyo, 1988, p. 178.
[44] Michael Hanel-Green, 'The Rarotonga South Pacific Nuclear-free Zone Treaty', in Walker and Sutherland (eds), *The Pacific: Peace, Security & the Nuclear Issue*, p. 93.
[45] Walter Nash, cited in Dewes and Green, *Aotearoa/New Zealand at the World Court*, p. 9.
[46] *Evening Post*, 12 May 1982, cited in McKinnon, *Independence and Foreign Policy: New Zealand in the World since 1935*, p. 279.
[47] David Lange, *my life*, Viking, Auckland, 2005, p. 165.
[48] McKinnon, *Independence and Foreign Policy: New Zealand in the World since 1935*, p. 282.
[49] David Lange, *Nuclear Free—The New Zealand Way*, Penguin Books, Auckland, 1990, p. 33.
[50] Lange, *Nuclear Free—The New Zealand Way*, p. 35.
[51] Lange, *my life*, p. 205.
[52] Richard Kennaway and John Henderson, *Beyond New Zealand II: Foreign Policy into the 1990s*, Longman Paul, Auckland, 1991, p. 68.
[53] *Defence of New Zealand, Review of Defence Policy 1987*, Government Printer, Wellington, 1987, pp. 14–17.
[54] Lange, *Nuclear Free—The New Zealand Way*, p. 161.
[55] *The Defence of New Zealand 1991, A Policy Paper*, GP Print Ltd, Wellington, 1991, p. 5.
[56] Jim Bolger, *A View From The Top*, Viking, Auckland, 1998, p. 149.

[57] *New Zealand in the Security Council: 1993-94*, Information Bulletin no. 52, Ministry of Foreign Affairs and Trade, Wellington, March 1995, p. 4.
[58] John Crawford, *In the Field for Peace: New Zealand's contribution to international peace-support operations: 1950-1995*, New Zealand Defence Force, Wellington, 1996, p. 62.
[59] Paul Bensemann, 'The War with no Enemy', *NZ Defence Quarterly*, Summer 1994, p. 2.
[60] UMR Insight Limited, *Ministry of Defence Quantitative Summary*, Wellington, April 1995, p. 3.
[61] *The Shape of New Zealand's Defence, A White Paper*, Ministry of Defence, Wellington, November 1997, p. 27.
[62] *The Shape of New Zealand's Defence, A White Paper*, Ministry of Defence, p. 8.
[63] *New Zealand Herald*, 11 September 1999.
[64] John Crawford and Glyn Harper, *Operation East Timor: The New Zealand Defence Force in East Timor 1999-2001*, Reed Books, Auckland, 2001, pp. 177–211.
[65] *The Government's Defence Policy Framework*, Ministry of Defence, Wellington, June 2000, p. 4.
[66] *Defence Review 1983*, Government Printer, Wellington, 1983, p. 23.
[67] The Ministry of Defence website, available at <http://www.defence.govt.nz/about-us/divisions/acquisition.html>, accessed 4 November 2008.
[68] Margaret Blunden, 'British Defence Decision Making; the Boundaries of Influence', in Margaret Blunden and Owen Greene (eds), *Science and Mythology in the Making of Defence Policy*, Brasseys Defence Publishers Limited, London, 1989, p. 211.
[69] Rolfe, *Defending New Zealand: A Study of Structures, Processes and Relationships*, p. 21.
[70] Jonathan Boston et al, *Reshaping the State: New Zealand's Bureaucratic Revolution*, Oxford University Press, Auckland, 1991.
[71] Hon. D.F. Quigley, *New Zealand Defence, Resource Management Review 1988*, Strategos Consulting Limited, Wellington, 1988, p. 1.
[72] Phillip McKinnon, 'New Zealand reviews defence structure', *Jane's Defence Weekly*, 26 September 2001, p. 10.
[73] Don K. Hunn, *Review of Accountabilities and Structural Arrangements between the Ministry of Defence and the New Zealand Defence Force*, Wellington, 30 September 2002, p. vi. The implications of this comment shall be explored more fully in relation to the acquisition of HMNZS *Charles Upham*, the F-16 decisions, and the LAV IIIs.
[74] *New Zealand Herald*, 27 March 2003. See Appendix 1 for the respective listing of responsibilities.
[75] Rolfe, *Defending New Zealand: A Study of Structures, Processes and Relationships*, p. 57.
[76] *Force Development Processes, Defence Planning System*, First Edition New Zealand Defence Force, Wellington, 23 November 1994, p. 1.
[77] Report of the Controller and Auditor-General, *Ministry of Defence: Acquisition of Light Armoured Vehicles and Light Operational Vehicles*, Ministry of Defence, Wellington, August 2001, p. 59.
[78] Report of the Controller and Auditor-General, *Ministry of Defence and New Zealand Defence Force: Further report on the acquisition and introduction into service of Light Armoured Vehicles*, Ministry of Defence, Wellington, December 2004, p. 32.
[79] *Statement of Intent of the New Zealand Defence Force (NZDF) Te Ope Kaatu o Aotearoa, for the year ending 30 June 2005*, Headquarters New Zealand Defence Force (HQNZDF), Wellington, 3 May 2004, p. 38.
[80] *Defence Long-Term Development Plan, Update*, November 2004, p. 3.
[81] *Army News*, no. 298, 21 October 2003.

Chapter 2

The ANZACS, Part 1 — The Frigate that wasn't a Frigate

As long ago as 1954 the cost of replacement frigates had been an issue. Almost a quarter of a century later, the 1978 *Defence Review* made the observation that 'the high costs of acquiring and maintaining modern naval ships and systems compounds the difficulty of reaching decisions which will adequately provide for New Zealand's future needs at sea'.[1] Indeed 'extensive enquiries to find a replacement for HMNZS *Otago* made it clear that the cost of a new frigate had gone beyond what New Zealand could afford'.[2] This observation led to the serious consideration of converting the Royal New Zealand Navy (RNZN) to a coast guard service, but the Government rejected the notion on the basis that, although a coast guard could carry out resource protection tasks, it would mean the end of any strategic relationship with our ANZUS Treaty partners, and the RNZN would no longer be able to operate as a military force. The Chief of Naval Staff, Rear Admiral Neil D. Anderson, said that the New Zealand Government's commitment to maintaining a professional fighting navy was 'a magnificent shot in the arm for everyone in the Navy'.[3]

The Government remained committed to a compact multi-purpose navy, and calculated that a core operational force of three ships would be the minimum necessary force. These ships were to be the *Leander*-class frigates HMNZS *Waikato* and HMNZS *Canterbury* (commissioned in 1966 and 1971 respectively), and the older Type 12 frigate HMNZS *Otago*. The fourth existing frigate at the time, HMNZS *Taranaki* (a type 12), was to undertake the roles of resource protection and basic sea training. There was some concern though about the sort of vessel that would ultimately replace the *Otago* and how and when that replacement should happen. In May 1979 a project review team, led by Commander Somerford Teagle, examined a wide range of vessels. One of these, an American frigate, would have met every requirement set out in the Defence White Paper, but even in 1979 it was priced at NZ$400 million, and therefore ruled out. Consideration was then given to purchasing rejuvenated British frigates at a cost of NZ$44 million each, before plans were submitted for the possible conversion of *Taranaki*, *Waikato* and *Canterbury* late in 1979.

A decision on frigate replacements was expected to have been made before the end of 1979, but was deferred in February 1980, with a request from the Government to the Ministry of Defence to explore further options. Later that year the Government decided not to replace the ageing *Otago*, rejecting the RNZN's replacement proposals for the second time in a year.

It was the British defence review of 1981 which allowed the possibility of a 'bargain buy' which helped resolve the issue for at least a decade. The decision was made to purchase two *Leander*-class frigates, HMS *Dido* and HMS *Bacchante*, which dated from the early 1960s. This allowed the naval combat force to remain with a core of four operational vessels, albeit with oil-fired boiler power. The Minister of Defence, David Thomson, commenting upon the purchase said: 'In the existing financial circumstances it was plainly necessary to seize any opportunity to acquire effective operational part-life vessels as an alternative to the purchase of a new ship.'[4] Whilst there was concern expressed that this would lead to the RNZN facing block obsolescence in the early 1990s, the Government nevertheless concluded a deal in October 1981. *Bacchante* was transferred to New Zealand in October 1982 and renamed HMNZS *Wellington*, but did not enter service until mid-1986. *Dido* was refitted in Southampton and transferred to New Zealand as HMNZS *Southland* in December 1983.

Public concerns about the cost of defence had heightened significantly by the beginning of the 1980s, and the Government was keen to consider novel ways of reducing the costs involved in maintaining a combat fleet. The 1983 *Defence Review* reinforced the findings of the previous *Review* that a reduction in capability to a coast guard role was not acceptable, and that a combat force should be maintained.[5] However, fiscal concerns were to the fore, and the Government's dilemma about a future replacement for the frigates was clearly spelt out in the *Review*. Because of the political and economic implications surrounding the frigate replacement question at the time, and the debate which has ensued for over two decades since, it is worthwhile quoting fully from the *Review* to highlight Government thinking at the time:

> The frigate's main attraction lies in its flexibility of employment and its ability to offer a graduated range of responses in varying circumstances particularly in times of tension short of war. New Zealand's frigates have been configured essentially as anti-submarine escorts best suited to operations within a fleet environment. They are however versatile and will give scope for deployment on a wide range of duties for the rest of their operational life. Given the range and capability of modern weapons and sensor systems, frigates could remain a viable combat force option for New Zealand into the indefinite future—if the financial problems of providing them with an effective self-defence capability and for their eventual replacement could be overcome. However, at this time there appear no realistic prospects of the future defence budget being able to accommodate the costs that would be involved. *Financial considerations alone therefore demand consideration of an alternative force structure for*

the Navy. The period during which the present frigate force is available must accordingly be used to determine a new operational concept for the RNZN.[6]

The novel solution that was being explored at the time was to introduce a fleet of submarines; they were seen potentially as being cheaper to introduce and to operate than the frigate force. Robert Miles, an outspoken and passionate defence commentator, called MP Doug Kidd's suggestion that the RNZN become a submarine force 'misguided'. He went on to roundly criticise the concept, drawing attention to the limited utility of submarines for the range of roles the RNZN was expected to fulfil. Instead, he suggested that New Zealand expand its naval patrol force with the purchase of ships such as the British *Castle*-class offshore patrol vessels.[7] He would not be the only one to make that suggestion. Initial investigations suggested that a submarine might cost NZ$140 million, rather than the NZ$240 million cost for a new frigate. However, the plan never did proceed; further evaluation indicated that it was not as cost effective an option as originally thought, and the project was finally cancelled by the Labour Government in February 1985.[8]

The Impact of the Fourth Labour Government, and the Frigate that wasn't a Frigate

As previously discussed, the election of the Fourth Labour Government and the subsequent 'nuclear ships' dispute led to the need to review defence policy. The ANZUS dispute had become the major controversy of the decade, and left the Labour Party with the question of the future direction of defence policy. To help inform this next step, the Government convened a Defence Committee of Enquiry in 1985, the first time that a New Zealand Government had sought out public opinion on defence planning.[9] This Committee was to hear public submissions and report on public attitudes towards strategic and security issues. The report and its recommendations were to be taken into account in the preparation of the anticipated 1986 *Defence Review*.[10] Public debate and controversy surrounded this period, and the question of frigates was to the fore once more.

Another discussion paper, *An Alternative Defence Policy*, put forward by the Peace and Justice Forum in March 1985, challenged the need for frigates and also supported the purchase of the *Castle*-class vessels,[11] and this recommendation was reinforced by the 'Just Defence' submission to the Defence Committee of Enquiry in February 1986.[12] Such sentiments were echoed by the Labour Party's Wellington regional conference, held in May 1986, when it passed two remits calling for the adoption of a civilian-based defence policy, and the replacement of the frigate fleet by smaller boats suitable for fisheries protection.[13]

Early in 1987 the debate heated up. The Australian Chief of Naval Staff, Vice Admiral Michael Hudson, was in New Zealand meeting top Navy and Defence officials during February. The 23 February issue of the *Evening Post* carried a story stating that 'the New Zealand Navy is considering joining Australia in a frigate deal as part of a long-term plan to replace New Zealand's ageing vessels'. It went on to say that 'one frigate type of particular interest was a light patrol vessel with ocean-going capabilities'. The report brought a sharp rebuke immediately from the New Zealand Prime Minister, David Lange, which was reported in the *Dominion* the following day. Lange criticised by inference the Secretary of Defence, Denis McLean, commenting:

> The prospect is that we have a vessel, drummed up with Australia, providing exactly what we need. *But it won't be a frigate.* ... It is unfortunate that there has been the impression gained, from certain statements in certain quarters, that we are in the frigate business. *We are not in the frigate business.*[14]

The report went on to say that defence specialists suggested that Lange was talking about a frigate hull, but without the high-tech installations of a fully fitted frigate, perhaps to appease the peace groups who were becoming increasingly vociferous in their opposition to any replacement for frigates. It was further suggested that replacing the frigates with patrol boats would have meant the end of a blue-water role for the RNZN, but that Lange's comments made it clear that the Government intended to maintain a blue-water capability.

The 1987 *Defence Review* was published two days later, on 26 February 1987. In the introduction to the 1987 *Review*, emphasis was placed on the comprehensive nature of the review of defence policy which had taken place since the Labour Party had come to power and introduced New Zealand's nuclear-free legislation. As a result of the ending of the security relationship with the United States, greater emphasis was to be placed on the importance of New Zealand's relationship with Australia:

> The New Zealand—Australia defence relationship has always been close and remains a key element in New Zealand's defence strategy. Defence cooperation is one of the strands of the evolving trans-Tasman relationship that also covers political, commercial and personal links. The ANZAC military ties have a long and honourable history. ... The withdrawal of United States military cooperation with New Zealand has made our defence relationship with Australia more important, but it has not substantially changed its nature.[15]

The importance of this relationship was underscored with a clear acknowledgement that New Zealand forces needed to be trained and equipped to operate jointly with Australian forces, and that:

The security of either New Zealand or Australia would be at severe risk if the other was seriously threatened and it is inconceivable that a joint response would not be forthcoming. For both security and military reasons, as well as economic and political considerations, we need to maintain our close defence relationship with Australia.[16]

The central defence objective of developing greater self reliance and working closely with Australia to meet the defence needs of the region was clearly stated. Some joint developments and purchasing had already begun to take place, with the setting up of identical defence communications networks in both countries, the purchase of an artillery field gun, and the potential purchase of new rifles which would be manufactured in Australia. None of these, though, were on the scale envisaged in the involvement of New Zealand in the planning and potential purchase of the 'Australian Ocean Combat Ship'.

The Labour Government had two clear and interlinked objectives—the development of naval capability, with the replacement of the surface combatants; and the development of the relationship with Australia. With the tenor of the times, neither objective was going to be easy to achieve.

The *Defence Review* highlighted the importance of maintaining flexibility in New Zealand's naval forces. It confirmed that there was a longstanding need for replacement of the current frigates, and pointed to working together with the Australians to see 'if a mutually acceptable and cost-effective ship can be constructed which will meet both countries' needs'.[17] Two weeks later, the Australian Minister for Defence, Kim Beazley, was reported as saying that a blue-water navy with a capacity to contribute significantly in the area of submarine warfare was seen as an essential ingredient in the trans-Tasman relationship: 'Provided those capabilities are maintained ... the co-operation between our two countries will be close.'[18] Significantly, the new vessels were being called 'new surface combatants' in the official title of the Australian project—supporting Lange's insistence that New Zealand would not buy any more frigates. John Henderson, at the time Head of the Prime Minister's Department, emphasised that great care was taken in those early stages to avoid the term 'frigate' completely.[19]

The press release by Lange on 15 July 1987 confirmed the Government's plan to proceed with the projected replacement of the frigates during the 1990s. Notwithstanding this confirmation, the same month the *International Defence Review* drew attention to the political atmosphere in New Zealand, which it suggested could seriously obstruct the procurement of any warships. It quoted one source 'close to the programme': 'The Prime Minister needs educating, although that's the New Zealand Navy's job, not ours. Even "frigate" is a dirty word there, and to be politically acceptable the ship will have to be called something like an "ocean surveillance vessel".'[20] However, the descriptive term could not be avoided, and when Beazley released a statement on the project in July, he welcomed the New Zealand announcement to join Australia in buying a 'new class of frigate'.

Initial estimates gave an indicative figure of up to NZ$300 million as the sail-away cost for each of the first two ships delivered. Opposition to the frigates closely followed the announcements, with Just Defence concerned that the Government had not seriously considered cheaper non-frigate alternatives, again mentioning the *Castle*-class patrol vessel. Sylvia Bagnall, its spokesperson, said that at, a total cost of $1 billion, New Zealand would get four frigates designed to suit Australia's and not New Zealand's needs.[21] The following week the Minister of Defence, R.J. Tizard, responded to clarify aspects of the project in the light of the criticisms that were being reported:

> Since we have no defined enemy, we need vessels that can perform the functions of the various roles we see for ourselves. These include maintaining a role in the South Pacific and building co-operation with Australia. Contact and co-operation with Pacific Island countries is paramount, as is protection of our own economic zone and help to Pacific Island countries to do the same. Obviously an increased search and rescue response will be a very significant part of our contribution.
>
> There is a certainty that we will have these roles. By contrast there is no certainty our ships will have to perform a wartime function. They must have that capacity of course, but their use for most of their lifetime will be in the roles set out above. That may not be how the Australians see their ships' role.[22]

The Minister's words were carefully crafted, emphasising those roles that would be most politically acceptable at the time. Jim Anderton, the new Chair of the Foreign Affairs Select Committee, was only too well aware of the issues involved in upgrading the Defence Forces. Anderton drew attention to the trade-offs involved:

> Now that the nuclear policy is in place, the reality is that we are going to have to bear the cost. There is a cost, and if we are to carry on with any kind of conventional forces, we're going to have to give them the wherewithal.[23]

The trade-offs and controversy were only just beginning.

Evaluating the Alternatives

Paradoxically perhaps, the anti-nuclear policy of the Labour Government provided the greatest opportunity in many years for the purchase of new ships for the RNZN. The commitment to maintaining a blue-water navy and to ongoing cooperation with Australia, that was to be spelt out in the 1987 *Defence Review*, ensured that the New Zealand Government took seriously the opportunity to purchase ships jointly with the Australians. Whilst the South Pacific was intended to be the major focus for Defence, the Government did not wish to see New Zealand distanced from its closest ally. A Defence Review Officials Committee had been exploring the possibilities for surface combat ship replacements throughout 1986, and published their report in November of that year. They noted that, as a consequence of ongoing close liaison between the navies of each country, it was found that 'the independently desired ship characteristics for the RAN new Surface Combatants and the RNZN Replacement Combat Ship are virtually identical'.[24] (See Appendix 2, Ship Characteristics.) The *Review* Committee indicated that significant operational and logistical advantages would be possible if New Zealand and Australia were to select a common design. They went on to say that, in collaboration with the RAN, two options had been identified. The first was to pursue a joint program based on building all of the ships in Australia. The second option was to pursue a cooperative program where New Zealand would have ships built to the same design, but in the country of origin. To pursue the first option, they advised, it would be necessary to sign a Memorandum of Understanding by mid-1987. The Memorandum of Understanding was subsequently signed on 6 March 1987, noting that the Australian Government was seeking eight new Surface Combatants, and that New Zealand would have an option to purchase two, with the possibility of a further two at a later stage.[25]

The *Review* Committee had noted that the cost of the vessels was likely to be up to 30 per cent more if they were built in Australian yards, yet felt that the net benefit to Australia was such that the Australians could be expected to offset the cost penalty to New Zealand. Notwithstanding this observation, the Committee also noted that it was likely that potential European shipbuilders might offer a package that was more fiscally attractive, and that therefore building the ships in their country of origin was the most likely option. Nevertheless, they recommended proceeding with the first option in the interests of closer relationships with Australia, and to provide the maximum opportunity for New Zealand industry involvement. The Memorandum of Understanding recognised this dilemma, and was crafted in such a way that it allowed for New Zealand participation up to the stage of selecting the design and shipbuilder evaluations. At that point New Zealand could choose whether it wished to proceed with the acquisition of the ships. This allowed for significant opportunities for New Zealand to be involved in the choice of design and for potential New Zealand industry involvement. It also allowed the opportunity for a significant period of public debate about the acquisition itself. These two elements developed alongside each other in an unparalleled fashion which was to impact significantly on the decision-making process. At stake were political futures; the nature of the trans-Tasman relationship; developments for New

Zealand industry; and the future shape of the RNZN. The 'Frigate Debate', as it became known, was of such significance that it shall be examined separately in a following section.

The *Review* Committee's observations

In developing its report, the *Review* Committee took the opportunity to look broadly at what ships or designs were available at the time which might meet the need of the RNZN to fulfil the tasks required of it. It reviewed a range of vessels which would give an indication of a cost/capability balance, looking at vessels which ranged from 1000–4000 tonnes, from Offshore Patrol Vessels (OPVs) to Destroyers. It commented on a UK Ministry of Defence review which examined an initial 13 OPV proposals, and narrowed that down to three—the *Skeandu*, 84 metres; VT (Vosper Thornycroft) Mk19, 78 metres; and Yarrow OPV at 95 metres. It noted that all three could be offered as 'stretched' versions at 90 and 91 metres for the first two, with the Yarrow OPV being available at 101, 105 and 115 metres. On the grounds of inadequate capability (having made the observation that the minimum length to allow sufficient space for a hangar for helicopter maintenance as well as adequate space for weapons and sensor separation was approximately 110 metres), the Review team rejected the notion of all of the OPVs with the exception of the Yarrow 115 metre OPV III. This ship it considered alongside those falling into the Corvette/Light Frigate category.

The ships in the Corvette/Light Frigate category which they examined were the Yarrow 115 metre OPV III; Vosper Thornycroft Mk 18; 'M' Type (Netherlands); and F2000 (France). From this group of four, they noted that there would be no compatibility of weapons systems on the French ship with those in service with the RAN, and that, as the Yarrow OPV had been designed to merchant ship standards, the vessel would not have the same survivability as a conventional warship, yet would cost as much. The *Review* Committee also looked at two larger vessels—the Yarrow Type 23 Frigate and the Vosper Thornycroft Type 21, but felt that both vessels exceeded the capability requirements of the RNZN, and were too costly.

Proposals to the Joint Project Management Team

Following the signing of the Memorandum of Understanding, a Joint Project Management Team was set up in the Australian Department of Defence. Twelve proposals were initially received by the team, including three which had been reviewed by the RNZN. These 12 designs were the 'M' Type (Netherlands); Meko 200P (Germany); F2000 (France); the Italian *Maestrale*; Type 23, (Yarrow and Swan Hunter); Type 122 (Germany); *City*-class frigate (Canada); a modernised *Leander* (Vosper Thornycroft); *Nordkapp* 'coast guard frigate' (Norway); *Ulsan*-class frigate (Korea); and an airship proposal from Airship Industries. A reduced Type 122; Light Patrol Frigate, (Yarrow); Light Frigate, (Hall and Russell); and FFG-7, (Unysis Corporation) were also proposed.

In September a supplement to the original Memorandum of Understanding was signed, spelling out in greater detail the Collaborative Project Management Arrangements.[26] (That same month the New Zealand Labour Party's Annual Conference voted for withdrawal from the frigate project.) By October three designers had been selected to develop their designs further; these were Royal Schelde of Holland for the 'M' Type; Yarrows Shipbuilding for the Type 23; and Blohm and Voss for the Meko 200P. It was indicated by the respective Ministers of Defence that the three had been chosen from a total of 19 who had responded to the request for proposals, and that two of the three would be chosen to join consortia to bid for the tendering of the ships by March 1988. Later that month the Ministers announced that the 13 groups who had registered in the project would be invited to reconsider their original plans; and that from the final proposals two consortia would be invited to tender for the ships to be built in Australia.

By the end of 1987 the designs had been narrowed to two—the Type 'M' and the Meko 200. Blohm and Voss had not only paired with Australian Marine Engineering Corp (Amecon), based at Williamstown in Victoria, to build the Meko 200, they had purchased a 25 per cent shareholding. Royal Schelde meanwhile had paired with Australian Warship Systems (AWS), based at Newcastle in New South Wales. Both consortia presented their tenders to the Department of Defence on 19 January 1989, with an expectation that the successful bidder would be announced in August. New Zealand would at that time make its decision on whether or not to proceed with the project.

The Frigate Debate

The potential purchase of the ANZAC frigates was possibly the most strongly debated defence purchase of the century, generating significant public discussion and media coverage. It was clear almost from the outset of the frigate debate that the Government was intent on maintaining a blue-water capability, just as their predecessors had determined in 1983 and 1978. 'One key point is clear: as an island nation we need a navy,' said the Minister of Defence in a December 1988 discussion paper.[27] What was less clear was what form of vessel would replace the frigates and form the core of the RNZN's capability. At the centre of the debate were arguments about cost and utility. Members of the peace movement, politicians and service personnel, both serving and retired, produced a plethora of articles.

This debate about the frigates raged throughout 1988 and 1989, quickening pace as it went along. Members of the peace movement and others opposed to the frigate purchase were quick to raise their concerns, whilst the New Zealand Government seemed slow to rebuff its critics.

Lieutenant Commander David Davies (a retired RN and RNZN officer) was strongly critical of the Government's stance, and wrote a lengthy paper arguing against the frigate purchase, fundamentally on the basis of their lack of utility for New Zealand's needs.[28] He argued that the current four frigate force had been used in much the same way as frigates had been used throughout the 1950s, 1960s and 1970s, with an emphasis on overseas deployments and very little time on active service in New Zealand.[29] With the introduction of a new *Fisheries Act* in 1976, New Zealand had indicated its intention to declare a 200 mile Exclusive Economic Zone (EEZ) and, through his experience as Fisheries Controller at the Ministry of Agriculture and Fisheries, Davies felt certain that the resulting 1.4 million square miles of ocean had inadequate protection. Furthermore, he suggested it never could have as long as the deep-sea navy consisted of four frigates. His concern centred on reports that he had received from several different sources about the illegal activities of longliners fishing north of the Kermadecs. If these reports were accurate, he suggested, this activity would lead to significant depletion of stocks of juvenile fish:

> I am very strongly of the opinion that the deep-sea resources of the EEZ are not only under threat but are under attack and have been from the earliest days of the declaration of the 200mile Exclusive Economic Zone. I would also speculate that unless we get our defences in place to combat this situation very soon, irreparable damage will be caused.[30]

Davies was concerned that the RNZN should have sufficient vessels, of sufficient capability, to ensure adequate protection of New Zealand's EEZ, and to undertake the other tasks spelt out in the 1987 *Defence Review*. He suggested that six ships was the smallest possible working group, and discounted any meaningful role for the *Lake*-class patrol boats which were still nominally in Navy service at the time.[31] Whilst not specifying the type of vessel which would best meet New Zealand's needs, he suggested specifications which were similar to a well equipped OPV.

When the arguments against the ANZAC frigates were put forward by the peace movement, they drew attention to the highly sophisticated nature of the proposed vessels. 'What you see here is a very sophisticated modern warship, one of the most sophisticated armaments in the world today,' is how David Knox of the Meko 200 consortium described their proposed ship.[32]

In August 1988 Peace Movement Aotearoa published its case against the frigates. They highlighted that the issue should not just be seen as a military or Government spending issue, but also as a moral issue. They reflected the feeling that few in the Labour Government supported the project, and that if the project went ahead it would be 'purely for short term political reasons', and that 'most of the pressure is coming from the Australians whose shipbuilding industry is operating under-capacity and who are keen to build a defence export industry'.[33] The cost of the project was viewed as preposterous when spending was being squeezed in so many other crucial areas, and this was seen as the biggest single reason for not proceeding with the purchase. The point was carefully made that Treasury had emphasised that the need to reduce the deficit should take financial precedence over other Government objectives, and quoted an *Evening Post* editorial which had asked: 'Can the Government seriously be contemplating expenditure of nearly $2 billion, or more, at a time when gas reserves are being sold off to pay off part of the national debt?'[34] The RNZN was attacked for driving the project for historical reasons—a continuing wish for an anti-submarine capacity and an ANZUS role, and for pushing through a project 'they know isn't reasonable'.[35]

Peace Movement Aotearoa proposed a new concept navy, based also on six ocean-going vessels—two multi-purpose support ships, and four resource protection ships. Whilst it did not specify that these should be *Castle*-class vessels, they did comment that the approach from the Whangarei Engineering and Construction Co. to the Ministry of Defence, indicating that it had the capacity to build the *Castle*-class OPVs, should have been taken more seriously. They also suggested that the RNZN's priorities should be completely re-assessed, and that the current emphasis on anti-submarine warfare training be replaced by training for tasks which were actually needed. The following month, the Labour Party's Dunedin conference rejected the ANZAC ship program, and in October a Heylen poll conducted for the television program *Frontline* indicated that 76 per cent of the population was against the frigate deal.

The Government was slow to respond to criticism, but in October Tizard indicated that the Government was serious about the project, and that from then on criticism would be met with a Government publicity campaign. He began this himself with a presentation to the Tawa Rotary Club in November. Here he commented that the project had been very much in the media spotlight over the previous six months, and that it had been 'subject to an intense, emotional campaign by the New Zealand peace movement'.[36] Tizard wished to take the opportunity to 'blow the logic back into the debate'.[37] He went on to summarise the reasons for the purchase of the ANZAC frigates, highlighting the block obsolescence of the *Leanders*, and the requirements of the 1987 *Review*. In addition to the baseline characteristics, he emphasised the 'fitted for, but not with' weapons capability of the vessels, which would allow for 'equipment such as anti-ship missiles, towed array sonar, and close-in weapon systems (to) be fitted later if circumstances demand'.[38] Tizard emphasised that the frigates would come with an adequate level of equipment to protect themselves in low threat environments, responding to critics who had expressed concern that the vessels would have insufficient self-defence capabilities. Echoing his comments of the previous year, he once more stressed the resource protection, disaster relief and search and rescue, and the low-level military roles of the vessels, adding: 'If these ships never fire a shot in anger, then I shall be pleased, because throughout their lives these vessels will be busy performing peacetime roles.'[39]

Peace Movement Aotearoa and others had been highly critical of the cost of the frigates, but the Prime Minister sought to put the deal in perspective at a press conference in November 1988:

> Now I believe that people will gradually get the whole thing into context when they recognise that there is going to be no whipping out there and asking for $2 billion. That it is accommodated within the vote. That at the maximum projection it reaches $100 million a year. Now we are spending about $16.9 billion—not million, but billion dollars a year—on health, education and social welfare.[40]

Alexander Fry, the Assistant Editor of the *New Zealand Listener* also sought to give some sense of proportion to the debate when he commented:

> Aggregating the expenditure on ships over 20 years and coming up with a figure of $2 billion is itself a cheap shot. We could do the same for education ($60 billion in twenty years) and frighten ourselves off education. The fact is that New Zealand spends less on defence than most developed countries. Nobody wants to increase that dramatically, so we need intelligent debate before the final decision on ships is made.[41]

The debate was set to continue. The publication in December 1988 of *New Zealand Defence, Resource Management Review* (which was to become known as The Quigley Report) saw another step taken in the process of major state sector reforms, which were the hallmark of the Fourth Labour Government. Whilst many of the reforms suggested were focused on structural and fiscal concerns, opportunity was nonetheless taken to comment on the ANZAC frigate proposal

> The ANZAC ship project is seen by Australia as a litmus test of New Zealand's commitment to the trans-Tasman relationship. But in our view, this project involves much more than a decision to purchase or not to purchase frigates. The Australians have made it clear that if New Zealand opts out of the project, this will be regarded as raising questions not only about our defence credibility but about our overall commitment to closer relations with Australia generally. Failure to purchase the frigates will be interpreted by the Australians as an unwillingness on New Zealand's part to play a credible role as a defence partner in the region and signal that we are in the process of withdrawal from the 'community of friends'. It will also be interpreted as a clear sign that we are not

prepared to recognize that Australia is itself prepared to pay a substantial price in monetary and non-monetary terms to ensure that New Zealand remains a credible defence partner. The 'price' which Australia is prepared to pay has already been extended to a commitment that New Zealand will not find comparable ships which cost less from other sources.[42]

Also in December 1988, the Minister of Defence released a discussion paper which provided a clear critique of previous defence planning. It drew attention to the exaggerated view previously held of the direct threat to New Zealand, and the lack of planning for more likely contingencies. It highlighted equipment weaknesses in each of the services, and the lack of logistical resources needed for regional operations. As the paper discussed the specific requirements for the replacement of the frigates, it highlighted one of the biggest dilemmas facing the Government—that of specification: 'On the face of it our requirements are simple. For most of the situations New Zealand ships might expect to face the question of "threat" does not arise.'[43] Much criticism had been raised about the level of equipment with which the ships were to be fitted, driving the price. The Minister squarely raised the question of what self-defence capabilities were appropriate, pointing to the RNZN's recommendation for specifications close to those of NATO vessels; however, he indicated that the New Zealand Government would pursue a lesser specification. Nevertheless, he acknowledged that the vessels would have to be suitably equipped to take account of the possibility that they might be used in coming to the defence of Australia. The tenor of the times was reflected in the Minister's careful use of language: 'The question of a military role for these ships is not an easy area for public discussion.'[44] Nevertheless, the Minister once again spelt out the Government's commitment to maintaining New Zealand's naval forces so that the country could make a contribution to international security, and would not limit the RNZN to the role of coastguard:

> That is not the Government's intention. Current defence policy is founded on a wider regional view of New Zealand's defence interests and responsibilities. The decision to take the coastguard route would be difficult to reconcile with those commitments. In some circumstances it could prevent the use of New Zealand ships in situations where they were needed.[45]

Fears about the possible roles for the ships, and the possibility that they might draw New Zealand back into the ANZUS alliance remained strong, as did the opposition to the ships from within the Labour Party. The same month as the Minister released his paper, the Labour Party president, Ruth Dyson, commented that 'buying the frigates is not inevitable',[46] and later that month the Party was reported to be working on a package which would outline a range of cheaper alternatives to the Government.

The debate about the frigates continued to rage into 1989. The year began with a major seminar in Wellington, hosted by the Pacific Institute of Resource Management. Terence O'Brien, at the time Assistant Secretary at the Ministry of External Relations and Trade, ended his presentation thus:

> My conclusion is simply that the case for alternatives has not yet really been made. The case for proceeding along the road that the Government set two years ago remains undisturbed in terms of hard-nosed NZ national and external interests.[47]

Kevin Hackwell from Just Defence responded in his presentation:

> In his paper, Mr O'Brien stated that for anyone to argue for an alternative ship to the ANZAC frigate they would first have to rewrite the 1987 Defence White Paper ...
>
> It is Just Defence's belief that an accurate reading of the White Paper leads inevitably to the conclusion that New Zealand should be buying alternative ships that are very different from the ANZAC frigates.[48]

It *was* the case that the baseline characteristics approved by the Labour Cabinet on 15 July 1987 provided for a significantly higher level of capability than had been intended by the White Paper.[49] The baseline specifications set for the frigates to be acquired by New Zealand were exactly the same as those earlier set by the Australians for their own frigates:[50]

> New Zealand requirements could not be said to have been arrived at independently. Mr [Frank] O'Flynn agreed, pointing out that as the Minister of Defence who had signed the Memorandum of Understanding with Australia, he had had no control over the provision of baseline characteristics for the New Zealand ships.[51]

David Lange couched his observations about the ships specifications quite carefully when he addressed the 73rd Dominion Council Meeting of the Returned Services' Association on 12 June 1989:

> I think it is fair to say that the ANZAC design is toward the higher end of the spectrum envisaged by the 1987 White Paper. ... We set out in the 1987 Review the sort of characteristics we had in mind. ... It is no secret that we originally expected to end up with something more like a patrol boat.[52]

The Australians, however, were determined that New Zealand would not end up with just patrol boats.

What's in a name?

External sources of influence were quite apparent when it came to New Zealand narrowing down the alternatives, and deciding whether it would pursue the opportunity to join the Australians for the 'Australian Ocean Combat Ship' option. Those influences were both subtle and not so subtle, impacting from the time of the naming of the project, through to New Zealand's decision to proceed with purchasing two ANZACS:

> The glorious name of ANZAC (Australia–New Zealand Army Corps) of WW1 and WW2 fame has been adopted for the programme, despite perhaps being incongruous for a naval project, in that it is a traditional symbol of virtually all forms of military co-operation between the two countries.[53]

In June 1989, the Strategic and Defence Studies Centre at The Australian National University published a paper by former New Zealand Defence Secretary Denis McLean, and Desmond Ball, at the time Head of the SDSC, titled simply *The ANZAC Ships*.[54] They also sought to draw on the ANZAC connection in their support for the joint project:

> The ANZAC connection is, in terms of its breadth, intimacy and longevity, a rare phenomenon in the modern world. ... But a common cultural heritage overlapping geostrategic interests and a long tradition of close cooperation in the defence field mean that it would be folly radically to diverge in our regional defence policies and military programmes.[55]

The peace movement was not impressed:

> It's clear why the name 'ANZAC' was chosen for the new frigates. It's easier for the Navy to appeal to sentimental, backward-looking associations with past wars rather than think through what a real role in the South Pacific would mean today.[56]

Rear Admiral David Campbell was Secretary to the Australian Chief of Naval Staff at the time, and recalls the emphasis accorded to the ANZAC connection:

> Minister Kim Beazley was very keen in the early days of this project that NZ should be involved, and the more the better. He was of the view that every encouragement and assistance should be given to NZ to remain fully engaged in regional defence. All sorts of bad vibes were seen as coming from NZ after the ANZUS split. CNS knew full well from his political master that he had to exercise as much influence over his RNZN counterpart as possible. I recall special pressure being placed in the lead-up to and the conduct of the inaugural Western Pacific Naval

Symposium in '86. Part of the pressure was the selection of the name of the ship class.

Naming ships in the RAN is a very serious business. There is a Ships' Names Committee whose secretariat sifts and sorts the many hundreds of submissions that come in each year. Ship Associations are the most vociferous but ideas come from city councils and individuals as well. The Committee also looks after ships' badges and other naval heraldry. The new frigates attracted their share of nominations and *Tribal* and *Bathurst* class were prominent, after their WW2 and Korean forebears. In the end, CNS (Vice Admiral M.W. Hudson) personally decided on *Anzac*. Not only was she an honoured name in the RAN (with two predecessors) but there was very powerful symbology in the New Zealand connection and that, I believe, was uppermost in CNS's mind. (All of which, I'm bound to say, was against the expert and earnest advice of his Secretary, who urged *Tasman*. There had been an earlier ship of that name and the same NZ connection was there. Better, indeed, since it was a maritime connection and not just a khaki, Army thing. The Secretary still sulks over the decision. Naming ships is a very serious business indeed.)

In the event, the name was well received in NZ. But it's interesting that it was such a calculated thing. I don't know whether in fact it had any influence on the NZ decision, but it was certainly hoped and intended that it would.[57]

Admiral Hudson commented;

I cannot recall the precise date on which the term 'ANZAC' was made public, but its origin lay in a single cross Tasman telephone conversation between RADM Doug Domett and myself. We needed some symbolism that this would be a truly joint project and I suggested 'ANZAC' as one that politicians on both sides would be hard put to ignore. He agreed immediately and, as we anticipated, it was quickly taken up. This possibly was the easiest part of the whole project.[58]

Whether the naming of the project did or did not have any influence on the decision, Australian politicians were determined that they would have.

Throughout the two and a half years leading up to New Zealand's decision about whether to sign up to the ANZAC shipbuilding program, the Australians made it very clear that they wanted New Zealand involvement. As previously indicated, Kim Beazley made it apparent at the time of the release of the 1987 White Paper, that if New Zealand expected close cooperation with Australia it needed to maintain its blue-water and anti-submarine warfare capability.

In June 1988 Senator Gareth Evans reinforced the need for New Zealand to maintain its capability; 'New Zealand has to decide whether it wants the common security defence relationship with Australia. If it wants it, it's going to have to bring something worthwhile to that relationship.'[59] That something, as it turned out, was expected to be the purchase of up to four ANZAC frigates.

Whilst there were many denials of apparent Aussie bullying ('Senator Denies Australian Pressure Over Frigates' read a headline in the *New Zealand Herald*),[60] the leaking of a Cabinet paper to the press in November 1988 made clear what the Australians expected:

> The *Anzac* ship project, as Mr Beazley's own pet project, is something he is determined to see come to fruition. In Mr Beazley's view the region required the protection of a frigate force of some 20 ships. ... Without New Zealand's help Australia would be three or four ships short of this essential requirement. For these reasons Beazley stressed that Australia was willing to 'go overboard' to ensure that New Zealand got the ships at a price it could afford.[61]

Apart from the additional naval capability that the ANZAC ship project promised, the addition of a nominal extra four ships made the unit cost per vessel much more attractive for the Australians, who were determined to redevelop their ailing shipbuilding industry: 'In announcing the programme, the Australian Minister for Defence, Kim Beazley, described it as "the largest naval shipbuilding programme in Australia's peacetime history" and commented that "the navy is offering the salvation of Australia's shipbuilding industry".'[62]

For reasons of both regional security and domestic politics, Australia wished to ensure that New Zealand committed to the project. Perhaps this was another reason why Australia was willing to 'go overboard'. John Henderson commented: 'I worked a lot with Beazley's office. Beazley was determined we'd have four frigates. Why was he so keen? Because it was make-work for the Australian shipbuilding industry.'[63]

That same day in November 1988 that the Cabinet paper was leaked, David Lange was reported in the *Evening Post* as saying that New Zealand could not 'decouple' its security interests from those of Australia. He went on to say that:

> there was no 'real, practical, logical alternative' to the joint Anzac frigate building programme. If New Zealand was to withdraw from its joint commitment to Australia, it would 'tear apart the fabric of a relationship built up over the years that covers everything from politics, law and business to a whole mass of personal and family ties'.[64]

Earlier that day at a post-Caucus press conference, when asked if it was inevitable that New Zealand would be buying from Australia, the Prime Minister replied: 'Now as I've said before, we won't be buying anywhere else and I have the view that we will be buying ocean combat vessels from Australia.'[65]

The first two issues of the *New Zealand International Review* in 1989 contained a total of five articles, putting both sides of the issue—and again the question of alternatives was raised.[66] So what were the other alternatives?

The Other Alternatives

The alternative that had perhaps had most press space by the beginning of 1989 was the *Castle*-class, having been suggested by Robert Miles in 1983, and by Just Defence since 1985. This class of offshore patrol vessel had been designed for the Royal Navy, to provide a ship capable of resource protection, policing Britain's 200 mile EEZ. The first of class, HMS *Leeds Castle*, was completed in 1981. Together with its sister ship HMS *Dumbarton Castle*, the vessel quickly saw active service in the Falklands War, being despatched there in April 1982. The vessels gained a reputation for excellent sea-keeping, and an ability to embark helicopters in rough conditions. They were 81 metres long, and displaced 1630 tonnes. Maximum speed was 19.5 knots, with a range of up to 10 000 miles. Whilst the original vessels did not have hangars for helicopters, the manufacturers indicated that design provision had been made for hangar space. Just Defence made much of their relative cost and capability when comparing them with the ANZAC frigates, citing the Whangarei Engineering Company managing director Kelvin Hardie giving a price of about NZ$40 million for construction (admittedly without weapons systems), as opposed to NZ$500 million for an ANZAC frigate.[67]

The suggested alternative of the *Castle*-class was given short shrift by the Minister of Defence. In a press release issued in July, Tizard was again on the offensive, saying that the RNZN had never considered the *Castle*-class as replacements for the *Leanders*. They had been considered as replacements for the *Lake*-class patrol vessels prior to the development of the 1987 White Paper:

> The reference to the Navy wanting to purchase or build Castle class patrol vessels is based on information that was produced prior to the 1987 White Paper. ... What it comes down to is the Castle class vessel was a contender for the patrol craft and nothing else. ... The 1987 White Paper did not include a strong priority for replacement patrol craft so funding for it was never sought in the indicative capital equipment plan.[68]

The following month Captain Ian Bradley (Ret.) sent a letter to John Matthews, the Managing Director of Technic Group—an engineering firm in New Plymouth which was keen to see new vessels built in New Zealand—responding to a request for comment on the *Castle*-class. He compared it to the IS-86, a Danish designed ship which had by now entered the fray, championed by Harry Duynhoven,

Labour MP for New Plymouth. 'Either of these ships could have a role in the RNZN', commented Captain Bradley. Duynhoven had been intent to see that the IS-86 was chosen.

In March 1989, two months after the tenders for the ANZAC frigate project had been delivered, Peter Glente, the managing director of Svendborg Shipyard in Denmark visited New Zealand. Subsequently he wrote to Gerald Hensley (at that time in the Prime Ministers' Department) offering details of his firm's frigate—the 4000GRT (subsequently referred to as the IS-86). This was a vessel of 112 metres, with a displacement of 3500 tonnes, and a top speed of 21.4 knots. It had a large helicopter deck, hangar and a double skinned hull designed for breaking ice up to a metre thick. The vessel was offered at an indicative price of NZ$70 million, or on very favourable finance terms.

Glente made the point that four such ships had been ordered by the Royal Danish Navy, and the first would go to sea trials the following year. His letter was forwarded on to Tizard, to whom Glente subsequently wrote on 5 April 1989. By this time Svendborg had made contact with Duynhoven who was on holiday in Europe, and had persuaded him to visit the shipyard. Duynhoven returned in time for the central North Island Labour conference in Wanganui on 9 April, and helped ensure this conference voted against the ANZAC frigate proposal. He said:

> I believe we can get ships that can easily do what we require for New Zealand, and that are completely capable of coping with the seas, that are quite similar in size to the frigates, for less than $100 million.[69]

The Government was unmoved, with the Minister of Defence responding in May to a letter from John Matthews requesting a meeting, by saying that there was no good reason for having a meeting at that stage, and emphasising that the review of potential ships had been closed some two years previously. This response was reinforced by the Prime Minister the following month in a written reply, when he wrote: 'I would not at this point wish to pursue your offer to build "any type of frigate you require" here in New Zealand.'[70] Unwilling to take 'No' for an answer, the Danes sent a delegation in July, with Glente, and Captain Niels Ottesen of the Royal Danish Navy, but Lange still remained unmoved, once more 'pouring cold water' on the idea. Lange commented that the proposal could pass quite a high degree of commercial and technology risk on to the New Zealand Government, and he was also critical of a number of purported technical deficiencies with the vessel. Not to be deterred, Matthews wrote an open letter to the New Zealand Government on 20 August 1989, and on that same day Duynhoven also wrote to all Cabinet members, urging them to once more consider the IS-86. Duynhoven worked hard to use political influence to help shape a change in the decision-making process, but to no avail. David Lange made that very clear:

> Once we got the word that the frigates were the price of Australian goodwill, it became a matter of extracting the best possible deal. We mused publicly about alternative purchases. We acted coy about making up our minds. We haggled over details. But in the end we signed on the dotted line and bought two Australian ships.[71]

Later he was to comment:

> Yes, the other designs didn't get a look in; they didn't get a fair hearing. We went through the motions but I made it abundantly clear that there was no way those designs were going to succeed. I mean, I told Harry Duynhoven that he could produce them for nothing and we still wouldn't take them. ... We ended up being told they were going to be built in Australia. There is no doubt about that. ... But in 1988 I said we wouldn't be buying anywhere else and that was the truth of it. There was no point in mucking around—that was what we had to do.[72]

Geoffrey Palmer had a different perception:

> Yes Harry's ships were never a goer. But we had them analysed incessantly, and they were never going to be interoperable with the Australians. Interoperability with Australia is essential, and we needed to have the equipment to make that possible.[73]

Despite Duynhoven's protestations, by August 1989 the decision on the ANZAC frigates was well in train.

The Frigate Decision

August 1989 was a pivotal month in the ANZAC frigate decision-making process. Already in July, Tizard had indicated that the Government had the support of the majority of Cabinet ministers. This however was insufficient to save the political career of David Lange, who resigned as Prime Minister during the first week of August. The US-based publication *American Defense & Foreign Affairs Weekly* was quick to comment on the significance of this resignation, suggesting that it would seriously delay any decisions on the joint ANZAC program. They noted that Deputy Prime Minister Geoffrey Palmer, who was to take Lange's place, and Helen Clark, who was to become Deputy Prime Minister, had been quiet on the frigate issue, and would in all probability not support the proposal. They were unequivocal in their comments on Lange's departure: 'Lange, known for never being able to make a decision, took the easy way out—almost predictably, according to the cynics—and retired on "health grounds" before the tough frigate decision was to be made.'[74]

The Australians were going to wait no longer, and took the decision on 14 August to accept the Amecon consortium bid to build the Meko 200 derivative. The issue remained a potentially divisive one within the Labour Party with the

Party president, Ruth Dyson, reminding MPs that the national conference the previous year had rejected the frigate deal. Nonetheless three days later the Prime Minister, Geoffrey Palmer, publicly announced his support for the project, and on 7 September 1989 announced that the Government had decided in principle also to accept the Amecon tender and purchase two ANZAC ships, with an option for two more at a future date, envisaging 'a one-for-one replacement of the Royal New Zealand Navy's existing four ships'.[75] The Prime Minister acknowledged the influence of societal concerns, saying:

> And I know the Peace Movement will not be happy with it. But about that matter, what I want to say is that we have considered very carefully everything that the critics have put up. We've been through a lengthy consultative process about it. And we've come to the conclusion in the end that in the best interests of New Zealand we needed to commit to this project.[76]

He spelt out the cost of the project—$942 million for two ships and the total project, with project costs some 20 per cent less than Australian costs, as New Zealand was to carry a lower share of project and infrastructure costs. The sail away cost of each ship had been kept to NZ$299 million, with an overall project cost some 30 per cent less in real terms than the 1986 dollar price. In considering the question of whether to commit to two or four frigates, the Prime Minister added that the cost for a further two vessels would be an additional $867 million, 'but I should say to you that that decision does not need to be taken for nearly a decade'.[77]

A change of leadership in New Zealand clearly helped the decision-making process. According to John Henderson, 'in the first month after the change of leadership, Palmer drove the frigate decision through. ... It was the honeymoon period.'[78] Palmer himself acknowledged the place of both timing and political influence when facing the challenge of having the decision approved:

> When David Lange left the decision was far from a done deal. Timing is everything in politics and the change of leadership probably made things easier. Russell Marshall, Bob Tizard and myself were never in any doubt about the importance of acquiring the ANZACS. But I had to work extremely hard to get it through Caucus.[79]

The editorial in the *New Zealand Herald* the day after the decision was announced concluded that 'the country, meanwhile, will gratefully close the issue and await with interest a start on shipbuilding'.[80] Such sentiment subsequently proved unduly optimistic.

Implementation of the Project

How well did the decision to go ahead with the ANZAC project work in practice for New Zealand? What were the difficulties that had to be surmounted? There was a delay to the final signing of the heads of agreement contract for the two frigates, when it became apparent that the Australians wanted New Zealand to commit to pay for parts for the second, optional, pair of frigates. The contractual issues were eventually settled and the contract signed on 10 November 1989. That was not, however, the end of the matter.

The Labour Party had had a particularly difficult term of office between 1987 and 1990, with three Prime Ministers in that period. When it seemed clear that Labour was likely to lose the 1990 election, the then Prime Minister, Mike Moore, suggested that the frigate deal might be cancelled.[81] Trade-offs and judgement of political side effects were to the fore. As the secretary of the Metal Workers Union in Victoria said: 'It seems to me the statement of a man desperate for votes'[82] In the event, the votes were not forthcoming, and the Labour Party lost office. The uncertainty over the frigates though remained.

In July 1992 the Foreign Affairs and Defence Select Committee was critical of several aspects of the frigate project in its report which examined progress on the frigate contract. In particular, it was critical of Treasury not ensuring greater certainty in costs through foreign exchange management (by this time the dollar cost for the frigates had risen 31 per cent to $1219.5 million[83]), and they were concerned about whether industry participation levels would be met. The criticism brought a stinging rebuke from the Australian Shadow Minister for Defence, Alexander Downer: 'So much of this New Zealand report just sounds like whingeing. We offered New Zealand a situation where they could buy one frigate and practically get the other one free at the Australian taxpayer's expense.'[84]

New Zealand industry participation rates did improve, and the promised trade off of greater New Zealand involvement in Australian defence work contracts did begin to materialise. By July 1993 New Zealand companies had secured NZ$340 million of some NZ$800 million earmarked for New Zealand industry. By December 1995 that had only increased to NZ$382 million, but by February 1997 that amount had risen to NZ$470 million, placed with some 417 firms. Ultimately, the total value of work awarded to New Zealand firms was in excess of NZ$800 million.

Before any of this work was undertaken, the final weapons specification had to be decided. The November 1992 issue of *Asia Defence Journal* noted that, besides a vertical launch point defence missile system, each of the new frigates would carry an FMC Mk45 127mm gun under a technology transfer contract. The article began: 'It seems that the 'politics' of the 'ANZAC' frigate project are well in the past. There are no longer demonstrations against the frigate acquisition outside the New Zealand Parliament. ... It is now business as usual.'[85]

The 'politics' of the project had though been alive and well, and yet again it was necessary to contend with external sources of influence. Rear-Admiral David Campbell of the RAN again commented:

> I was the Australian Naval Attaché in Washington from January 1989–February 1992. It was an interesting and difficult time in US–NZ relationships. It's hard to appreciate now, but NZ was treated as a pariah state. Australia and New Zealand were bound by treaty over the frigate acquisition, i.e. something enforceable under international law. In effect, the RNZN would have an exact copy of the RAN ships—guaranteed by treaty. The catch was that nobody had consulted Uncle Sam. The RAN enjoyed a pretty-well unrestricted access to US technology, but it was a presumptuous assumption that this was transferable to NZ—yet this is precisely what was entailed in the treaty. Soon at issue were the Mk 49 radar, the Mk 41 vertical launch system, and the 5"Mk 45 Mod2 gun. The US was not at all happy to see these going to NZ and soon made its objection known.

> I initially knew nothing of this. The first thing I knew was when I was summoned by the Secretary of the Navy (The Hon H. Lawrence Garrett III) to explain myself. Why was I going around saying that the Kiwis ought to get/were going to get the radar? Why was I stirring up the Navy International Program Office clearly in the face of US policy? Apparently, that's what the NZ Defence Staff were doing—taking my name in vain. I pleaded innocence and outrage and Garrett accepted that. It happened again a few weeks later, this time over the Mk 41, and again later over the gun. Both times I was again summoned and Garrett was really getting annoyed, accusing me of duplicity, and worse. After the third occasion, I had a blazing row with my NZ counterpart and threatened serious consequences.

> A little later, I was being directed by Canberra to try to get the USN to relent but that was something that had to be done without NZ 'assistance'. Given all that had gone before, that was not easy to accomplish. Looking back upon it, I really can't decide whether I was a brilliant negotiator or whether Uncle Sam was simply making us all sweat a bit. But, either way, it was hard work. In the end, everything worked out alright.[86]

In the end, as far as delivery of the vessels was concerned, everything was resolved, though with several teething problems along the way.

The first steel was cut for ANZAC ship 01 in March 1992, and it was commissioned as HMAS *Anzac* on 18 May 1996. Ship 02 was to be HMNZS

Te Kaha. The first steel for the vessel was cut on 11 February 1993, and it was launched in Melbourne on 22 July 1995. The vessel's arrival in New Zealand, due for May 1997, was delayed after problems were discovered with the propulsion system—calcium buildup from marine growth on the bearings around the ship's propeller shafts. *Te Kaha* crossed the Tasman Sea in early July, and was commissioned into the RNZN on 22 July 1997. Whilst there were some modest delays in the build program, the early concerns about significant delays and cost over-runs in Australian yards were largely unfounded. The RNZN's second ANZAC, HMNZS *Te Mana*, had its first steel cut in February 1995 and was launched on 10 May 1997. Due for commissioning in March 1999, *Te Mana* was actually commissioned on 10 December 1999.

The ANZAC Frigates in Service

Since being commissioned, both ANZAC frigates have been working at a heavy operational pace. Initially there were some further equipment failures, with *Te Kaha* having its gas turbine propulsion unit replaced under guarantee in September 1998. The following July it once more had problems with the propshaft bearings, and these were replaced in dry dock in Devonport, Auckland. The final build problem was discovered when *Te Kaha* was once more in dry dock for its Annual Maintenance Period in May 2002. Microscopic cracks had been found in the bilge keels of several of the Australian ANZAC frigates, and similar cracks were discovered in *Te Kaha*. Design solutions were supplied by both the shipbuilder and the designer. *Te Mana* had fewer reported faults, a broken camshaft in one of the diesel engines being one of them.

'Fitted for but not with' was one of the catch-phrases of the time, leading to charges that the vessels would not be adequately armed. In 1996 the RAN instituted proposals to improve the warfighting capabilities of its vessels, with the introduction of its Warfighting Improvement Program, but the RNZN had no involvement. However, by the time the frigates were in service, there had been a number of additions to the weapon systems.

Original costings had been based on one medium calibre (76mm) gun and one battery of anti-aircraft missiles. Plans were underway at an early stage to fit refurbished Mk32 ship-launched torpedo tubes from the *Leanders*, and *Te Kaha* was fitted with the tubes from *Southland*. Provision was also made, and the vessels subsequently fitted with, the *Phalanx* close-in weapon support system, *Te Kaha* inheriting the system from HMNZS *Waikato*. The vessels were also designed to accommodate a towed array sonar system, with which they have been fitted from time to time.

Perhaps the most significant weapons upgrade was the addition of the SH-2G *Super Seasprite* helicopter, built by Kaman Aerospace in the United States. The maximum initial cost of four new-build helicopters was set not to exceed

NZ$274 million in 1997—a decade after the frigate debate had begun in earnest. Whilst the new aircraft were being built, Kaman loaned the RNZN four SH-2Fs from the US Navy, the first of these flying in February 1998. Ultimately a decision was taken to acquire five new aircraft. The first two new aircraft were accepted in Auckland on 18 August 2001, with deliveries of all five due to be completed by 2003. Despite their not inconsiderable cost, they arrived with a minimum of fuss.

These aircraft added significantly to the capability of the vessels. They were fitted with advanced radar and electronic support measures equipment, and could be fitted with *Maverick* air-to-surface missiles, or Mk 46 torpedoes or Mk 11 depth charges, considerably extending the reach of the frigates. By the time the ANZAC frigates were sent in harm's way, they were significantly better armed than might have been anticipated. A decade previously Lange had said:

> We're stuck with them now. Sometimes you win Lotto and sometimes you don't, and we didn't win on that one. I cannot see any justification for the frigates continuing. I just can't. I cannot get anyone in Defence to tell me what they're going to be used against. They cannot tell me how things of that specification are to be used. I come back to what we need. We need a logistic support ship to support the army and we need to have a platform to take to the Pacific for the sort of support work that needs to be done, but the frigates don't do it.[87]

However, history has once again proven that it is never possible to predict future defence scenarios. True to the original intent of having vessels that would undertake resource protection close to home, *Te Kaha* sailed to the Ross Dependency amidst much media publicity in February 1999, to deter Patagonian Toothfish poachers. Later that year though, she was dispatched to provide support to International Force East Timor (INTERFET), and then to the Persian Gulf to join the Multinational Interception Force. In June 2000 *Te Mana* was sent to Honiara in the Solomon Islands for guardship duties, and was relieved later that month by *Te Kaha*. Both vessels were to return—*Te Kaha* in September, and *Te Mana* in May 2001. For five months in 2002 *Te Mana* was deployed to Asia, returning in July, and *Te Kaha* left the following month for a four month tour of duty in Asia. During the return voyage to New Zealand *Te Kaha* was diverted to the Persian Gulf once more, to take part in Operation *Enduring Freedom*, and was replaced on station in February 2003 by *Te Mana*. During the 2002–2003 reporting year, the two frigates were programmed for a total of 251 days at sea. In fact they worked a total of 337 days at sea. In April 2004 *Te Mana* once more deployed to the Persian Gulf for a four month period of Maritime Interdiction Operations (MIO). During the 2003–2004 reporting year, the two frigates were programmed for a total of 287 days at sea, yet worked a total of 307 days.[88] This high level of activity continued to be maintained over the next four years. In the 2006–2007 reporting year programmed activity was to be a minimum of 272 days at sea, yet the two frigates achieved 290 sea days. In April 2008 *Te Mana* once more left Auckland for a five month period to undertake operations in the Persian Gulf as part of the Coalition Task Force. Such a pace of operations in distant waters was not what was envisaged as New Zealand's area of direct strategic interest when the ANZAC debate first began, and yet again reinforced the role of external sources of influence in the life of the ANZAC frigates.

Summary

The ANZAC frigate project was one of the most controversial major defence projects of recent times and the decision-making process long and tortuous. Indeed, when making the announcement about the decision to proceed with a two frigate purchase, Geoffrey Palmer said:

> I can't remember a decision which the Cabinet and the Caucus have gone into in greater detail and argued the merits of for longer or more extensively than this one. It is certain that these issues have been thrashed out in complete detail.[89]

History has proven the first assertion to be correct; undoubtedly the merits for and against were argued extensively. However a question mark was to remain over the second comment as will be examined in chapter 4, which focuses on the decision of whether or not to purchase a further ANZAC frigate.

In identifying key decision-making influences with regard to the purchase of the frigates, it is clear that the essential break-up of ANZUS and the need for closer relationships with Australia played a major part. Reflecting the pre-eminent place of external sources of influence, in his interview with Lange, Squadron Leader Forrest asked: 'If they said jump, would we jump?' Lange's response was: 'That's right, and that's the guts of it.'[90] However, Geoffrey Palmer disagreed, indicating both that he felt that the view of Australian pressure was overstated, and that there was a clear need for four frigates:

> I was Prime Minister and I can tell you they did not lean on us. I had one telephone call from Bob Hawke. But I didn't need any convincing. I felt then that we needed a four frigate Navy, and I still feel that now. I couldn't have lived with myself if we hadn't bought them. It never occurred to me that we'd not end up buying the four.[91]

Whilst it is apparent that the role of Australia was pivotal, how New Zealand saw its role in the world, public opinion, the judgement of political side effects and opportunity costs, and politics and political influence were also influential throughout the whole frigate debate and decision-making process. New Zealand's role in the world was redefined by New Zealand's anti-nuclear stance and the subsequent ANZUS split. The refocusing of New Zealand's Defence effort had to squarely face public opinion, which revolved around both the cost of the frigates, seen by some critics as obscenely expensive, and their warfighting potential which was strongly opposed by the peace movement. Taking account of politics and political influence, advocates such as Palmer were only too well aware of opposition among many in the Party to the purchase of the frigates. In undertaking its judgement of political side effects and opportunity costs, the New Zealand Government sought to make the decision more acceptable by emphasising the potential NZ$800 million worth of work which was forecast to come to New Zealand, and by highlighting the 'fitted for but not with' nature of the vessels. Other influencing elements which had a strong bearing were bureaucratic politics (evident particularly during the evaluation period, as the RNZN sought to maximise the utility of the vessels), whilst timing and political influence were acutely important as a final choice was made.

There were therefore a number of clearly identifiable factors that weighed in the decision to proceed with the purchase of the ANZAC frigates. Whether or not such factors were vital in other acquisition case study decisions will be explored in the following chapters.

ENDNOTES

[1] *Defence Review 1978*, Government Printer, Wellington, 1978, p. 23.

[2] *Defence Review 1983*, Government Printer, Wellington, 1983, p. 23.

[3] 'Navy going shopping overseas for frigate', *Evening Post*, 12 March 1979.

[4] Ministry of Defence Library vertical file , 'Leander frigates for NZ', news release, 19 October 1981, in Matthew Wright, *Blue Water Kiwis*, Reed Books, Auckland, 2003, p. 193.

[5] *Defence Review 1983*, p. 23.

[6] *Defence Review 1983*. [my emphasis]

[7] *National Business Review*, 28 November 1983, pp. 7–8.

[8] Wright, *Blue Water Kiwis*, p. 194. Admiral Sir Somerford Teagle had been part of the project team investigating the submarines, and added that another reason for not pursuing them was that 'they were a one-shot weapon'. (Personal interview, 20 September 2003)

[9] Dr Kate Dewes, Personal interview, 21 February 2004.

[10] *The Defence Question: a discussion paper*, Government Printer, Wellington, 1985, p. 3.

[11] Peace and Justice Forum, *An Alternative Defence Policy*, Wellington Labour Regional Council, Wellington, March 1985, p. 15.

[12] 'Just Defence', *Submission to the Defence Committee of Enquiry*, Just Defence, Wellington, February 1986, p. 30.

[13] *Dominion*, 10 May 1986 (The same conference was also reported to have called for the Government to pull out of ANZUS and lead the country into 'an acceptance of positive neutrality.')

[14] *Dominion*, 24 February 1987. [my emphasis]

[15] *Defence of New Zealand, Review of Defence Policy 1987*, Government Printer, Wellington, 1987, p. 14.

[16] *Defence of New Zealand, Review of Defence Policy 1987*, p. 16.

[17] *Defence of New Zealand, Review of Defence Policy 1987*, p. 35.

[18] David Baxter, 'Beazley did for Labour what Hayden didn't', *National Business Review*, 13 March 1987, p. 13.

[19] Squadron Leader A.J. Forrest, 'The Anzac Frigate Decision: The Rationale of David Lange', No. 34 Staff Course, Whenuapai, October 1993, p. 3.

[20] R.J.L. Dicker 'Renewing the Australian surface fleet', *International Defence Review*, vol. 20, no. 7, July 1987, pp. 887–88.
[21] *Evening Post*, 9 September 1987.
[22] Office of the Minister of Defence, Press release, Wellington, 18 September 1987.
[23] Gordon Campbell, 'The Frigates of Oz', *New Zealand Listener*, 21 November 1987, p. 38.
[24] *RNZN Replacement Surface Combat Ships*, Report of the Defence Review Officials Committee, Wellington, 18 November 1986, p. 4.
[25] *Memorandum of Understanding between the Government of Australia and the Government of New Zealand Concerning the Collaboration in Acquisition of New Surface Combatants*, 6 March 1987.
[26] *Supplement to the Memorandum of Understanding between the Government of Australia and the Government of New Zealand Concerning the Collaboration in Acquisition of New Surface Combatants*, 9 September 1987.
[27] Minister of Defence, The Rt. Hon. Robert James Tizard, *The Naval Question*, Ministry of Defence, Wellington, December 1988, p. 8.
[28] Lieutenant Commander David Davies, RNZN (Ret.), *The Case Against the New Zealand Frigate*, David Davies, Karori, 1988.
[29] Davies, *The Case Against the New Zealand Frigate*, p. 5.
[30] Davies, *The Case Against the New Zealand Frigate*, p. 7. In 2003 the world was barely moved by the revelation that 90 per cent of the world's large fish stocks had been destroyed. Research in Canada, undertaken by Ransom Myers (fisheries biologist) and Boris Worm, published in *Nature* magazine, confirmed that the world's fish stocks were under attack, and that irreparable damage would be caused unless immediate measures for conservation were put in place. The resource base was said to have been reduced to less than 10 per cent of what it had been in 1950, 'not just in some areas, not just for some stocks, but for entire communities of these large fish species from the tropics to the poles'. *National Geographic News*, 15 May 2003, available at <http://news.nationalgeographic.com/news/2003/05/0515_030515_fishdecline.html>, accessed 12 December 2008.
[31] The *Lake*-class patrol boats had been another compromise decision which left the RNZN with a boat which was totally unsuited for New Zealand waters. Designed as an inshore craft to work out to a 12 mile limit, its short length meant that it was incapable of dealing adequately with the rough sea states so common around New Zealand, and caused seasickness and injuries even amongst experienced sailors. Four craft had been bought in 1975, HMNZS *Pukaki*, *Rotoiti*, *Taupo* and *Hawera*. HMNZS *Pukaki* and *Rotoiti* were placed in reserve in the mid-1980s and they were all eventually unceremoniously disposed of in 1991.
[32] David Knox, AMEC consortium, Presentation to the Wellington MoD frigate industry briefing, 18 May 1988, cited in Nicky Hager, *The case against new frigates*, Peace Movement Aotearoa, Wellington, August 1988, p. 4.
[33] Hager, *The case against new frigates*, p. 1.
[34] *Evening Post*, 15 April 1988, in Hager, *The case against new frigates*, p. 1.
[35] Hager, *The case against new frigates*, p. 6.
[36] Minister of Defence, The Rt. Hon. Robert James Tizard, Address to Tawa Rotary Club, 1 November 1988.
[37] Tizard, Address to Tawa Rotary Club.
[38] Tizard, Address to Tawa Rotary Club, p. 4.
[39] Tizard, Address to Tawa Rotary Club, p. 7.
[40] David Lange, Post Caucus Press Conference. Extracts. 3 November 1988 in. Forrest, 'The Anzac Frigate Decision: The Rationale of David Lange', p. 11.
[41] Alexander Fry, Editorial, *New Zealand Listener*, 3 December 1988.
[42] Strategos Consulting Limited, *New Zealand Defence, Resource Management Review 1988*, Wellington, 4 December 1988, pp. 234–35.
[43] Tizard, *The Naval Question*, p. 7.
[44] Tizard, *The Naval Question*, p. 9.
[45] Tizard, *The Naval Question*, p. 10.
[46] *New Zealand Herald*, 7 December 1988.

47 Pacific Institute of Resource Management, *The Anzac Frigate Debate*, Pacific Institute of Resource Management Inc., Wellington, February 1989, p. 13.

48 Pacific Institute of Resource Management, *The Anzac Frigate Debate*, p. 32.

49 Forrest, 'The Anzac Frigate Decision: The Rationale of David Lange', p. 4.

50 Policy Committee on Foreign Affairs and Security of the New Zealand Labour Party, *Opportunity for New Vision*, Response to Conditional Proposal on ANZAC frigates submitted to Policy Committee by Prime Minister Geoffrey Palmer, Minister of Defence Robert Tizard and Foreign Minister Russell Marshall. Unpublished typescript, 5 September 1989, p. 7.

51 PACDAC [Public Advisory Committee on Disarmament and Arms Control] Minutes, 30 May 1989.

52 David Lange, Address to the 73rd Dominion Council Meeting of the Returned Services' Association, 12 June 1989, p. 8, cited in Forrest, 'The Anzac Frigate Decision: The Rationale of David Lange', p. 4.

53 Ezio Bonsignore, 'The ANZAC Programme: Frigates for "Down Under"', *Military Technology*, vol. 13, no. 3, 3/89, p. 17.

54 Denis McLean and Desmond Ball, *The ANZAC Ships*, SDSC Working Paper no. 184, Strategic and Defence Studies Centre, The Australian National University, Canberra, June 1989.

55 McLean and Ball, *The ANZAC Ships*, p. 2.

56 Hager, *The case against new frigates*, p. 4.

57 Rear-Admiral David Campbell, Correspondence, 15 September 2003.

58 Admiral Michael W. Hudson, Correspondence, 15 May 2004.

59 *Evening Post*, 26 June 1988.

60 *New Zealand Herald*, 23 September 1988.

61 David Lange, Leaked Cabinet paper cited in the *Dominion*, 3 November 1988.

62 Bonsignore, 'The ANZAC Programme: Frigates for "Down Under"', p. 19.

63 John Henderson, Personal interview, 21 August 2003.

64 *Evening Post*, 3 November 1988.

65 David Lange, Post Caucus Press Conference, cited in Forrest, 'The Anzac Frigate Decision: The Rationale of David Lange', p. 7.

66 *New Zealand International Review*, vol. XIV, nos. 1 & 2, 1989.

67 Kevin Hackwell, 'The Case for Corvettes', *New Zealand International Review*, vol. XIV, no. 2, 1989, p. 9. In a subsequent letter to Kevin Hackwell, (21 August 1989), Alastair Lambie, the Managing Director of A&P Appledore (Aberdeen) Ltd (who had purchased the assets of Hall and Russell) indicated that a standard *Castle*-class vessel without weapons fit would cost £16 million; if fully fitted with significant ASW capability, it would cost £127 million.

68 Office of the Minister of Defence, *Press Release*, Wellington, 31 July 1989.

69 *New Zealand Herald*, 10 April 1989

70 Letter from David Lange, Prime Minister, to J.B. Matthews, 6 June 1989.

71 David Lange, *Nuclear Free—The New Zealand Way*, Penguin Books, Auckland, 1990, p. 167.

72 David Lange interviewed by Squadron Leader A.J. Forrest. See Forrest, 'The Anzac Frigate Decision: The Rationale of David Lange', p. A-2.

73 Rt. Hon. Sir Geoffrey Palmer, Telephone interview, 2 May 2005.

74 'Lange's Resignation Delays ANZAC Frigate Design', *Defense & Foreign Affairs Weekly*, vol. XV, no. 32, p. 1 and pp. 4–5.

75 Geoffrey Palmer, *Press Statement*, 7 September 1989.

76 Rt. Hon. Geoffrey Palmer, Post-Caucus Press Conference, Wellington, 7 September 1989, p. 2.

77 Palmer, Post-Caucus Press Conference, Wellington, 7 September 1989, p. 4.

78 John Henderson, Personal interview, 21 August 2003.

79 Palmer, Telephone interview, 2 May 2005.

80 *New Zealand Herald*, 8 September 1989.

81 *New Zealand Herald*, 16 October 1990.

82 *New Zealand Herald*, 16 October 1990.

83 *New Zealand Herald*, 1 July 1992.

84 *Evening Post*, 8 July 1992.

[85] P. Lewis Young, 'The Progress of the Australian and New Zealand Navies "ANZAC" Frigate Project', *Asia Defence Journal*, vol. 18, no. 11, November 1992, p. 35.
[86] Rear-Admiral David Campbell, Correspondence, 15 September 2003.
[87] Squadron Leader A.J. Forrest, 'The Anzac Frigate Decision: The Rationale of David Lange', p. A-5.
[88] New Zealand Defence Force, *New Zealand Defence Force Annual Report 2004*, NZDF, Wellington, p. 63.
[89] Palmer, Post-Caucus Press Conference, Wellington, 7 September 1989, p. 2.
[90] Forrest, 'The Anzac Frigate Decision: The Rationale of David Lange', p. A-4.
[91] Palmer, Telephone interview, 2 May 2005.

Chapter 3

Oranges and Lemons—HMNZS *Charles Upham*

As long ago as the 1970s the need had been identified for the purchase of a sealift ship to support the implementation of New Zealand's defence and foreign policy in the South Pacific, and to support New Zealand's involvement in UN operations. The proposed ship was to have an ice-strengthened bow for Antarctic operations, and helicopter facilities, but the cost at the time was seen as putting such a vessel beyond New Zealand's reach. The 1978 *Defence Review* noted the need for 'a general purpose logistic support capability. The adaptation of a suitable commercial vessel…is not discounted'.[1]

The need for a Logistic Support Ship (LSS) continued to be recognised, and the 1987 White Paper drew attention to the need to purchase some form of sealift vessel for New Zealand forces as an essential part of the New Zealand Defence Force (NZDF)'s ability to mount effective operations in the region. With the impending withdrawal of the New Zealand battalion from Singapore, and the clear shift in focus to the South Pacific signalled in the White Paper, the Army's Ready Reaction Force (RRF) had no means of moving quickly around either the Pacific or to Southeast Asia—there was insufficient transport to deploy and sustain a battalion group away from New Zealand. The White Paper commented: 'A further and essential part of our ability to mount effective operations in the region is the purchase of a logistic support ship—probably a converted merchant ship.'[2]

Subsequent studies undertaken in 1988 suggested that a purpose-built LSS, initially with a displacement of up to 12 000 tonnes, be built. The vessel would have the capacity to transport up to 200 troops and heavy equipment, and be capable of unloading onto a beach, or onto conventional wharves.[3] Such a specialist ship, with landing craft and helicopters, could have cost up to NZ$240 million, and was ultimately seen as exceeding the necessary credible minimum.[4]

The 1991 Defence White Paper defined three security scenarios in which there might be a call for a limited deployment of forces in the South Pacific region: the need for evacuation of New Zealand nationals; a terrorist threat; or requests for assistance to respond to threats to law and order. The desired capability to respond to these tasks was seen as being able to deploy a sizeable force to those islands which have seats of government or significant centres of population. Once again the gap in transport and force projection capabilities was identified, and a call was made to review possible ways of closing the gap.

The 1991 White Paper did set up a number of reviews and one of these saw the need for a vessel that would primarily move troops and equipment around the Pacific, and be available to provide support for peacekeeping operations. The *Air and Sea Transport Review* team concluded that there was no doubt that a military sealift capacity was a core capability element if the NZDF was to meet the defence tasks specified in the White Paper.[5] The team had a clear concern about the limitations of chartering, observing that the time taken for a vessel to be delivered to Auckland could not be quantified with any certainty. With few suitable vessels available for charter in Australia, New Zealand or the South Pacific, it was likely that a vessel would have to come from Europe, taking 36 days to get here. Whilst the *Review* team noted that there appeared to have been some reservations about the need for military shipping for strategic transport, they were of the opinion that 'sea-lift is essential; otherwise the lack of a credible deployment capability should call into question the New Zealand Army's present force structure'.[6]

The new vessel was to be capable of carrying supplies to the Islands in times of civil emergency, or to evacuate New Zealand citizens at times of civil unrest. The review saw a sealift ship deploying up to a company of personnel with their equipment and supplies, to provide reconstruction, rehabilitation or medical assistance. The vessel would also be expected to be able to provide sealift to offshore islands, especially the Chatham Islands, when other transport was unavailable, and to maintain the continuity of Cook Strait transportation between the North and South Island when other services were restricted or were unavailable. Importantly, the type of gap to be filled was re-defined, and it was suggested that the less ambitious task of operating into those ports which had wharf facilities might be sufficient. It was ultimately recommended 'that the NZDF obtain a military sealift ship (MSS) based on a commercial medium size roll on/roll off ship as a matter of priority'.[7] This chapter traces the events that led to the purchase of such a ship, HMNZS *Charles Upham*, then its subsequent lease and ultimate sale.

Evaluating the Alternatives

During 1991, the *Review* team considered a number of possible vessel types as solutions. They acknowledged that a *Mercandian* 1500 vessel could deploy 50 per cent of the vehicles and stores required by the RRF, and considered this size of vessel as the credible minimum. However, they believed the purchase of a vessel such as the *Union Rotorua* would be a more attractive option. Whilst it was somewhat larger than the minimum requirement, the *Review* team felt it would be 'an economical and effective solution to the NZDF's *greatest current capability deficiency*'.[8] It noted that the *Union Rotorua* almost exactly matched the dimension specification to deploy the RRF vehicles and equipment. The *Union Rotorua* was one of the first vessels to be considered for the task of providing logistic support. This vessel could have deployed all of the RRF's vehicles and equipment in one lift. Admiral Sir Somerford Teagle recalled seeing the vessel in Sydney Harbour, looking large and imposing. He said to his Australian Defence Force (ADF) counterpart, 'that could be our new Logistic Support Ship',—though personally he was not wedded to any particular vessel type, more the capability any such vessel would bring to the NZDF. The *Review* team also saw the vessel as imposing, and thought that the perception of the size of the ship might be its only real disadvantage. With a length of 205 metres and a maximum laden weight of up to 24 000 tonnes, the ship did have a large profile. Whilst in international shipping terms it was only a medium-sized vessel, it was amongst the larger ships to visit New Zealand ports regularly, and would have been by far the largest ship operated by the Royal New Zealand Navy (RNZN):

> There was a perception that she was too big—I don't know why. There was no issue of her being too big in the maritime sense. As for the requirement that the chosen vessel should fit the Calliope Dock, that was just one of many criteria. I don't believe that this on its own would be sufficient reason to reject the *Union Rotorua*.[9]

In all of the documentation that I have reviewed, there is no clear, rational explanation as to why the *Union Rotorua* was dropped from the short-list. The vessel was gas-turbine powered, and it was noted that the prime mover would soon need an overhaul.[10] However, its sister ship the *Union Rotoiti* was diesel-electric, and Teagle saw no reason why the *Union Rotorua* could not have been easily converted.

The estimated through life costs were NZ$10.02 million per year, as opposed to an estimated NZ$7.1 million for a Mercandian 1500, but the *Review* team were clear that the greater capability, capacity, speed and flexibility offset the increase in operating costs.[11] Perhaps with the benefit of hindsight, the *Review* team's observation of the vessel's apparent lack of problems as regards stability or motion at sea with a light load should have been given more weight. Of particular note was the *Review* team's observation about a Mercandian vessel already plying New Zealand's waters. *The Spirit of Freedom*, a Mercandian 610 had been trading between Auckland and Lyttleton for four years and the *Review* team noted that, 'designed for trade in the North Sea, this vessel, unless fully laden, is very uncomfortable at sea in the South Pacific'.[12] These were to be words of portent.

The 1997 NZDF Report, *HMNZS Charles Upham: Review of acquisition and proposed conversion*, went into some detail about the steps which led up to the purchase of HMNZS *Charles Upham*. In summary, the steps reported to have been undertaken were as follows:

1. In November 1991, the NZDF undertook an appraisal of the roll on/roll off vessel *Union Rotorua*. The ship was available for sale, and the *Review* team

considered that, with suitable modifications, it would provide the minimum capacity required for sealift operations. In May of 1992 Cabinet authorised the investigation of costs to bring the *Union Rotorua* into service.

2. In June 1992 further studies within NZDF led to a refinement of the requirements for a new vessel, and the *Union Rotorua* was considered to be slightly too large for the these new requirements, and Cabinet authorised comparison with at least one other vessel.

3. In July 1992 the shipbroking firm of Rugg and Co. in the United Kingdom was engaged to investigate suitable ships on the second-hand market. Defence staff received a total of 33 available ships in 20 different classes, which they narrowed down to 21 ships in 9 classes, plus the *Union Rotorua*. In October 1992 this list was further refined down to 4 classes, and the option of building a new ship was considered, with yards in Korea, Poland and Spain being asked for indicative prices. (The Polish yard was slow to respond and not pursued further.)

4. In November a team of Defence personnel inspected the four second-hand class of ships, and held discussions with the Spanish and Korean shipyards, with the outcome being that either a new or second-hand ship would be suitable. Of the second-hand ships, the Mercandian 2-in-1 class was the preferred option.

5. In December 1992 BMT Defence Services Limited in the United Kingdom was selected to review Defence's estimates for the conversion cost for a Mercandian 2-in-1 class vessel, comment on the practicality of the conversion, and also to carry out comparisons with a new vessel. During that month a specification was also drawn up which was to be used for the evaluation and subsequent purchase of the chosen vessel (see Appendix 3, User Requirement). At the end of January 1993 BMT Defence Services concluded that a conversion was feasible, but indicated that the vessel class failed to meet specification in a number of areas including a narrow quarter ramp and low deck height, and that stabiliser tanks would be required for helicopter operations. There were also concerns about vessel motion. In addition it commented that there was very little difference in cost between a second-hand and new vessel.

6. In April 1993 Defence sought Cabinet approval for the purchase of either a second-hand or a new vessel. Cabinet, though, decided to defer a decision until it had reviewed the forthcoming Defence Consolidated Resource Plan. The 1997 *NZDF Review* notes that officials were surprised that, at this point, Cabinet stressed that the main rationale for acquiring the vessel was to be able respond to natural disasters and other emergency situations in the South Pacific region. Cabinet at this time also invited the Minister of Defence to investigate the possibility of cooperating with Australia in the financing and use of a military sea-lift ship.

HMAS *Tobruk*

In late 1993, the Australian Government offered to lease the heavy landing ship, HMAS *Tobruk*, to the NZDF. In November a brief was developed for the Chief of Naval Staff to assist with discussions. It was noted in the brief that there were some important shortfalls against the user requirement, most notably that the ship had only half of the cargo capacity of a Mercandian vessel, and that the vessel required significantly more crew—144 as against 65. (This was potentially a concern for the RNZN at the time, though it was noted that the RFA operated with a crew of 65, so some personnel savings were likely.) Discussions were held with several senior Royal Australian Navy (RAN) officers during the period 14-18 February 1994 and 'the general feeling was that the ADF wished to lease the vessel to New Zealand rather than have us buy it'. Significantly, it was stated that 'the RAN ... obviously do not wish to be put in a position where they make an offer which we might turn down'.[13]

The NZDF assessed its suitability and initially was supportive of pursuing this option. The *Tobruk* still had significant cargo and personnel carrying capacity, with the ability to land resources across the beach. However, it was apparently not clear at this stage what the costs involved would actually be.[14] Nevertheless, it was recommended that this option be pursued, and on 11 May 1994 the Australian Minister for Defence, Senator Robert Ray wrote to his New Zealand counterpart, Warren Cooper, with a firm offer of a lease for the ship. Later that month, Cabinet gave approval for discussions to proceed with a view to acquiring the vessel, which Australia would retain some access to each year. At the time, an officer, not part of the team claimed: 'The team is going through the motions. We will have a look at her, but the politicians have already decided to take her.'[15] Senior Defence personnel agreed that it would be politically beneficial for the New Zealand Government to take the *Tobruk*, but the *Tobruk* was described as a 25 year old ship in a 10 year old body. An engineering officer was reported to say: 'The country will pay dearly. She's an orphan, so parts will be expensive. She will be a nice little earner for the dockyard's new operators.'[16] However, a meeting held on 9 June with representatives from the Ministry of Defence and the NZDF, agreed that the *Tobruk* offered an acceptable interim solution to meet the MSS requirement; and that the aim should be to obtain a Cabinet decision in time to agree a lease with the Australians in Darwin on 28–29 July 1994.

Within less than two weeks the situation seemed to have markedly changed. In a Position Paper, approved by the Secretary for Defence, attention was drawn to the original reasons why agreement had been given for pursuing the lease of the *Tobruk*. Of some importance was the continuing requirement by the ADF for the capabilities of a New Zealand crewed and operated *Tobruk* for exercises and contingencies, which was an important Closer Defence Relations (CDR) consideration. The avoidance of capital costs was also seen as an advantage, though not decisive.

In the event, on 21 June 1994 the Australians advised that they wished to sell the *Tobruk*, offering a deferred purchase or lease to purchase option. (In a Minute to the Cabinet Subcommittee, the price of A$58 million was mentioned as the current value of the ship.[17]) It was observed that the purchase of the *Tobruk*, based on the Australians having no further use for it, had no inherent advantages for New Zealand. This removed any CDR benefits for New Zealand and, coupled with an availability date which kept slipping, Defence in New Zealand decided that the purchase was not the right decision. A negotiating team was still nevertheless due to leave for Australia; they were advised clearly by the Secretary of Defence that they were 'to ensure that our Australian colleagues have a full appreciation of the new position in respect of acquiring an MSS capability ... and that other than for CDR considerations, New Zealand has no interest in *Tobruk*'.[18]

In the Alliance Report of 1998, *The Biggest Lemon Ever To Leave Auckland*, it was reported that New Zealand was offered the vessel at the then cost of about NZ$18.57 million. The Audit Office was told by the NZDF that while the *Tobruk* was offered in May 1994 at a price of A$7 million, plus a quantity of spares at a further A$7 million, these were preliminary estimates only and subject to negotiation.[19]

Rear-Admiral David Campbell was at the time Deputy Chief of Naval Staff (DCNS) in the RAN. His recollection was that 'the Minister said the Kiwis could have the ship for nothing'. Campbell went on to say that the principal reason was that whilst the RAN could no longer afford the *Tobruk* (with two replacement ships arriving), the Minister 'was very anxious that her capability not be lost to the alliance in the SW Pacific'.[20] So keen was Senator Robert Ray on retaining the capability that he was prepared to give the ship away. With an offer like that on the table, coupled with the very strong political pressure Ray was exerting, the New Zealand Government had to examine the proposal very seriously. The planned visit mentioned above went ahead, and Campbell received an official visit from representatives of the RNZN and the MoD:

> It was plain to me from the outset that they had no intention of taking the ship. Before the visit there had been some trans-Tasman enquiries and preliminary negotiations. I recall one such item being 'Would we include the ship's inventory of spare and repair parts?' Reluctantly, I agreed. They were probably worth more than the ship herself, but I understood the Minister wanted the transfer to go ahead and so I was prepared to forego the revenue. In my office, they wanted to know (actually it was stronger than a question; it was more like a demand) whether Australia would pay for her next scheduled refit? Absolutely

not, I said—an answer that they knew perfectly well was the only possible one. It was evident to me that they were genuinely worried about her relatively high manning and the cost of the forthcoming refit, but at the same time they were desperate to get other reasons why they should not accept her. The negotiations, on their part, were perfunctory and dutiful and I never thought that they were sincere.[21]

In November 1997 the then New Zealand Minister of Defence spoke to this decision:

After several months of discussion the RAN recommended that New Zealand should buy the vessel, but that it would not be available for two years (i.e. by 1996) and the cost of this would be considerably higher than New Zealand had anticipated. In view of this, and taking into consideration the very high operating costs for the vessel, the NZDF determined that it was not worth continuing with further discussions.[22]

In reviewing the correspondence of the time, it seems as if there was an initial willingness to seriously consider the *Tobruk* despite the vessel's shortcomings. As noted previously, the potential benefits to CDR were seen as being important: 'On balance we considered the CDR contribution New Zealand could make by taking on the *Tobruk* were worth these disadvantages.'[23] In this minute, Gerald Hensley, the Secretary of Defence, commented that leasing the *Tobruk* was seen as an acceptable interim trade-off solution because it meant New Zealand could have made a significant contribution to CDR. The change from a lease proposition to a possible purchase was seen to change that considerably. Yet two elements do not quite fit: Rear-Admiral Campbell's recollection that the Minister was willing to give the ship away to maintain the capability in the region (which was confirmed by Dick Gentles—'Yes, they did offer it to us free of charge');[24] and Campbell's response to my question as to whether there would have been a likely ongoing CDR requirement? 'With *Tobruk* do you mean, whether donated, leased or sold? Yes, most certainly.'[25]

Were bureaucratic politics an issue with the *Tobruk*? The memo from the Secretary of Defence was very clear in the message it sent to officials who were going to Australia. Or was the *Tobruk* really a vessel that was going to be too expensive to run and maintain? Undoubtedly the *Tobruk* would have been an expensive vessel to man and operate, costing perhaps NZ$4 million per annum more in operational costs. This is though quoted as a maximum cost, and again like the *Union Rotorua* it was observed: 'The *Tobruk* can do many things that even a converted *Charles Upham* will not be able to.'[26] It was suggested by the Alliance Party in 1998 that 'the real additional operating costs had we purchased the *Tobruk* would probably have come in at much less than this figure'.[27] The Alliance Party went on to suggest that, in retrospect, not proceeding with the acquisition of the *Tobruk* was probably a mistake. The Audit Office report argued with these sentiments, saying that there would have been a delay with the vessel entering NZDF service; that further delays would have been incurred because of the necessity to refit the engines; and that, as with the *Charles Upham*, there was no guarantee that funds would be available to complete the necessary work. Nevertheless, despite the decision not to take the *Tobruk*, the vessel has continued to prove useful in combined regional operations 'turning up like that nautical nemesis the *Flying Dutchman*'[28] —providing logistic support in the Bougainville operation in 1994, subsequently visiting Wellington on 30 May 1998 to unload Army equipment used in Bougainville, and taking New Zealand troops to East Timor in 1999. In 2005 the vessel transported troops and equipment to Iraq. Although concerns had been raised in 1994 about the ship's longevity, the HMAS *Tobruk* was still in service in 2009.

HMNZS *Charles Upham*

The prospect of a LSS had been under consideration for 15 years by the time Defence asked Cabinet in 1993 for approval to purchase a vessel. However, at this point the consultants preparing the 1997 *Review* commented that they understood that the Prime Minister's Department had given indications that the Military Sea-lift Ship project should not be promoted. Officials prepared a new report for Cabinet but it wasn't considered because of the forthcoming 1993 General Election.

In July 1994 the decision was made within Defence to proceed with the purchase of a second-hand ship. Four issues were identified which led to this decision; a vessel could be acquired quickly (it was already almost three years since the first potential vessel had been inspected); cashflow would be improved; no large initial outlay would be necessary, and the smaller sum spent and shorter lifespan of this initial ship would allow for experience to be gained which would better inform requirements over the longer term. The Ministry then asked the broker who had previously handled the earlier enquiry to update them on the availability of Mercandian 2-in-1 class vessels, rather than review the market again. Following protracted discussions the *Mercandian Queen II* became available, approval was sought from Cabinet to purchase the vessel and this approval was given on 28 November 1994.

In the supporting documentation to the Cabinet Subcommittee from the Minister of Defence, the caution was made: 'If we decide against sealift, the Australians could perceive us as not being serious about maintaining a credible defence effort.'[29] In a further memorandum to the Cabinet Subcommittee dated 22 November 1994, the Minister of Defence spoke to Treasury's concern about the financing of the proposed acquisitions that were to be discussed at Cabinet, including the MSS. He noted that Treasury acknowledged that the MSS would be a flexible and desirable asset and that, in Treasury's view:

the decision on whether to purchase a ship involves a trade-off between three key factors:

Cost: A fully capable MSS costs $60m being $25 million for the initial capital and an additional $34m required to upgrade for the ship (sic) for carrying troops and helicopter. The additional operating costs of $7m annually are significant. No compensating or offsetting capability is proposed. The operating costs are to be met by unspecified internal efficiencies and adjustments.

Risk: The likelihood of a major deployment of military forces without sufficient warning time to charter commercial shipping is a critical factor in assessing the case for the MSS.

Priority: Ministers will need to assess whether providing this new capability should proceed when there are other pressures on defence resources to maintain existing capabilities such as the *Orion* fleet.[30]

Cabinet approved the expenditure of up to NZ$26 million for acquisition and initial modification of a MSS, and noted that the updated Defence Consolidated Resource Plan (DCRP) was to include provision for further expenditure of up to NZ$34 million for phase 2 modifications. The sale was finalised on 16 December 1994 at a purchase price of Danish Kroner 55 000 000, or NZ$14.15 million. A Defence official reportedly said: 'There is a feeling of relief around defence that the project has been finally realised.'[31]

Once the purchase was completed, the vessel was to be delivered after carrying a cargo to defray costs, and it sailed as a merchantman under the New Zealand flag. The vessel arrived in New Zealand on 14 March 1995, and was delivered to the RNZN the following day. It was formally commissioned into the RNZN in October 1995, being named, by his widow, after one of New Zealand's most famous war heroes, Charles Upham. The Minister of Defence, Warren Cooper, said at the time that he expected that the vessel would be well used in exercises, UN peacekeeping deployments, and in emergency relief work.

From the outset it had been clear that the vessel would need modification. The initial modifications were to be limited to essential work to bring the ship into immediate service, but even at this stage the vessel was said to be useable and able to carry a full range of freight: 'The MSS will be able to meet its primary function without the follow on modifications and it will also to a large degree be able to perform effectively its assigned ancillary tasks.'[32]

The *Charles Upham* was 133 metres in length with a displacement of 7220 tonnes. It had a single engine and single screw. As a commercial vessel, the *Charles Upham* carried a merchant crew of seventeen. Refitted for a helicopter, she would have permanent accommodation for up to 65, with the capacity to accommodate an additional 150. In a four page *New Zealand Defence Quarterly* article, much was made of the arrival of the new ship, the contribution she would make to the NZDF, and the modest alterations necessary:

> The helicopter deck apart, most modifications are not likely to be structural or expensive. Even so, the Defence Force is in no tearing hurry because, says Ministry of Defence Project Director, Peter Ware, they 'want to get it right.' No firm decision will be taken on major alterations for some months, during which crews will be able to get operational experience of the ship. ... Many decisions have yet to be taken before the *Charles Upham* is fully operational, but at this stage the future of New Zealand's military transport looks bright. Certainly the ship will give a much needed boost in an area that has long been lacking, and it looks set to do so at a minimum cost to the taxpayer.[33]

During the next several months the crew was able to get operational experience of the ship, and the above bright predictions were to be proved sadly wrong.

The 1997 *Review of the Charles Upham* drew attention to the *Air and Sea Transport Review* which followed the 1991 White Paper, and recommended an '80/20' solution for the purchase of a MSS. That is, acquiring most of the capability needed to meet most of the likely operational circumstances. Having the ability to unload at an unimproved wharf was therefore one of the fundamental requirements. Nevertheless, the *Review* itself pointed out that cargo handling equipment 'appears to be an area not fully considered at the time (late 1992)'.[34] It went on to say that part of the proposal was to use a forklift for large container handling; however, the vessel had a weight limit of 17 tonnes per single axle, whilst the forklift had a weight of 20 tonnes per axle, even when not loaded. This seems to have been a major oversight, especially when no requirement was made for the vessel to have its own lighterage facilities. The *Review* expressed surprise about this, saying that it seemed inevitable that there would be some missions where wharves were either damaged, or non-existent. It seemed increasingly as though the ship could not achieve the 80/20 solution, and that reaching some of those islands which had seats of government or significant populations was not as possible as had been hoped. The vessel was reportedly unable to access Rarotonga, and there were fears that fitting it with cranes to unload heavy cargo would cause it to roll.

Entering Service — The (sea) Trials of HMNZS *Charles Upham*

HMNZS *Charles Upham*'s main task was to deploy the Royal New Zealand Army's RRF on overseas operations. This would require transporting up to 150 troops, armoured personnel carriers, trucks, field artillery, and associated equipment such as field kitchens and surgery. An opportunity to test this ability was to present itself in 1996 as part of a 'Limited Operations and Evaluation' period.

The vessel made two operational sea trips, from Napier to Lyttleton and, from 24 June–3 August 1996 from Auckland to Fiji on Exercise *Tropic Dust*, with plans to visit Tonga, Niue, Western Samoa and Fiji. The author went on board the ship in Apia harbour in Samoa in July, and was struck first of all by how high she was sitting out of the water. The vessel had some light equipment on board, and a number of containers carrying shingle to add ballast, but by all accounts the trip so far had been one of the most uncomfortable many of the seasoned sailors had ever experienced. Commander Gary Collier, Director of Naval Force Development, spoke about the difficulties the following year:

> Unfortunately, the ship struck some very rough weather and, not helped by an engine defect, she ended up beam on to some fairly heavy seas—not much fun for the ship's company, let alone the army personnel and cargo onboard especially when a roll of 37° was recorded. This was a similar motion to that experienced by some of the senior member's of the ship's company when, also lightly laden, a cyclone was encountered during the delivery voyage.[35]

The commanding officer, Commander Ian A. Logan, was reported as being at times fearful for the safety of the ship. So great was this concern that the ship was withdrawn from service in August 1996 in order to undertake modifications to reduce the motion problem of the ship and improve the reliability of the propulsion system. At the same time the Minister of Defence was told that a submission seeking Cabinet approval for Phase 3 modifications was in the process of preparation.

The main reason why the *Charles Upham* was kept tied up alongside at Devonport in Auckland was its propensity to roll when at sea. The BMT Defence Services report in January 1993 had drawn attention to the probability of uncomfortable motion when the ship was lightly loaded: 'The technical staff involved in the selection process were aware of these points, and the other advantages ... were sufficient to override any concerns on this point.'[36] The vessel had been designed to carry up to 7000 tonnes of cargo, and thus loaded sat low in the water, slowing the period of roll. Lightly loaded, the ship rolled hugely, making life on board distressingly uncomfortable, threatening the safety of cargo lashings, and preventing altogether any possibility of helicopter operations. Whilst there was no initial decision on whether the ship would have a helicopter of its own, in light of the observation about the possibility of operating in areas with limited wharf facilities, the limited ability for a helicopter to operate even after stabilisation work would seem to be of concern. Subsequent calculations predicted that the vessel would need to carry at least 3500 tonnes of cargo or ballast in order to produce suitable ship motion.

The Calliope South Windbreak

By the beginning of 1997, the reputation of the ill-fated vessel had plummeted. It was reported that there had been a whispering campaign instigated against the quality of the RNZN's project management, and it was suggested that the priority for the *Charles Upham*'s conversion had been unexpectedly downgraded. In April the first formal review of the vessel's purchase was published, HMNZS *Charles Upham: Review of acquisition and proposed conversion*, finding that the vessel was bought for a fair market price and was suitable for conversion. In May of that year, the *New Zealand Herald* ran a front page article with the headline 'Huge bill for defects in Navy vessel'. In June of 1997 Commander Gary Collier wrote an update article in *Navy Today*—referring to the ship as 'the Calliope South windbreak'—explaining some of the reasons for the hold up in further development work on the *Charles Upham*. He suggested that there were three factors contributing to the delay: the financial position of the NZDF had necessitated a Defence Assessment; there was an ongoing review of operational requirements; and the Government had called for an independent audit into the acquisition process and the ship's suitability for conversion. Collier postulated:

> I would be cautiously optimistic that, once detailed design work has been completed, we could see some real activity in the latter half of next year (it takes about 12 months to complete the drawings and the subsequent contract process anyway). ... I will finish this hopefully helpful article by emphasising that *Charles Upham* is an important element to the NZDF and that it is receiving a high priority amongst the corridors of power.[37]

The need for sealift capacity was once again highlighted in the 1997 *Defence Review*:

> Modern armed forces have a large logistical tail. Troops can be moved by air but their kit and supplies must come by sea. New Zealand has not traditionally maintained a military sealift capability. Instead it has relied on others, most recently the United Nations, to provide transport for our heavy equipment. The risks of continuing to do so are rising.[38]

Nevertheless, the White Paper of that year indicated that 'the Government will consider whether to convert HMNZS *Charles Upham* in about two years time'.[39] (In fact, on 20 October 1997 Cabinet had agreed it would consider modifications to the *Charles Upham* towards the end of the three year planning cycle in 2000.) By this stage, the vessel had been tied up alongside at Devonport in Auckland for 16 months, and had cost some NZ$22 million. In November 1997, the recently formed Alliance Party published its first booklet on the vessel, *The Scandal of The Charles Upham*, and described the formal April report as being 'widely regarded both inside and outside the Defence Force as a whitewash'.[40]

In April 1998 the RNZN indicated that the funding priority to convert the ship could not be maintained in the face of a stringent Defence budget, and that the ship would be offered for lease anticipating funding becoming available. The Minister of Defence, commenting on why the vessel could not be converted said: 'This is simply not our most important need…funding for the conversion of HMNZS *Charles Upham* is scheduled for 2000/01.'[41]

The ship subsequently sailed on 12 May 1998 on a delivery voyage to Spain, for a bareboat charter of two years and two months, to deliver citrus fruit in the Mediterranean. Immediately on completion of the charter, it was said, the vessel would undergo the modification program necessary to allow the ship to operate effectively in all load conditions: 'The ship will be a significant asset for New Zealand's responsibilities in the Pacific Region.'[42] In July 1998 the Alliance Party produced their second booklet, *The Biggest Lemon Ever To Leave Auckland*, describing the vessel then as 'doing a passable imitation between a lemon and a white elephant'. It then commented that both the field commander in Bougainville, Brigadier Roger Mortlock, and the Chief of Naval Staff, Admiral Fred Wilson, had been as critical as serving officers could be of the logistical and cost implications of not having the *Charles Upham* available for use for Bougainville. Following this, the Foreign Affairs, Defence and Trade Committee, asked the Audit Office to comment on both the quality of advice the New Zealand Government had received and the implications contained in the Alliance Party booklets. The Audit Office report was released in September 1998.

With the degree of controversy and public concern that had been raised by this stage, requests for information were being received by both the Ministry of Defence and Treasury. The Minister of Defence felt that the public interest would be best served by as full a disclosure of official information as possible, and asked for information held by both the Ministry of Defence and the NZDF pertaining to the acquisition of the *Charles Upham* to be made available. The result was a 690 page document, *Official Information Pertaining to the Military Sealift Project HMNZS Charles Upham*, released in November 1998. In a statement made to the Foreign Affairs and Defence Select Committee at the time of the release, the Minister said:

> Contrary to speculation based on misinformation that is being fed to the public, the *Charles Upham*, once modified, is the right ship to meet New Zealand's military sealift requirement. While it is unfortunate that the current financial squeeze has resulted in a delay to these modifications, there are no reasons not to proceed with the work in two years time. We will then have a fully capable ship that will give us at least 15 years service.[43]

Later in November, the Minister recommended that Cabinet endorse the Defence 10 Year Capital Plan, and noted that it would take 18 months for the design work to be completed and tenders let for the conversion of the *Charles Upham*.

Finally, in July 1999, five years after Cabinet had given initial approval for the purchase of a second-hand vessel, it gave approval in principle for the conversion progress to begin. The conversion was expected to be finished by 2002, some 15 years after the 1987 *Defence Review*.

Controversy continued and, in early November 1999, following the deployment of New Zealand troops to East Timor, Geoff Braybrooke, Labour's defence spokesperson, attacked the Government saying: 'The troop carrier capability has had such low priority under National that the botched purchase, HMNZS *Charles Upham*, is carrying oranges and lemons in the Mediterranean.'[44] Later that year there was an election, a change of Government, and the beginnings of the third formal review of HMNZS *Charles Upham*.

The Decision to Dispose of HMNZS *Charles Upham*

Following the election in 1999 and the subsequent change to a Labour led government, a Strategic Assessment[45] and a report, *New Zealand's Foreign and Security Policy Challenges*,[46] were completed in 2000, each of these helping to inform *The Government's Defence Policy Framework*[47] released in June 2000. In this policy document it was made clear that the Government would complete reviews by November 2000 which would identify options for effective military sealift for deployment and support of troops. Later that month the Secretary of Defence wrote to the Minister, noting that the Prime Minister had asked to be briefed on those capability projects identified in the Framework. The Secretary reported that a contract had been let to BMT Defence Services for the production of the design for the conversion to be undertaken; this was to be done in three phases, two of which had already been completed. The options put to the Government were to accept that the conversion to the *Charles Upham* provided the cheapest way of providing an acceptable sealift solution, and allowing the design work to be completed; or to review the project specifications for generic military sealift taking 'consideration of the advantages of an across-the-beach capability, and identify available alternatives'. The Secretary added: 'The Defence Policy Framework points in the direction of the generic review.'[48]

In a briefing to Caucus in October 2000, the Minister indicated that in fact lessons had been learned from East Timor:

> The primary reason we need a sealift ship is to deploy the heavy equipment of a committed Army group within a reasonable period. The lessons of East Timor demonstrated the importance of sealift and the need for us to address this.[49]

The *Sealift Review* was completed in November 2000, and made a number of observations and recommendations. Firstly it highlighted the distinction customarily made between strategic and tactical sealift. Strategic sealift is the delivery of heavy equipment from New Zealand to an assembly area, usually a fixed port, where vehicles and equipment are married up with personnel, who are most likely to have been flown into the area. Tactical sealift is the delivery of equipment and personnel into an operational area; and tactical sealift ships are designed to operate in areas without formal port facilities. The *Review* makes the point that, in the case of East Timor, both requirements were demonstrated, with strategic sealift transporting equipment to Darwin by roll-on, roll-off vessel; and a French tactical sealift ship completing the journey and off-loading over the beach. The *Review* indicated that a limited over the beach capacity would be useful, and could be provided by a modified *Charles Upham*. The *Sealift Review* examined four options:

1. Reliance on commercial chartering;
2. Acquisition of a used military sealift ship;
3. Purchase of a new purpose built ship; and
4. Modification of the *Charles Upham*.

It defined the capacity needed as the requirement to transport equipment to support a battalion group, and therefore the specification was almost exactly the same as that originally proposed in the User Specification of 1992.

The reliance on commercial chartering was seen as carrying some risks—particularly the concern about the possible delays at a time when a rapid response might be needed, but also the lack of a tactical capability. The used military sealift ship was seen as a high-risk option in terms of cost, whilst the new, purpose-built vessel was seen as high in tactical utility, whilst only being able to match half of the strategic capacity of a modified *Charles Upham*. The *Review* concluded that, whilst the *Charles Upham* had some limitations in its ability to off-load cargo across the beach, and limited utility for other duties when not undertaking sealift, it was nonetheless 'the most cost effective option for meeting the core requirement for assured strategic sealift'.[50]

Earlier that month the Cabinet Policy Committee had invited a group of Ministers, including the Prime Minister, Deputy Prime Minister, Minister of Finance and Minister of Defence, to explore how to progress defence options more rapidly. One month later, 21 December 2000, a Sustainable Defence Plan was submitted to Ministers from both the Department of the Prime Minister and Cabinet and Treasury. The Plan stated:

Officials' conclusions at this stage are that:

1. Any immediate requirement for strategic sealift should be provided by charter arrangements;

2. The *Charles Upham* should be sold next year when it comes off charter; and
3. Any further requirements for sealift or a ship with a multipurpose role can be examined in the context of a replacement for HMNZS *Canterbury*.[51]

Following discussion at the Cabinet Policy Committee meeting in March, Cabinet decided on 2 April 2001 to endorse the above recommendations, and the decision was announced in the *Government Defence Statement* of 8 May 2001.[52] In July the Minister of Defence announced that the vessel had been sold to a Spanish shipping company saying that the NZ$35–40 million needed to modify the vessel was not considered to be a prudent use of defence resources.

Reflections on the Purchase and Disposal of HMNZS *Charles Upham*

As has become already apparent, the major concern about the *Charles Upham* was that it did not work in the way that was intended. After the ship had been bought, the intention was to make it ready in three steps. The first of these were the initial modifications and commissioning; the second was the period of sea trials; and the third was to have been the more expensive full modification stage. Timing and political influence were important influencing elements from very early on in the ship's development.

It is important here to recall that the 1997 *Review* had commented that the Prime Minister's Department had given indications in 1993 that the MSS project should not be promoted. Cabinet had given approval for the purchase of the ship on 28 November 1994, and the sale was finalised very quickly, on 16 December 1994. After a Mercandian had first been identified as a suitable ship, some six vessels had come up for sale. By the time Cabinet approval had been given all had been sold, but one sale fell through and a vessel was again available. However, the sale needed to be actioned quickly. Dick Gentles, former Deputy Secretary, Policy and Planning noted: 'There was a feeling of conspiracy that because we'd bought the vessel so quickly after Cabinet approval that the deal was cooked up; politicians were suspicious.'[53] Political influence then came into play. Warren Cooper, the Minister of Defence at the time said: 'I formed the impression that Jim Bolger wasn't enthusiastic about the deal and that impression grew subsequently when we had purchased the vessel.'[54] Robin Johansen confirmed the concern: 'I had a visit shortly afterwards from the Prime Minister's Department, and was told I shouldn't put up any plans for the conversion of the vessel because "it won't happen."'[55] Jim Bolger, Prime Minister at the time, was forthright in his comments: 'I was never persuaded that we needed it; when we got it, it couldn't do its job; and subsequently it was moved on pretty quickly.'[56]

At the time of commissioning in October 1995 it was proposed that no firm decisions on major alterations would be taken for some months, to allow for operational experience. The second step began on 2 November 1995, with the ship virtually unchanged from its original condition, except for the addition of communications equipment and increased accommodation.

As has become clear, the first stage of sea trials for the ship was dangerous, and disastrous for the ship's image. At this point it seems as though there were two factors operating in tandem to make development of the *Charles Upham* difficult—fiscal and operational. In looking at trade-offs, the decision had been made to bring the vessel out from Europe with a commercial crew. When the RNZN had commissioned the fleet replenishment ship HMNZS *Endeavour*, the crew had been sent to the Merchant Navy Training School in Launceston, and some to the Royal Fleet Auxiliary (RFA) in the United Kingdom for training. An RFA Chief Officer joined the *Endeavour* as an advisor: it was recognised that operating merchant vessels required different skills from those required for combat vessels. Again the question of bureaucratic politics was raised. Peter Cozens noted: 'The Navy didn't use the same principles for the *Upham* as they had with the *Endeavour*—a huge lack of judgement. At first I thought it was plain stupidity; but it was strategy.'[57] Teagle gave a different view:

> There was never the opportunity to train the crew the way we did with *Endeavour*. With the *Endeavour* we had time to plan. We learnt from the RFA for *Endeavour*; that specialist training they had provided needed to be provided for the crew of the *Upham* and it wasn't. I had retired shortly after the decision to purchase the ship was taken, so why, I don't know.[58]

The issue of bureaucratic politics was also raised by the Audit Office Review:

> We could not establish why the evaluation of the *Charles Upham* by sea trials was not reactivated after the propulsion system was fixed. When the ship was leased it was sailed to Europe in a light-load condition.[59]

These two elements, together with the history of policy decisions which were part of ongoing political influence, combined to ensure that the necessary funding which had been identified at the beginning of the project was never forthcoming. The ship was withdrawn from service in August 1996, and a freeze on unapproved capital expenditure was already in force. In October 1996 the first Mixed Member Proportional (MMP) election returned a Government led by the National Party, with the support of New Zealand First. Winston Peters, the leader of New Zealand First, was appointed as Treasurer, and once again no funds were forthcoming for the progress of the *Charles Upham*.

The Reviews

As indicated, there were three formal reviews of the *Charles Upham*, in 1997, 1998 and 2000, and two reports, by the Alliance Party, in 1997 and 1998. The 1997 *Review* concluded with:

> The consultants have reviewed the acquisition process. They consider that the process of evaluating the options and the purchase was carried out in a professionally responsible manner. The steps taken were, for the most part, those that one would normally expect.[60]

The Alliance Party report of 1997 said that the 'conclusions are most kindly described as surprising. ... Unkinder critics have called the conclusions a whitewash'.[61] The 1998 Report from the Office of the Controller and Auditor-General was wide-ranging in its review. It examined the DCRP, which covered a 10-year period and was reviewed on an annual basis. It was told by Treasury that the latter's former manager had been concerned about the lack of priorities in the plan. It also noted that the Plan was reviewed at least annually, with resulting changes to priorities. The DCRP for 1994–95 had a note attached regarding the *Charles Upham* which stated: 'Potential upgrades have been identified at $34 million. The cash requirement will be confirmed in light of operating experience and funded out of underspends and programme slippage on an opportunity basis.'[62]

The Report team was clearly concerned that the commitment to fund modifications was secondary at this stage to other projects. They highlighted that Treasury commented: 'It is not clear at this stage what would be the value of an unmodified sealift ship, in the event that Ministers do not wish to commit to the additional expenditure necessary to upgrade it.'[63]

It would seem that right from the beginning of the proposal there was a question mark hanging over any future major funding for conversion. Members of the External Relations and Defence Committee were asked in their deliberations to note that the purchase and initial modification of the vessel would provide an adequate basic capability, and that future modifications would happen only if money was available which did not mean prejudicing other projects. The Report team was of the opinion that, even at this stage, it meant that the upgrade of the MSS was the lowest of priorities. Once more highlighting the place of bureaucratic politics, it concluded that the Government of the day made its decision 'on assurances from both NZDF and the MoD that proved in the event not to be valid'.[64] The Audit Review Team summarised its major findings succinctly: 'The adequate basic MSS capability promised to Cabinet has never been realised. The statement that capital equipment procurement would not require a capital injection has proved to be incorrect'.[65]

Was HMNZS *Charles Upham* a lemon?

HMNZS *Charles Upham* ended up being the butt of many jokes, particularly when it went off to Spain to become a citrus fruit transporter. There are many varied opinions about why the vessel turned so sour. Robert Miles, a radical defence commentator from Timaru, suggested that it was likely the RNZN knew they were buying a lemon; that if this had not been the case, they might have had a new amphibious assault ship, or the *Tobruk*.[66] In February 2000, in an open discussion on the lessons of East Timor, Major General Piers Reid, former Chief of General Staff, spoke in impassioned fashion about the *Charles Upham*:

> For the third time in the past six years, after Bosnia and Bougainville, the mistaken purchase of the totally unsuitable Charles Upham has come back to haunt the Defence Force. I cannot overstate the need for a suitable vessel; for deployments, for services protected evacuations and for disaster relief. The internal Defence politics, which saw the cheapest near-enough cargo ship purchased, to preserve funds for the frigates, has worked entirely against the national interest.[67]

The Admirals, contended Robert Miles—echoing Major General Reid—wanted to concentrate on a blue-water fighting force. Such sentiments were echoed by Peter Cozens, Director of the Centre for Strategic Studies, Victoria University of Wellington: 'The Navy simply did not want it, and did everything in their power to ensure they didn't get it.'[68] Robin Johansen, former Deputy Secretary—Acquisitions added: 'The Navy didn't see the acquisition of the Upham as being of strategic value to them.'[69] Rear Admiral Jack Welch however commented: 'The Navy was given the task of fulfilling a national requirement to buy a ship to transport the Army. Had we followed through with the conversion she would have been quite suitable for the purpose.'[70] On this aspect Peter Cozens agreed and thought the concept of conversion was 'brilliant, spot-on. The Corps of Naval Constructors said it was feasible and would produce an excellent outcome. It would have done.'[71] His sentiments were reflected by Admiral Sir Somerford Teagle: 'It could have been a good ship. It was a tragedy—a missed opportunity. It seems it was never really given a chance.'[72]

Once again, Jim Bolger responded in direct fashion: 'The terminology that it could have been a good ship tells you everything you want to know. It wasn't.'[73] There were other commentators who suggested that the ship was never really given a chance, and provided interesting feedback of their own. The following letter appeared as part of ongoing correspondence in the *New Zealand Listener* in 2001:

> (The) reference to the much-maligned HMNZS *Charles Upham* assumed that the ship was lacking in stability by inferring that she could only cart lemons 'without rolling over and going glug'. That ship, and many

others of her class, sail the world's sea lanes daily. One of their many attributes is that they possess a surfeit of positive stability, which makes for uncomfortable seakeeping qualities, but in turn provides a tremendous margin of safety if the ship is ever damaged. This fact seems to have been overlooked.

As a military materiel carrier, she was superb, but the RNZN did not appreciate her capabilities. Some of the published figures for her to be made 'serviceable' in RNZN terms were ludicrous. One wonders why she was never given a fair go. Merchant naval personnel are conversant with such ships and had she been manned by them, she might have performed her allotted duties admirably.[74]

The RNZN continued to work on a solution for the poor sea-keeping qualities of the vessel throughout the 1990s but, with a change of Government following the election in 1999, the opportunity for correction was to be lost.

Summary

Whilst external sources, and in particular the value placed on CDR, had some influence in the early stages of the decision to purchase the ill-fated HMNZS *Charles Upham*, the most consistently apparent influencing elements during the early phases of the decision-making process were New Zealand's role in the world, geographical priorities, and the judgement of short-term versus long-term payoffs. Although the National Party and the Labour Party each had different views of New Zealand's role in the world, they both recognised the need to be able to deploy troops and equipment overseas. Geographical priorities as spelt out in the 1987 White Paper required Defence to be able to respond to regional crises. With the debate about a LSS having begun in earnest in 1978, and having been reinforced by the recommendations of the 1987 White Paper, the impact of judgements of short-term versus long-term payoffs and the trade offs this entailed was to nevertheless ensure that some 30 years later New Zealand was still waiting for a fully functioning Multi-Role Vessel to become available. Here one would have to wonder about the difference in the order of magnitude of committing several hundreds of millions of dollars for a replacement frigate, the lease of the F-16s, the upgrading of the *Orions* or the purchase of new armoured vehicles for the Army (each of which will be explored in subsequent chapters), with the original estimate of NZ$34 million to upgrade the *Charles Upham*.[75] Undoubtedly bureaucratic politics had their place, as the New Zealand Army and the RNZN pursued their own priorities. Timing and political influence, though, were ultimately the crucial features in the decision-making process, the resistance to completion of the conversion work proving to be the death knell for HMNZS *Charles Upham*.

ENDNOTES

1 *Defence Review 1978*, Government Printer, Wellington, 1978, p. 28.

2 *Defence of New Zealand, Review of Defence Policy 1987*, Government Printer, Wellington, 1987, p. 35.

3 *HMNZS Charles Upham: Review of acquisition and proposed conversion*, NZDF Report No. 210, 14 April 1997.

4 *The Defence of New Zealand 1991, A Policy Paper*, GP Print Ltd, Wellington, 1991, p. 80.

5 *Review of Defence Air and Sea Transport*, Report of Review Team, Volume 1, Wellington, 1991, p. vii.

6 *Review of Defence Air and Sea Transport*, Report of Review Team, p. 32.

7 *HMNZS Charles Upham: Review of acquisition and proposed conversion*, p. 1.

8 *Review of Defence Air and Sea Transport*, Report of Review Team, p. viii. [my emphasis]

9 Admiral Sir Somerford Teagle, Personal interview, 20 September 2003. The requirement that the vessel should fit the Calliope Dock, as was specified in the 1992 User Requirement (see Appendix 3), effectively meant that HMNZS *Union Rotorua* could no longer be considered.

10 *Review of Defence Air and Sea Transport*, Report of Review Team, p. 40.

11 *Review of Defence Air and Sea Transport*, Report of Review Team, p. 40.

12 *Review of Defence Air and Sea Transport*, Report of Review Team, p. 14.

13 Minute NA 11925-0002 from DPPR to CNS, 23 February 1994, p. 5, contained in *Official Information Pertaining to the Military Sealift Project HMNZS Charles Upham*, Ministry of Defence, Wellington, November 1998, p. 6.

14 See answer to written question 15929 of 26 November 1997, quoted in *The Scandal of The Charles Upham*, Alliance Party, Wellington, November 1997, p. 2. This says that the Royal Australian Navy indicated 'that the ship could be leased at a very attractive rate (sum not disclosed)'. Whilst lease costs were not discussed in detail, expressions such as 'at a price you can afford' were apparently used. (See Minute NA 11925-0002 from DPPR to CNS, 23 February 1994.)

15 Ric Oram, 'Defence rethink on troop ship', *New Zealand Herald*, 25 July 1994.

16 Oram, 'Defence rethink on troop ship'.

17 Minute PF/3310-16, 28 June 1994, p. 3, contained in *Official Information Pertaining to the Military Sealift Project HMNZS Charles Upham*.

18 Minute PF/3310-16, 28 June 1994, p. 5.

19 *HMNZS Charles Upham, Report on Concerns Raised by the Foreign Affairs, Defence and Trade Committee*, Office of the Controller and Auditor-General, Wellington, 24 September 1998, p. 36.

20 Rear-Admiral David Campbell, Personal correspondence, 15 September 2003.

21 Campbell, Personal correspondence, 15 September 2003.

22 See answer to written question 15929 of 26 November 1997, quoted in Alliance Party, *The Biggest Lemon Ever To Leave Auckland*, Wellington, July 1998.

23 Minute PF/3310-16, 28 June 1994, p. 5.

24 Dick Gentles, Personal interview, 12 November 2003.

25 Campbell, Personal correspondence, 15 September 2003.

26 Alliance Party, *The Biggest Lemon Ever To Leave Auckland*, p. 5.

27 Alliance Party, *The Biggest Lemon Ever To Leave Auckland*, p. 5.

28 *HMNZS Charles Upham, Report on Concerns Raised by the Foreign Affairs, Defence and Trade Committee*, p. 4.

29 Memorandum from Minister of Defence to Chair, Cabinet Sub-Committee for Defence, Security and External Relations, 31 October 1994.

30 Memorandum from Minister of Defence to Chair, Cabinet Sub-Committee for Defence, Security and External Relations, 22 November 1994, pp. 7–8.

31 Ric Oram, 'New ship to work her passage carrying cargo', *New Zealand Herald*, 3 January 1995.

32 Memorandum from Minister of Defence to Chair, Cabinet Sub-Committee for Defence, Security and External Relations, 22 November 1994, p. 4.

33 Matthew Wright. 'Sealift for Soldiers', *New Zealand Defence Quarterly*, Number 8, Autumn 1995, pp. 21–22.

34 *HMNZS Charles Upham: Review of acquisition and proposed conversion*, p. 19.

[35] Gary Collier, 'HMNZS Charles Upham—what's happening?', *Navy Today*, No. 12, June 1997, p. 15.
[36] *HMNZS Charles Upham: Review of acquisition and proposed conversion*, p. 21.
[37] Collier, 'HMNZS Charles Upham—what's happening?'
[38] Quoted in Alliance Party, *The Scandal of The Charles Upham*, p. 7.
[39] *The Shape of New Zealand's Defence, A White Paper*, Ministry of Defence, Wellington, November 1997, p. 45.
[40] Alliance Party, *The Scandal of The Charles Upham*, p. 1.
[41] See Question for Written Answer 2670 of 4 April 1998, quoted in Alliance Party, *The Biggest Lemon Ever To Leave Auckland*, p. 2.
[42] 'Charles Upham departs on charter', *Navy Today*, No. 23, June 1998, p. 18.
[43] 'Sealift Ship Charles Upham', available at <http://www.defence.govt.nz/scripts/press/index.asp?page=34>, accessed 23 January 2002.
[44] 'Labour-a sensible defence policy', available at <http://www.scoop.co.nz/mason/stories/PA9911/SOO167.htm>, accessed 20 September 2003.
[45] *Strategic Assessment 2000*, External Assessments Bureau, Department of the Prime Minister and Cabinet, Wellington, 24 March 2000.
[46] *New Zealand's Foreign and Security Policy Challenges*, Ministry of Foreign Affairs and Trade, Wellington, May 2000.
[47] *The Government's Defence Policy Framework*, Ministry of Defence, Wellington, June 2000.
[48] Note and Annexes from the Secretary of Defence to the Minister of Defence, 20 June 2000, p. 4.
[49] Cover sheet and letter from Secretary of Defence to the Minister of Defence attaching the Notes to Brief Caucus, 30 October 2000, p. 4.
[50] *New Zealand Defence Force Capability Reviews, Phase One-Land Forces and Sealift*, Ministry of Defence, Wellington, November 2000, p. 83.
[51] *Sustainable Defence Plan*, Department of the Prime Minister and Cabinet, Wellington, 21 December 2000, p. 5.
[52] *Government Defence Statement: A Modern, Sustainable Defence Force Matched to New Zealand's Needs*, Ministry of Defence, Wellington, June 2001, p. 7.
[53] Gentles, Personal interview, 12 November 2003.
[54] Warren Cooper, Telephone interview, 1 May 2005.
[55] Robin Johansen, Personal interview, 29 April 2005.
[56] Rt.Hon. Jim Bolger, Personal interview, 15 December 2005.
[57] Peter Cozens, Director of the Centre for Strategic Studies, Victoria University of Wellington, Personal interview, 27 August 2003.
[58] Admiral Sir Somerford Teagle, Personal interview, 20 September 2003.
[59] *HMNZS Charles Upham, Report on Concerns Raised by the Foreign Affairs, Defence and Trade Committee*, p. 29.
[60] *HMNZS Charles Upham: Review of acquisition and proposed conversion*, p. 27.
[61] Alliance Party, *The Scandal of The Charles Upham*, p. 4.
[62] *HMNZS Charles Upham, Report on Concerns Raised by the Foreign Affairs, Defence and Trade Committee*, p. 19.
[63] *HMNZS Charles Upham, Report on Concerns Raised by the Foreign Affairs, Defence and Trade Committee*, p. 19.
[64] *HMNZS Charles Upham, Report on Concerns Raised by the Foreign Affairs, Defence and Trade Committee*, p. 21.
[65] *HMNZS Charles Upham, Report on Concerns Raised by the Foreign Affairs, Defence and Trade Committee*, p. 28.
[66] Robert Miles, *Scuttling the Army, The Charles Upham Scandal*, Black Diamond Press, Timaru, 1998, p. 8.
[67] Piers Reid, 'The Lessons of East Timor', in *Defence Policy after East Timor*, New Zealand Institute of International Affairs, Wellington, 2000; and personal interview, 3 September 2003.
[68] Cozens, Personal interview, 27 August 2003.
[69] Johansen, Personal interview, 29 April 2005.

70 Rear Admiral Jack Welch, Telephone interview, 31 May 2005.
71 Cozens, Personal interview, 27 August 2003.
72 Teagle, Personal interview, 20 September 2003.
73 Bolger, Personal interview, 15 December 2005.
74 G.T. Nichol, Letter to the *New Zealand Listener*, 6 October 2001, p. 9.
75 Cabinet Minute CAB (94) M 46/16.

Chapter 4

'No, Minister....' — The ANZAC Frigates, Part II

The Second Frigate Decision

In 1989 the decision on whether to buy the third and fourth ANZAC frigates seemed a long way off; indeed as previously indicated, Geoffrey Palmer had said the decision would not need to be taken for almost a decade. Before the next decision was due to be made, major changes to New Zealand's electoral system were to take place, with the introduction of Mixed Member Proportional (MMP) representation in 1996, and the need for the formation of a coalition government. It was the need for retaining coalition support that was to have a decisive influence on the National-led Government's decision not to proceed with the option to purchase the third and fourth ANZAC frigates.

As early as 1992, the Minister of Defence, Warren Cooper, suggested that New Zealand might not take up the option to buy the third and fourth ANZAC frigates. He was to reinforce his opinion, if not that of his leader, in an interview with the *Australian Defence Magazine* in 1994: 'We've got two *Leander*-class frigates that will remain good for a few years. My guess is that we wouldn't be able to sign up confidently for another two ANZAC frigates, but that door is left open.'[1] In January 1995, whilst New Zealand's first ANZAC frigate was taking shape on both sides of the Tasman, Cooper fired a further broadside in the discussions on whether to purchase the third and fourth ANZAC frigates: 'Two frigates enough for NZ: Cooper', read the headline in the *New Zealand Herald*. The article went on to say that the Minister did not believe that New Zealand needed to buy more ANZAC frigates: 'I am not fully committed to the third and fourth frigates. ... Quite frankly there are other priorities the Government will want to address.'[2] The decision on whether to buy more ANZAC frigates was due to be taken by the end of 1996. That timing was to coincide with the first MMP election, and the Minister indicated that defence spending would need to compete against other demands in the areas of education, health and welfare.

During the early 1990s, although there was little public debate about the frigates, public opinion nonetheless remained important. During 1995, the Foundation for Peace Studies published a report of a survey which had sought to establish up-to-date public opinion on a range of matters related to peace and defence issues. Two questions in the survey had particular relevance for the upcoming debate on the purchase of further frigates—one about the level of defence spending; the other about how many, if any, ANZAC frigates should be purchased.

With regards to attitudes on defence spending, there was a clear message that there was no mandate for increased spending, with results as follows: [3]

Does defence spending need to be:

		(%)
(i)	Increased	12
(ii)	Decreased	31
(iii)	About the same	38
(iv)	Undecided	19

Should the New Zealand Government:

		(%)
(i)	Purchase 3 frigates	8
(ii)	Purchase 2 frigates	36
(iii)	Purchase 1 frigate	18
(iv)	Cancel	28
(v)	Don't know	10

As can be seen, a large percentage of respondents wished to maintain the status quo, holding defence spending at current levels and pursuing the purchase of two frigates. However, a significant minority, 31 per cent, wished for a decrease in defence spending, and 28 per cent wished for cancellation of the frigate purchase, whilst only 8 per cent supported the purchase of a third frigate. It was against such a backdrop that the first MMP election was to be fought.

The 1996 MMP Election, the Impact of Coalition Government, and the Second Frigate Decision

In the run-up to the election, the Labour Party launched its foreign affairs and defence policy in August 1996. Whilst remaining committed to a blue-water navy, Labour would buy only two ANZAC frigates. Foreshadowing changes that would start to take place at the beginning of the twenty-first century, the policy stated that Labour would 'ensure that we [New Zealand] have a fleet of a minimum of four vessels that will perform the essential South Pacific blue water navy roles at a more appropriate level of sophistication and technology'.[4]

Reinforcing the research findings of the Foundation for Peace Studies Aotearoa-New Zealand's the previous year, and speaking to public sentiment, the leader of the Opposition, Helen Clark, commented that 'there is but a small constituency for defence-related expenditure in New Zealand'.[5] This was apparently reflected in the Defence budget which, according to New Zealand Defence Force (NZDF) spokesperson John Seward, had decreased dramatically in real terms—some 35 per cent since 1989–90. The budget for the 1996 financial year was NZ$1.6 billion, and reportedly just 1 per cent of Gross Domestic Product (GDP). New Zealand's Australian neighbours continued to watch with concern.

Following the return of a National-led Coalition Government at the end of 1996, the thorny issue of the frigate purchase option was soon back on the political agenda. Ruth Laugesen reporting in the *New Zealand Herald* at the beginning of 1997 noted:

> After a softly-softly approach by the Australian government last year because of the New Zealand elections, Prime Minister John Howard is expected to apply renewed pressure on Jim Bolger when he visits New Zealand for three days from Saturday.[6]

She went on to comment that the representatives from Australia were expected to meet resistance from New Zealand First Cabinet ministers, as that Party's election policy had also opposed purchasing more frigates. New Zealand First MP and Associate Treasurer Tuariki Delamere has stated: 'Our overall stance is that we oppose it. We would need to be convinced and we have to work through the issue'.[7] Notwithstanding this expected opposition, National's new Minister of Defence, Paul East, supported the proposal to buy more frigates, saying that he could see clear benefits for continuing with the ANZAC frigate program.

With a decision on whether to pursue the option to buy two more ANZACS needing to be taken by November 1997, May of that year saw the Prime Minister, Jim Bolger, in Melbourne for the launching of the second New Zealand ANZAC, HMNZS *Te Mana*. In a speech he gave the day before the launch, Bolger offered strong support for the frigate project. He indicated that the New Zealand Government would not reduce the size of the planned fleet of four, despite indications that there was growing resistance both within his own Caucus, and within that of New Zealand First, to buying even one more frigate. Speculation was growing though that if further frigates were ordered, the air strike force might have to be abandoned. That same day, in a bid to hedge bets, Paul East indicated that the Government might opt for an alternative to buying the two proposed new ANZAC frigates. He noted that options included indefinitely deferring a decision; going for corvette-sized vessels; or exploring the possibilities of second-hand vessels.

By August 1997, with pressure growing from within, the Government confirmed that officials from the Royal New Zealand Navy (RNZN) and from the Ministry of Defence would visit the United States to check the prices of warships. The performance criteria for the ANZAC frigates had been set out at the time of the first frigate purchase decision-making process, and essentially remained unchanged. However, alternative vessels with comparable abilities were explored during the time of the first Coalition Government. In order to retain a four-frigate Navy, the Minister had asked officials to explore the possibility of replacing the *Leanders* with second-hand ex-US FFG-7s. However, taking all costs into account (see Table 4.1) it was clear that the purchase of two second-hand refitted FFG-7s would cost substantially more than a new ANZAC, and the Minister concluded that that option should not be further pursued.

Table 4.1: Comparison of Annual Costs for Mixed and ANZAC Fleets (1997 NZ$ million)

(Averaged over five years)

Averaged Annual Costs	2 ANZAC, 2 FFG 7	4 ANZAC	3 ANZAC
Personnel	$29.040	$26.080	$19.560
Operating	$69.330	$58.040	$43.530
Depreciation	$99.114	$107.100	$80.325
Total	$197.484	$191.220	$143.415

(*Source: Defence Assessment Paper*, Office of the Minister of Defence, Wellington, 17 September 1997, p. 5. Paper attached to ERD (97) 18.

Harry Duynhoven, the Labour MP for New Plymouth, was quick to suggest the Danish frigate option again, saying that by investigating the possibility of ex-US warships, the RNZN had 'blown out of the water' one of its main arguments against the Danish vessels—that running two classes of warship would be too costly. It was not an option that gained support.

It had been six years since a Defence White Paper had been published, and in June of 1997 the Cabinet Strategy Subcommittee on External Relations and Defence directed officials to complete the Defence Assessment by 31 July 1997. In the draft copy of the *Defence Assessment*, six force structure options were developed, the major features of which are shown in Table 4.2:

Table 4.2: Force Structure Options

Variables	Option A	Option C1	Option C2	Option C3	Option C4	Option D
Naval Combat Force	4 frigates	3 frigates	2 frigates	2 frigates	3 frigates	2 frigates
Air Combat Force	retained	eliminated	retained	eliminated	retained	eliminated
Infantry Battalions	2 with four rifle companies	2 with three rifle companies	2 with three rifle companies	3 with three rifle companies (deployable brigade)	2 with three rifle companies	2 with three rifle companies
Net Change in Funding ($ Million)	213	(26)	11	(57)	131	(50)

(*Source: Defence Assessment Paper*, Office of the Minister of Defence, Wellington, 17 September 1997, p. 3. Paper attached to ERD (97) 18.)

The recommendation of the Minister of Defence, Paul East, to the Cabinet Subcommittee, was to adopt a refined Option C4, resulting in:

i. A Naval Combat Force based on the ANZAC frigates, with the third to be ordered this year.
ii. A Land Combat Force based on two regular force infantry battalions with four rifle companies each.
iii. An Air Combat Force comprising the A-4 *Skyhawks*, these to be replaced by a suitable aircraft in due course.
iv. A Long Range Maritime Surveillance Force based on the *Orions*, re-winged and equipped with updated sensors and communications suites (Projects *Kestrel* and *Sirius*).
v. An Air Transport Force based on the one-for-one replacement of the current fleet of C-130 *Hercules* and B-727 aircraft. The C-130 fleet is to be replaced by the acquisition of five C-130J aircraft.
vi. The maintenance and development of the remaining capabilities in the existing force structure.[8]

The Minister also recommended upgrading the Army's combat capability, including the acquisition of armoured vehicles. In the covering paper, ERD (97) 18, of the Cabinet Subcommittee, it was proposed that:

> A proposal be brought forward before the end of 1997 to authorise officials to commence negotiations for the acquisition of a third ANZAC ship. The option available to New Zealand for the purchase of two

additional ANZAC frigates would not be taken up. The Navy would become a three frigate fleet from 30 June 1998.[9]

In fact, the prospect of buying any further frigates in the near future seemed increasingly unlikely. On 13 October Winston Peters, leader of New Zealand First, Deputy Prime Minister, and Treasurer, declared that his Party would not support the purchase of a third frigate—there was no mention of a fourth. Confronting his colleagues in Cabinet over defence spending, he suggested that any decision on buying more than the current two frigates should be deferred until after 2000, that is, until after the next election. (New Zealand First had slumped in the polls at this stage to 1.7 per cent support, and this stand was seen as an attempt to position New Zealand First, in the eyes of the electorate, as a compassionate party.) The following day, despite his own firm conviction that New Zealand needed a third frigate, the Prime Minister commented that the decision on whether to purchase a third frigate could wait until after the 1999 election. This time it was the Minister of Defence's turn to say that the decision had to be taken 'fairly soon', though the previous deadline of November 1997 no longer applied, and it would still be possible to purchase a frigate beyond the option date. Peters was firm in his resolve against the purchase of any further frigates, claiming that the first decision was wrong: 'It was the wrong decision to make; it was the wrong technology, enormously overpriced. That is still my view.'[10]

However, on 15 October the *New Zealand Herald* called for greater commitment on the part of the Government:

> A closer trans-Tasman defence relationship requires New Zealand to maintain a respectable fighting force and at least a modicum of military equipment compatible with that of its partner.
>
> Credibility on that score requires at the very least a four-frigate Navy. And having agreed to replace two of its ageing fleet with the Australian vessels there seems no sense in going elsewhere for the remainder.[11]

On this occasion it would seem that the *New Zealand Herald* was somewhat out of step with the over-riding public and political opinion of the times. The Government had taken note of the report commissioned by Treasury on *The Navy Critical Mass Argument*. Written by Professor G. Anthony Vignaux, he concluded: 'Based on the data provided...the logic of the "Critical Mass" argument is undeniable. A frigate force of 2 frigates cannot carry out the Government requirement. A force of 3 frigates is marginal.'[12] Despite this observation that three frigates would be marginal, at a meeting on 20 October Cabinet agreed that the Naval Combat Force would be based on a fleet of three surface combatants, and also 'agreed that the option available to New Zealand under the ANZAC Ship Treaty, which provides for the purchase of two additional

ANZAC frigates, will not be taken up'.[13] Cabinet deferred any decision on the content and timing of the release of the White Paper until 3 November. No comment was made about any possible acquisition of a third frigate.

At the time that Peters made his pronouncement about the third frigate, the long awaited *Defence Assessment* was in the final stages of completion; another assessment, the *Inquiry into Defence Beyond 2000*, had only just begun. The need for a broad deliberation on the future of defence had led the Foreign Affairs, Defence and Trade Committee to set up an enquiry to 'consider options for the development of New Zealand's Defence policy, structure and capabilities beyond 2000'.[14] The Chair of the Committee was the Hon. Derek Quigley, ACT MP and author of the 1988 *Resource Management Review*. Quigley suggested that the *Defence Assessment* be put on hold, pending the outcome of the inquiry: 'The Defence Assessment is more than a year late already. A short delay will give us the opportunity to have a broader look at defence requirements'.[15] The Government, however, were not going to wait.

In November 1997 the latest Defence White Paper, *The Shape of New Zealand's Defence*, was released.[16] The White Paper reinforced that the policy set out in the 1991 White Paper continued to be the most appropriate policy framework to guide defence policy, and spelt out, as expected, the future structure of the Naval Combat Force which, as indicated above, was to move from four frigates to three in 1998. Commenting on the White Paper, the Australian Minister for Defence said he hoped that the frigate decision was not final: 'We'll certainly be taking it up with New Zealand.'[17] Paul East suggested that the Government could 'revisit' the matter the following year.[18] His successor was to ensure that this happened.

The Third Frigate Decision

Maintaining a three frigate fleet was a clear objective; how to maintain it was not at all clear. Fighting a rearguard action against his coalition colleagues, the new Minister for Defence, Max Bradford, raised the prospect in March 1998 that the RNZN might have to merge with the Royal Australian Navy (RAN), unless a third frigate was ordered. It was suggested by Greg Ansley the *New Zealand Herald*'s Canberra correspondent, that this comment bore 'the marks of frustration and politicking, rather than serious thinking',[19] and the Australian Minister for Defence apparently shared little enthusiasm for the remarks. It was indicative of the tenor of the times.

Yet, it was to be the end of October and into November before the debate hit the headlines again. A year beyond the original deadline for making a decision on the purchase of further ANZAC frigates, Cabinet was asked to give authorisation for the purchase of a second-hand ANZAC frigate. In papers accompanying the memorandum to Cabinet, the Minister of Defence made a strong case for the purchase of a third ANZAC frigate, and highlighted that this would be the last opportunity to buy a third ANZAC.[20] The production line would be closed within two years, foreclosing the possibility of New Zealand buying a second-hand ship which the Australians would replace with a new-build.

However, along with this request, was another of the same date, asking for agreement in principle that the lease of 28 F-16s from the United States be negotiated. To seek two such requests at the same Cabinet meeting was perhaps, in light of the politics of the time, being a little optimistic. The Minister himself was only too aware of the difficulty of selling the proposals:

> But there is another affordability view, that of the public. There is little doubt that most people see the purchase of a third frigate as 'unaffordable'. Perhaps this has more to do with not understanding the role of the Navy, or of the role of the frigates in the Navy.[21]

The Minister was also aware of the views of some of his Cabinet colleagues: 'We had a relatively pacifist group of people within Cabinet. … The perception in Cabinet was that there wasn't support for a third new frigate. That's why I'd taken the precaution of organising a second-hand one.'[22]

Whilst Paul East had noted in the *Defence Assessment Paper* that no second hand ANZAC frigates were available, by the following year that had changed. Max Bradford said: 'The Australians bent over backwards' [to come up with a deal].[23] The Australian Department of Defence:

> offered [name deleted] a new ship as of today[24] … for delivery in four and a half years time. Modification would be required at a cost of up to [figure deleted]. The down payment would be 15% and the remainder would be paid over 5 years after delivery in 2003.[25]

Treasury seemed warm to the notion of a second-hand ship. Whilst a new ANZAC was considered and other classes of ship, such as the FFG-7 or UK Type 23 were also reviewed, Treasury felt that:

> The proposal to purchase a second-hand frigate from Australia is likely to be the most cost-effective means of maintaining a three-frigate Navy over the longer term, as it avoids the development and support costs that would be required with another class of ship. The second-hand purchase also minimises likely cost escalations.[26]

The release of the Interim Report of the Foreign Affairs, Defence and Trade Committee, *Inquiry Into Defence Beyond 2000*, in November 1998, the month in which the frigate decision was taken, added more fuel to the, by now, raging debate. The authors commented:

> The political, commercial and practical naval arguments ten years ago for purchasing the ANZAC ships were straightforward. ... The argument ten years ago has weakened with time, and has little force in relation to the purchase of a third ANZAC frigate. Both countries' businesses would have too much to lose by a winding back of the clock in the broader area of CER—not to mention the bad signals that any unilateral action by Australia would send to its other trading partners.[27]

However, the Minister made the point very clearly in the paper that this was a last-chance opportunity.

> This is the last opportunity to acquire a third ANZAC ship. Not taking a decision will risk the New Zealand Government not having a valid offer on the table for consideration from either TENIX or the Australian Government. The flow-on effect will mean that New Zealand would not be able to source an ANZAC replacement for HMNZS *Canterbury* prior to her withdrawal from RNZN operational service in 2005.[28]

By the fourth quarter of 1998 the country was officially in recession and unemployment rose. In November 1998 Jenny Shipley was Prime Minister and leading a minority Government. The coalition with NZ First had disintegrated in August of that year, and Shipley's Government relied on a 'mixed bag of 18 ACT, United and Independent MPs'.[29] In her 'Opening Remarks' in the book *Holyoake's Lieutenants*, Shipley noted: 'Sir Keith exemplified the virtues which subsequent New Zealand Prime Ministers have to strive for—magnanimity, calm assurance, good humour, team-building and, moreover, consensus-seeking as opposed to enforcing consensus.'[30]

In the lead-up to the decision on whether or not to purchase a third ANZAC frigate, Shipley was only too well-aware of the importance of seeking consensus and maintaining political support from a very varied group of MPs.

Labour Leader Helen Clark saw an opportunity to make significant political gains out of the situation, and pulled no punches:

> It is understood that the New Zealand Government has already indicated to Australia that it is likely to purchase a third frigate, but that Mrs Shipley does not want to make any public announcement before February. The coincidence of announcement in February, presumably after the scheduled vote of confidence, will not be accidental. Mrs Shipley and National know that there has been opposition in ACT to a frigate purchase, and that former Peace Activists like the Rev. Ann Batten, would have to reconsider their support for the Government if the frigate purchase went ahead.[31]

Helen Clark went on to say:

> The Rev. Ann Batten says she speaks for the other independent MPs involved in launching the new political party when she states that they will not back the frigate purchase … if National is determined on the purchase of the third ANZAC frigate, then this issue may well precipitate an election before Christmas.[32]

> What is outstanding about the proposed purchase is the persistent allegation that the Government is proposing to put down a $50 million non-refundable deposit for a third frigate in a bizarre attempt to commit future Governments to it. It is understood that no such deposit is required. Mrs Shipley and National Cabinet Ministers are fighting a losing battle in trying to sell the idea of another ANZAC frigate purchase. National backbenchers are said to be extremely concerned about the political implications for their Government, which is already on the rocks.[33]

Clark went on to comment on the issue of trade-offs, which Max Bradford commented on as bureaucratic politics. Clark said:

> The big losers from a spend-up on yet another frigate would be the NZ Army which currently is carrying the major burden of New Zealand's defence commitments overseas. The NZ Army is highly respected for its work around the globe. Yet it has been sent to a major commitment in Bosnia under-equipped to the extent that soldiers' lives were in danger.[34]

The pressure on the Government continued throughout November. At its meeting on 30 November, Cabinet noted that there were three options before it to secure a replacement for the frigate HMNZS *Canterbury*; to buy a new ANZAC frigate from Australian-based Tenix Corporation now; to buy a second-hand ship from Australia; or to wait for an opportunity to buy in two or three years' time. Nevertheless, despite the opportunity to purchase what appeared to be a bargain, Cabinet rejected the deal for a third ANZAC frigate. The decision was announced on 1 December 1998 that New Zealand would not be proceeding with a third ANZAC frigate, and a decision for a replacement vessel was to be delayed until 2002. Bradford put on a brave face in commenting on the decision, and said the Government would continue to look for a replacement third frigate, although he 'acknowledged that this was highly unlikely to be another ANZAC'.[35] In reflecting on the decision, Bradford commented:

> There was a huge stink and we weren't doing at all well in the polls. The issue never got a timely enough run to convince the public. It was a combination of a concerted campaign by the Opposition and a minority Government no longer in coalition. There was Deborah Morris and others

being fed misinformation by the Army, and there were those in our own Party who were against it.[36]

The following year there was to be another election and a change of Government, and this was to be followed by a significant change to the outlook for the RNZN. New frigates would no longer be on the agenda.

Summary

In examining the final (two) decisions not to proceed with the purchase of further ANZAC (or indeed any other) frigates, several features come to the fore. New Zealand's relationship with Australia, the ongoing requirement for a blue-water navy, and the recognition that there was one last opportunity to buy a third ANZAC frigate—all these factors played their part during the early stages of the decision-making process. Timing however, was once more to be a crucial factor. The 1991 and 1997 *Defence Reviews* reinforced the notion of 'Self-Reliance in Partnership', while at the same time requiring the maintenance of a balanced force which was militarily credible. Whilst naval combat credibility had previously been predicated upon the notion of a minimum of a four frigate Navy, the Government was only too well aware of the political and budget constraints of the time. These constraints, rather than military credibility, led to a decision by Cabinet to move the naval combat force from four frigates to three in 1998. Even this, however, was not to eventuate.

Whilst continued public opposition to the frigates, and bureaucratic politics, including the role of Treasury and the Army, were important as the decisions not to proceed were made, ultimately the two most important elements during these periods were politics and the judgement of political side effects. Reflecting the new power of MMP, the impact of these influencing elements was to lead to the Government backing down on a decision to purchase a further frigate in both 1997 and 1998. Having made a policy decision in the 1997 White Paper that New Zealand should have a three frigate fleet, National was just not able to ensure that this would actually eventuate.

ENDNOTES

[1] Warren Cooper, Interview, *Australian Defence Magazine*, vol. 2, no. 7, September 1994, p. 6.

[2] *New Zealand Herald*, 18 January 1995.

[3] Stephen Levine, Paul Spoonley and Peter Aimer, *Waging Peace Towards 2000*, Foundation for Peace Studies, Auckland, 1995 p. 44.

[4] *Labour's Foreign Affairs and Defence Policy: An Independent Foreign Policy*, New Zealand Labour Party, Wellington, August 1996, p. 23.

[5] Rt. Hon. Helen Clark, 'Labour's Approach to Foreign Affairs and Defence Policy', Address to the Dunedin Branch of the New Zealand Institute of Foreign Affairs, 9 August 1996.

[6] Ruth Laugesen, 'East favours buying more frigates', *New Zealand Herald*, 9 February 1997.

[7] Laugesen, 'East favours buying more frigates'.

[8] *Defence Assessment Paper*, Office of the Minister of Defence, Wellington, 17 September 1997, p. 3 and p. 10. Paper attached to ERD (97) 18.

[9] ERD (97) 18, p. 2.
[10] ERD (97) 18, p. 2, and *New Zealand Herald*, 15 October 1997.
[11] *New Zealand Herald*, 15 October 1997.
[12] G. Anthony Vignaux, *The Navy Critical Mass Argument*, Victoria University of Wellington, Wellington, July 1997, p. 2.
[13] Cabinet paper CAB (97) M 40/8A, p. 2.
[14] *Inquiry Into Defence Beyond 2000*, Interim Report of the Foreign Affairs, Defence and Trade Committee, House of Representatives, Wellington, November 1998, p. 84.
[15] *Sunday Star-Times*, 19 October 1997.
[16] *The Shape of New Zealand's Defence, A White Paper*, Ministry of Defence, Wellington, November 1997.
[17] *New Zealand Herald*, 12 November 1997.
[18] *New Zealand Herald*, 12 November 1997.
[19] Greg Ansley, 'Naval gazing shows up NZ defence', *New Zealand Herald*, 25 March 1998.
[20] 'Replacement Frigate Project'. Paper attached to Cabinet paper CAB (98) 852, pp. 6–7.
[21] 'Rebuilding New Zealand's Defence Capabilities'. Paper attached to Cabinet Paper CAB (98) 855, p. 3.
[22] Max Bradford, Personal interview, 10 November 2003.
[23] Bradford, Personal interview, 10 November 2003.
[24] By extrapolation, it would seem that the vessel under consideration was Ship No. 151, the second ANZAC delivered to the RAN, HMAS *Arunta*, which was commissioned on 12 December 1998. See 'HMAS Arunta', available at <http://www.navy.gov.au/HMAS_Arunta>, accessed 28 October 2008.
[25] *Replacement Frigate Project, Executive Summary*, Office of the Minister of Defence. Paper attached to Cabinet paper CAB(98) 852.
[26] *Replacement Frigate Project, Executive Summary*. Paper attached to Cabinet paper CAB(98) 852.
[27] *Inquiry into Defence Beyond 2000*, Interim Report of the Foreign Affairs, Defence and Trade Committee, p. 31.
[28] *Replacement Frigate Project*, Office of the Minister of Defence. Paper attached to Cabinet Paper CAB(98) 852, p. 8.
[29] *New Zealand Herald*, 2 December 1998.
[30] Jenny Shipley, 'Opening Remarks', in Margaret Clark (ed.), *Holyoake's Lieutenants*, Dunmore Press Ltd, Palmerston North, 2003, p. 11.
[31] Rt. Hon. Helen Clark, Leader of the Opposition, Media Statement, 'Labour: Bradford must come out of bunker on frigate issue', 28 October 1998. Derek Quigley noted however that 'Despite Helen Clark's comments, ACT was not opposed to a third frigate. When Bradford briefed our caucus, our response was that it and the F-16 decisions were matters for the Government'. Derek Quigley, Correspondence, 23 April 2007.
[32] Rt. Hon. Helen Clark, Leader of the Opposition, Media Statement, 'Labour: Henare party on collision course with National over frigate purchase', 28 October 1998.
[33] Rt. Hon. Helen Clark, Leader of the Opposition, Media Statement, 'Labour calls on Government to declare its intention on third frigate', 28 October 1998.
[34] Clark, 'Labour calls on Government to declare its intention on third frigate'.
[35] *New Zealand Herald*, 2 December 1998.
[36] Bradford, Personal interview, 10 November 2003.

Chapter 5

'The Deal of the Century' — The F-16s

In November 1998 the National-led Coalition Government, at the same time that it decided not to pursue the purchase of a third ANZAC frigate, made a decision to lease 28 F-16 A/B aircraft from the United States. That same month, the Interim Report of the Foreign Affairs, Defence and Trade Committee, *Inquiry into Defence Beyond 2000* was published.[1] In contrast to the Government's decision, the Report challenged whether it was necessary to retain an air combat wing at all. The following year the Labour Party returned to power leading a coalition government, and had already indicated that it would review the F-16 lease decision. In order to do so, it called for the Chair of the *Inquiry into Defence Beyond 2000* Report, the Hon. Derek Quigley, to undertake the review. The *Review* was published on 6 March 2000,[2] and the Government announced on 20 March that it would not proceed with the lease arrangements entered into by the previous Government.

This chapter traces the events leading up to the National-led Government's decision to lease 28 F-16s, and the subsequent decision by the Labour-led coalition to cancel the lease, highlighting the critical elements which came to bear as the decision to lease was made, and then unmade. Subsequently I report on the decision to abandon the Royal New Zealand Air Force (RNZAF) strike air combat wing, and the disbandment of No. 2, No. 14 and No. 75 Squadrons in December 2001.

History and Background

For over three decades, the McDonnell Douglas A-4K and TA-4K served as New Zealand's strike aircraft. The 1966 Defence White Paper reinforced the need for the RNZAF to continue to operate in combat, transport and maritime roles.[3] By this stage, the *Canberra* bombers of No. 14 Squadron, which had been introduced in 1959, were seen to need replacement by 1970. British fighter production had been axed by the 1957 White Paper, and attention turned to the United States, which had several aircraft which might be suitable. Types considered by the RNZAF during 1967 included the Northrop F-5E *Tiger*, McDonnell Douglas F-4E *Phantom* and A-4E *Skyhawk*, and the General Dynamics F-111. Ultimately the McDonnell Douglas A-4E *Skyhawk* was selected, and in April 1968 14 were ordered at a cost of $NZ24.65 million.[4] Designated A-4K (K for *Kiwi*), the aircraft were essentially the A-4E with minor changes as specified by the RNZAF. The 10 A-4K and 4 TA-4K aircraft arrived in Auckland on board the USS *Okinawa* on 17 May 1970, although the uninsured aircraft were almost lost at sea. After leaving Pearl Harbor in Hawaii, the aircraft carrier hit a storm with 80 knot winds. The captain considered rolling the aircraft into the sea to save his ship, but the storm abated just in time to save them.[5] The aircraft were officially taken into service in June 1970, with No. 75 Squadron.

The decision to purchase the A-4 *Skyhawk* met with some criticism within the RNZAF, but the aircraft, first flown in 1954, had demonstrated its capability by 1968 when New Zealand placed the order: it was at that stage still the mainstay of the US Navy and US Marine Corps attack wings, and had been well-proven in combat in the Vietnam War.[6]

The aircraft's general capability for close air support was sufficient for the tasks expected of it in 1970, but by the time of the 1983 *Defence Review* an extended range of tasks was anticipated, including maritime strike, counter-air, sea and land interdiction and close air support. The RNZAF considered three options at the time: the acquisition of more capable second-hand aircraft; new aircraft; or the upgrade of the A-4 *Skyhawk*. In 1983 the RNZAF evaluation group reviewed a number of new aircraft, and favoured the purchase of new F-16s. The program cost was to be NZ$900 million, including spares and equipment, and was seen as prohibitive. A decision was then taken to considerably upgrade the current aircraft. The 1983 *Defence Review* commented:

> The A4-K *Skyhawk* aircraft have served us well in the attack role. The 1978 Review identified a requirement to upgrade the aircraft's navigation and weapon delivery systems and planning to do so is well advanced. It has since been established that a structural refurbishment programme will also be necessary to extend the life of the aircraft.

The *Review* went on:

> In addition to the planned upgrading programme, consideration has been given to acquiring additional aircraft. Augmenting the present force would offset basic performance limitations, replace those lost in service and provide for attrition during the aircraft's remaining life.[7]

The Royal Australian Navy (RAN) had a number of A-4 *Skyhawks* which were surplus to its requirements after its aircraft carrier had been scrapped in 1982. In 1984 the New Zealand Government approved the purchase of eight single-seat A-4Gs and two TA-4G two-seat trainers. The package deal cost NZ$40 million, including spares and equipment, and No. 2 Squadron was reformed to accept the aircraft.

The avionics upgrade was to be extremely comprehensive. The Labour Government gave its approval for a NZ$140 million modernisation plan in May 1985. The upgrade was anticipated to give the aircraft an avionics suite comparable to an F-16C, significantly enhancing the aircraft's strike capability and intended to give it an operational capability of 90 per cent of an F-16C for 15 per cent of the cost—a variation on the classic Kiwi 80/20 solution.[8] Despite the cooling of NZ–US relations over the anti-nuclear ships debacle, the US Congress gave its approval for the technology transfer in December 1985, and the contract with Lear Siegler was signed in 1986 by the Minister of Defence, the Hon. Frank O'Flynn. The importance of this work was reinforced by the 1987 *Review of Defence Policy*, which said:

> The RNZAF must be able to respond immediately and, if it becomes necessary, to engage hostile ships and submarines, at some distance from New Zealand. Maintaining this ability is an important part of deterrence: ensuring this type of threatening situation does not eventuate. Work currently underway on modernising the *Skyhawks* will greatly increase effectiveness in this regard.[9]

The first 'Kahu' *Skyhawk* was returned to service and flown in June 1988, and the last in March 1991.

The value of the upgrade was immediately apparent. Wing Commander Ian Gore, who led No. 75 Squadron on a series of exercises with Australian, Malaysian, Singaporean, and Thai air forces in 1991 and 1992 said: 'The Skyhawk has gone from an aircraft with no systems you could rely on, to one with the capability of modern front-line fighters, at a fraction of the cost.'[10] Flight Lieutenant Murray Neilson, who also flew on those exercises, further noted: 'We were constantly surprised how well we performed in air-to-air combat against superior aircraft, especially the F-16 ... *Kahu* has brought the *Skyhawk* into the 1990s.'[11]

The aircraft however still had shortcomings; they were noticeably slower than their modern counterparts when fully laden with weapons, and the *Maverick* missiles were only effective for a range of five miles—insufficient for a realistic attack on a modern warship. Nevertheless, Gore still saw *Kahu* as a major success: 'Considering we did so well against aircraft we aspired to replace the *Skyhawk* with—the F-16 and the *Harrier*—the update was an inspired choice.'[12]

At the time of the 1997 *Defence Assessment*, the decision was made to maintain an Air Combat Force comprising A-4 *Skyhawks*, which would be replaced by a suitable aircraft in due course. The 1997 White Paper commented further: 'The aircraft are old but sturdy. They have been rewinged and seven years ago were given a major upgrade. They have sufficient life left to perform effectively into the next decade.'[13]

In commenting on the Government's decisions, the *New Zealand Herald* noted: 'It is understood there is no immediate plan to replace the Air Force's 19 elderly Skyhawk fighter-bombers, but longer-term purchases are not ruled out.'[14] It was, in fact, to be no time at all before new purchases were considered.

'The Deal of the Century'[15] — The Lease of the F-16s

'Since the publication of the White Paper, an opportunity to acquire F-16 aircraft has arisen,' said the Chief of Air Staff, Air Vice-Marshal Carey Adamson in an *RNZAF News Special* in December 1998.[16] The article went on to say that a joint RNZAF–MoD Team had conducted an evaluation of the aircraft and discussed issues around the potential lease of the aircraft whilst visiting the United States in September 1998, and a decision on whether to proceed with the acquisition was expected before the end of the year.

The United States Government had offered New Zealand the opportunity to acquire 28 F-16s, originally brought for Pakistan, but embargoed in 1990 because of US concerns over Pakistan's desire to develop nuclear weapons.[17] The planes on offer consisted of 13 single-seater F-16A-15OCU and 15 two-seater F-16B-15OCU, which had been stored at a desert US Air Force base in Arizona since they were built in 1991 and 1992. The planes were effectively almost new, with each of them having flown for only three or four hours.

Gerald Hensley, at the time Secretary of Defence, had originally been approached in 1996 about the possibility of the F-16s being made available to New Zealand:

> I was at the ASEAN Regional Forum Meeting in Kuala Lumpur. I recall Kurt Campbell, Deputy Secretary said to me over dinner, 'Why don't you buy the F-16s?—we'll give you a good price'. That was in 1996.[18] I regret saying it now, but I replied that we were in the middle of the latest Defence Review, and could do nothing until it was completed.[19]

Subsequently, in May of 1998, the Secretary of Defence approached Sir Wilson Whineray to chair the Air Combat Capability Study, the timing of which

> has largely been determined by the need for a decision on the opportunity to purchase second-hand, but little used F-16 fighter aircraft, the so-called 'Peacegate' aircraft. Before a decision can be made on these aircraft, Defence first needs to determine what type of air combat capability is required.[20]

The Report (the Whineray Report) went into some detail to determine what type of air combat capability was required, and explored a broad range of capability options to assess how each might fulfil New Zealand's requirements. The study was unequivocal in its findings that the range of operational roles able to be carried out by an air combat capability should remain Close Air Support, Air Interdiction and Maritime Strike. These three roles were said to stand out in terms of their high military and policy utility for a New Zealand air combat capability.

The study explored the capabilities of the current A-4K *Skyhawk*, F-16 C/D, F-16 A/B, Light attack Aircraft, and a combination of Attack Helicopter and P-3K *Orion*. These five options were subject to detailed analysis, and Sir Wilson Whineray commented:

> This very clearly showed that the type of capability New Zealand requires is of a modern multi-role fighter aircraft; the F-16 C/D was used to represent such a capability in the study. This was by far the best option. None of the other options performed nearly as well.[21]

Notwithstanding these comments, the Report went on to say:

> The initial production fourth generation multi-role fighter capability represented in the study by the F-16 A/B was found to be highly effective across almost all of the requirements New Zealand anticipates. While the F-16 A/B would need updating to meet New Zealand requirements, it is a fourth generation aircraft with upgrade potential to a capability standard similar to that of an F-16 C/D.[22]

Max Bradford, the Minister of Defence, was very keen to see the *Skyhawks* replaced by the F-16s, partly because of growing concern about their structural integrity: 'I was getting some disturbing reports from the RNZAF about the state of the airframes, and the expected life of the aircraft would be less than anticipated because of structural problems with their tails.'[23] In November 1998 the Minister proposed to Cabinet that New Zealand should agree in principle to the proposal to negotiate the lease of 28 F-16 A/B aircraft. That same month, it was reported that the *Skyhawk* fleet was to undergo Life of Type testing, to determine whether the aircraft could remain airworthy until their anticipated retirement around 2005. The proposal to Cabinet sought approval to bring forward the replacement of the A-4K *Skyhawk*, and commented that 'mechanical airframe systems such as the engine, hydraulics and fuel systems ... are subject to the effects of age, declining reliability and a lack of readily available support from equipment manufacturers'.[24]

Leasing the aircraft was proposed over two 5-year periods, with an average cost to lease all 28 aircraft of NZ$12.5 million per year. There was, in addition to the lease cost, a capital cost estimated at NZ$204.5 million to reactivate the aircraft and purchase spares and training. Savings of $54 million were anticipated if the purchase went ahead, as the update to extend the life of the A-4K *Skyhawks* would not be necessary. It was also expected that the sale of the *Skyhawks* would realise 'a meaningful return'.[25] In total, it was estimated that the leasing of the F-16s would save NZ$431 million over the life of the aircraft, compared to purchasing new aircraft early in the next century.

In making a case for the lease of the F-16s, Max Bradford introduced an updated Defence 10 Year Capital Plan.[26] Within this, the Minister recognised the issue of trade-offs and commented that the new plan necessitated a change in project timings, 'slipping C-130 replacement to smooth a potential funding bulge',[27] and requiring, 'an extended delivery of armoured vehicles.'[28]

Treasury's response to the Capital Plan was cool, indicating that 'the Plan does not fit within the envelope of increased capital and operating funding signalled by the Defence Assessment'.[29] Treasury went on and said that the planned upgrade for the Army, purchase of a third ANZAC frigate, leasing the F-16s and replacing the C-130 *Hercules* could not be undertaken within the funding envelope.[30] Taking account of external influences, the proposal paper for the lease of the F-16s advised:

> The US has asked us to make a ... stronger commitment to increased defence spending, and an acknowledgement that the unfinished business needs to be addressed. ... A decision in principle to lease the F-16s ... would be very well received by the US Government and it would be a positive factor in its consideration of forward movement in our defence relationship.[31]

Gordon Campbell was somewhat blunter when commenting upon the Australian viewpoint: 'The decision to get them is also meant to appease the Australians. ... If we hadn't decided to get the F-16s, the Australians would probably have gone completely ballistic.'[32]

Once the decision in principle had been made, Campbell asked Max Bradford when an 'iron-clad agreement' would be made, 'one that not even an incoming Labour government could overturn?'[33] The Minister replied: 'We would want to make pretty rapid progress on this ... February, March, early April.'[34] In the event it was to be July before the lease deal was signed—and it was not as iron-clad as some might have hoped for. Whilst the Minister was emphasising the potential savings involved in the lease deal, questions were being raised elsewhere about whether an air combat force was necessary at all. The *Inquiry into Defence Beyond 2000*, Interim Report of the Foreign Affairs, Defence and Trade Committee was also published in November 1998. Whilst the Report acknowledged that there were national interest arguments in favour of keeping an air combat force, it noted that in 28 years the A-4 *Skyhawks* had never been used in combat. The Report went on to say:

> Air combat forces are expensive to retain and operate (14 per cent of the NZDF budget), and possibly beyond New Zealand's economic capacity to keep up to date without detracting from other more necessary military capabilities. ... We believe that the NZDF has two options: either disband the jet training and strike capability, on purely financial grounds, or to replace the current A4s with more modern combat aircraft on the basis of their capacity to contribute to the advancement of the country's

national interest considered alongside other competing expenditure priorities.[35]

On 1 December 1998, having lost the battle over the third frigate, the Minister was nevertheless able to announce: 'The A-4K *Skyhawks* air combat force will be replaced with 28 F-16 A/B aircraft on lease from the United States. Final negotiations on lease terms, and on the purchase of spares and support equipment, have to be completed.'[36]

In the debate over the choice of the F-16, A/B Group Captain Ian Brunton, Assistant Chief of Air Staff, RNZAF, noted that the F-16 had been the workhorse of the 1991 Gulf War, and that there were now 4000 F-16s worldwide.[37] However, in commenting on the importance of up-to-date technology in contemporary conflict, one US analyst said:

> The most significant technologies in the (Gulf War) conflict were not necessarily weapons but those that allowed allied forces to identify and track targets rapidly; gather, process, evaluate and distribute information; decide priorities for targeting; navigate on the ground, in the air, and at sea; or command and control.[38]

Gordon Campbell, in an article entitled 'Pop Gun' in the *New Zealand Listener*, published a month after the lease deal was announced, highlighted that the F-16s were fitted only with 'secure UHF radios'[39] and were without the data-link modems that allowed the processing and distribution of information seen as essential in modern combat. The aircraft were fitted with the same radar as the A-4 *Skyhawks*, without the capability to identify multiple threats and decide the level of threat and order of response. Campbell asserted: 'One thing is clear ... although these Block 15 A/Bs outclass our venerable Skyhawks, they are themselves already outdated.'[40] Brunton responded: 'The article is technically incorrect and paints a very misleading picture of the F-16 acquisition.'[41] Nevertheless, he did acknowledge that 'the computers and display systems in our aircraft are, however, becoming dated and will require upgrading'.[42] Notwithstanding this comment, Brunton assured that the F-16s would be 'more than capable of defending themselves.'[43] Quigley remained to be convinced, saying some seven months later that 'the pilots who fly our F-16 A/B aircraft, if the acquisition were to go ahead, would face serious disadvantages in combat'.[44]

Once again, in responding to the *Inquiry into Defence Beyond 2000*, the Government argued that the aircraft would be capable of fulfilling the tasks required of them without further upgrading, but that they would 'eventually receive a mid-life upgrade'.[45] In his response to Campbell's article, Brunton added:

> It is unnecessary for us to proceed with MLU (Mid-Life Upgrade) at this time. Furthermore, it makes sense for us to gain experience operating

the aircraft for a period so that we are in a better position to choose the best update option in due course.[46]

It seemed to me that these were the very sentiments expressed at the time that an unmodified HMNZS *Charles Upham* was brought into service.

In noting that the aircraft were not due to arrive until mid-2001, Helen Clark, the Leader of the Opposition, commented that this '[gave] an incoming government plenty of time to review the position.'[47] The following year was to be an election year, and the opportunity to purchase the F-16s, whilst not as controversial as the issue of the third frigate, was nonetheless to be at the forefront as the election approached.

To Lease or Not to Lease—The 1999 Question

Not surprisingly, the Chief of Air Staff, Air Vice Marshal Carey Adamson, was delighted with the Government's decision. In an article in the December edition of *RNZAF News*, he commented:

> The F-16 will maintain the roles of maritime attack, air-interdiction and close air support and, in doing so, will continue to defend New Zealand's strategic interests far more effectively and capably than the *Skyhawk* has been able to. Our allies and regional neighbours will see this as a major increase in the credibility of our national commitment to peace and security in the region.[48]

Helen Clark was somewhat less enthusiastic about the proposed lease deal, saying that 'the whole thinking and strategy behind it is warped'.[49] However, the importance of maintaining an air strike capability was further highlighted by the Secretary of Defence Gerald Hensley the following year:

> Maintenance of an air strike capability in particular is critical to our role in the principle FPDA activity; that of the air defence of Malaysia and Singapore.[50] ... We see New Zealand and Australia as a single strategic entity. As with the FPDA, our air combat force plays an important role in this relationship.[51]

Approval for the lease deal was announced by the Minister of Defence on 26 July 1999. Although the lease costs were to be the same as those announced the previous December, at NZ$124.8 million (excluding GST) the start-up package had increased by NZ$34 million to NZ$238 million. Nonetheless it was still estimated that the deal would save some NZ$350 million compared with purchasing new aircraft the following century. The 10-year lease agreement was signed two days later in Washington, DC, by the Attorney General, the Right Honourable Sir Douglas Graham. In commenting on the deal, the Minister of Defence said: 'It gives us a new aircraft at a price we simply couldn't afford to pass up. ... The lease is seen by Treasury as being "the least cost option" to acquire this increase in air combat capability.'[52]

The following month the final version of *Inquiry into Defence Beyond 2000* was released. In this Report, the Committee echoed much of what had been indicated in the Interim Report:

> For us, the important criterion alongside affordability for setting priorities for investment in the NZDF is the utility of the force elements that New Zealand maintains. We see air combat forces as being of lesser utility, given competing demands for scarce NZDF resources, than the other force elements maintained by the NZDF.[53]

The Report recommended that, were the air combat force to be retained, the possibility of down-sizing to a smaller force of better armed aircraft should be considered, whilst reviewing the lease of the F-16s. Max Bradford, not surprisingly, was opposed to the majority findings of the Report, indicating that the recommendations, if implemented, would fundamentally change New Zealand's defence relationship with Australia, 'which would be a matter of serious concern'.[54] Helen Clark, on the other hand, was strongly supportive of the Report's findings, and indicated that a Labour Government would adopt the recommendations: 'I'd be surprised if our policy when released didn't fairly closely shadow (the report).[55]

At a pre-election seminar held on 21 October 1999, Phil Goff reinforced this view:

> Labour opposes the decision to invest what will amount to $700 million on the F-16 A/B jet aircraft. It also opposes the purchase of further ANZAC frigates. Neither can be considered a priority if peace keeping is to continue to be the focus of deployment of our armed forces.
>
> In opting for frigates and F-16s, the National Government has put display ahead of utility. It has been concerned more about pleasing military chiefs in Australia and the United States, than about meeting the practical needs arising from the responsibilities we are actually placing on our armed forces.[56]

When Wayne Mapp spoke at the same seminar on National's Foreign and Defence Policy, he portrayed National's diametrically opposing view, reinforcing the importance of the development of the relationship with the United States:

> The Air Force requirements are of a different character. Everyone accepts the need for new strategic air transport and upgraded maritime surveillance. The sharp differences settle on the lease of the F-16s. ... The Air Combat Force is not just about military utility. It is also about restoring our Defence relationships, particularly with the United States.

> If we had failed to accept the extremely favourable lease arrangements for the F-16s, our friends and allies would question our commitment to the security of the region. Our overall relationship with the United States would have been severely damaged.[57]

When Labour's defence policy was released in November, it did in fact closely follow the Report, and confirmed opposition to the lease of the F-16s. Geoff Braybrooke, Labour's defence spokesperson, said it was wrong to spend such a large proportion of the defence budget on 'showpiece' items like the F-16s, whilst the New Zealand Army was being sent into war zones such as East Timor with obsolete equipment. As the two major parties entered the election race, they provided the New Zealand public with two very clear and very different views on defence, reflecting two different views of New Zealand's role in the world. Later that month the New Zealand public endorsed Labour's view and Labour came to power with a new Coalition government. Following the first meeting of the new Cabinet in December, Helen Clark confirmed that there was insufficient money available for increased spending for defence, and that removing the F-16 lease deal would assist with meeting other priorities: 'We'd need to take advice on that. That could be enough.'[58]

The Death of New Zealand's 'Flying Falcon' — The Final F-16 Decision

In seeking advice on the lease deal, Clark turned to former ACT MP Derek Quigley, the former chair of the Foreign Affairs, Defence and Trade Committee, and author of *Inquiry into Defence Beyond 2000*. In that Report, Quigley raised concerns about the difficulty the Committee had had in accessing adequate information about the F-16 lease. On 20 December 1999, Cabinet determined the terms of reference for an independent review of the proposal to lease the 28 F-16 aircraft, and Quigley was to have access to a much wider range of information than had previously been made available to him. The *Review* was urgent as, amongst other things, in Quigley's own words, 'the meter [was] running'.[59]

Throughout the debate on the lease of the F-16s, the Labour Party had been opposed to their acquisition. However, there were many who were concerned about the impact that the cancellation might have on New Zealand's relationship with Australia and the United States. Associate Professor Stephen Hoadley from the University of Auckland commented that the F-16 lease deal was a cooperative step, showing 'both Washington and Canberra that Wellington is a good international citizen and a serious team player', and that 'its cancellation risks relegation of New Zealand to the margins of the diplomatic map'.[60] John Armstrong, the *New Zealand Herald*'s political editor, warned that 'the Coalition cabinet is on a collision course with Canberra and Washington'.[61] He went on to say that 'cancellation would go down badly in Australia'.[62] This sentiment was echoed on other pages of the *New Zealand Herald* that day, with Greg Ansley, the Canberra bureau chief indicating that a cancellation of the lease would lead to 'anger and dismay'.[63] Max Bradford of course felt the deal was essential to maintain credibility with New Zealand's neighbours.[64]

However, others were less concerned. The [Christchurch] *Press* saw the deal as 'ill-conceived in the first place',[65] and suggested that there should be no surprise if Quigley advised that the decision should be reversed. The Prime Minister indicated that she did not see any cooling in New Zealand's relationship with the United States.[66] Professor Desmond Ball, from The Australian National University in Canberra, said:

> I don't think anyone would worry about them getting rid of the F-16s because there was no point in having them in the first place. Most of the relevant areas in the (Australian) Department of Defence were dumbfounded when the F-16s were acquired. ... It was hard to understand to begin with.[67]

The editorial in *The Independent Business Weekly* the following week reinforced this view:

> As for the reaction in Australia ... let's not forget officials there were aghast when we announced the F-16 deal in the first place. Their belief ... is unlikely to be different now.[68]

The *Review* was published on 6 March 2000, and sought to provide advice which would help the New Zealand Government determine whether the lease deal should be cancelled, deferred, amended or confirmed. It also considered whether the F-16 deal would have an adverse effect on other urgent defence priorities, and whether the deal locked the NZDF into a capability that was of significant cost and limited utility.

From the start, Quigley made the point that the review of the lease proposal also 'inevitably involved a much more fundamental consideration of New Zealand defence policy and force capabilities'.[69] He went on to suggest that the process required the review to consider how New Zealand wished to see itself, and what sort of tasks the nation wanted New Zealand defence forces to undertake. That is, what was New Zealand's role in the world? Reflecting upon the role of external influences, Quigley observed:

> The F-16 package involves more than merely upgrading a major combat capability. It appears to reflect a conscious decision by the US Administration to redefine defence relationships with New Zealand and enable us to play—*in its eyes*—a more effective role in regional security.[70]

The Report noted that whilst funding had already been committed to the F-16 aircraft—which had not been signalled in the 1997 *Defence*

Assessment—there were still 11 outstanding projects which were deemed to be Priority One in November 1998, and to which funds had yet to be allocated. Of these projects, six were for the New Zealand Army, three for the RNZAF, and two for the RNZN. They were:

- The balance of the Army Direct Fire Support weapons
- Army Anti-Armour Weapons
- Armoured Vehicle Replacement
- Landrover Replacement
- Reconnaissance Vehicles
- Army Communications
- *Orion* Upgrade (Project *Sirius*)
- *Iriquois* Life Extension
- C-130 Replacement/Upgrade
- Replacement of HMNZS *Canterbury*
- Conversion of HMNZS *Charles Upham*

Quigley was highly critical that there was no adequate process in place for setting priorities, and that projects were approved, or not, when they came to the top of the list after tendering—or if they were the subject, such as the F-16s of an 'opportunity purchase'.

In the *Review*, he also sought to clarify the Select Committee's views on the Army, highlighting that:

> The majority of the Committee did not say that the Army should be given permanent priority ahead of everything else. It said that given the 'better shape' of some other force elements, deployable land force elements and the other capabilities needed to support that, should be the top priority.[71]

Quigley added that 'the (then) Government members on the Committee agreed that "the development of a well-equipped motorised infantry force is the top priority in the re-equipping of the NZDF"'.[72]

Whilst acknowledging that determining overall defence priorities was not within the terms of reference of the *Review*, he noted that determining the impact of the F-16 lease on other defence requirements was within the terms of reference. The summary of the *Review* clearly stated the dilemma that was being faced by the Government. At the time of the 1997 *Defence Assessment*, it suggested, an extra injection of NZ$509 million was foreseen for the following 10 year period. By the time of the *Review*, that figure had increased to NZ$1 billion, and did not include an extra NZ$583 million required over the following three years to proceed with replacing Army communications equipment, light armoured and light operational vehicles, and Project *Sirius*. The *Review* made the point: 'It is against this background that the F-16 project needs to be considered.'[73]

The *Review* went on to confirm the not-inconsiderable costs involved in the project—NZ$1 billion of capital injection if the aircraft were leased, then purchased, and received the recommended upgrades. Contrasted with this additional cost, up to NZ$140 million per annum could be saved if the air combat force was disbanded.

The recommendations that the *Review* made were significant. Quigley noted: 'Clearly, New Zealand does not currently need 22 operational aircraft. After all, the RNZAF coped with 14 *Skyhawks* from mid-1970 to the mid-1980s with no visible diminution of effect.' He further concluded:

> The air combat capability also needs to be seen in a broader context. On the one hand, it provides the Government with choice in responding to international security and peacekeeping operations, particularly if the capability is upgraded. On the other hand, the savings in operating and capital costs from disbanding the air combat capability could be applied to other more urgent NZDF priorities. What has become apparent, however, is the feasibility of acquiring fewer F-16s to retain a core combat capability.[74]

In light of this, and further analysis of the savings that could be made by leasing a smaller number of aircraft, the recommendations of the *Review* were:

1. That the New Zealand Government consider approaching the US Government with a view to renegotiating the current F-16 package to include a lesser number of aircraft.
2. That all Defence projects be reviewed as a matter of urgency, on a project by project basis, with a view to prioritising them on the basis of their capacity—judged from an NZDF-wide perspective—to advance New Zealand's national interests.
3. That steps be taken to implement, as soon as practicable, all those aspects of the 1998 *National Real Estate Consolidation Strategy* that are already agreed by NZDF, and that decisions be taken on the remainder.
4. That those parts of the 1991 *Review of Defence Funding* as yet unimplemented be urgently considered and, where relevant, adopted.[75]

On the day that the report was published, Helen Clark said it was clear where the report was headed:

> It will probably say something like this: "If major capital investment in the airstrike arm of the Air Force was your top priority right now, and if you could afford it, this might be a reasonable deal. But if neither of these ifs applies, then the Government has every justification of looking again".[76]

For several months Clark had made it clear that neither of the 'ifs' applied. Two weeks after the publication of the *Review*, following a meeting of cabinet, the Government announced that it would not be proceeding with the lease arrangements. Clark released a statement on Monday 20 March 2000 clarifying the reasons for the decision:

> Mr Quigley made four recommendations ... three of which the Government will act on. The fourth recommendation in his report was that the Government should consider approaching the United States Government with a view to renegotiating the current F-16 purchase to include a smaller number of aircraft. The Government has decided not to take that course. We will be exercising New Zealand's right to withdraw from the lease arrangement. ... While reducing the number of F-16s would have alleviated the immediate funding problem inherent in this acquisition, it would not have removed it. ... In addition, such a decision would have prejudged the broader question of whether New Zealand should retain an air combat capability. That is a matter the government wants to take more time to address.[77]

Whilst Clark did acknowledge that the lease arrangement for the F-16 seemed a good one, she reiterated that this would only be the case if upgrading the air combat capability was a priority: 'The mere existence of a bargain at a sale is not a reason for buying it.'[78] In speaking to the Government's decision, the Prime Minister went on to say:

> Mr Quigley's report describes the Defence Force's fiscal position as parlous. Its capital expenditure requirement is unsustainable. It is also experiencing cash flow problems which would require at least a doubling of the capital injection contemplated in 1997. Unfortunately there is no priority setting in the New Zealand Defence Force which effectively and consistently links individual activities or projects to the government's most pressing national security concerns. *Getting rationality and coherence into defence planning and priority setting is now at the top of the coalition government's agenda.*[79]

Planning for an affordable, well-equipped NZDF was clearly a priority for the new Government; the lease of the F-16s, just as clearly, was not.
the Basement (Cohen St, Belconnen)the Basement (Cohen St, Belconnen)

Disbanding the Air Combat Force

Interestingly, Derek Quigley had noted that in 1991 Wayne Mapp[80] had argued in an article entitled 'Restructuring New Zealand's Defence Force' that the air strike force 'must be the first element to be either eliminated or integrated into the Australian Armed Forces'.[81] Mapp was clear at the time about what he felt about the utility of the Air Combat Force:

> From the New Zealand perspective, the force most suitable for reduction is the air force. The strike role of the A4 *Skyhawks* is almost of no relevance except in medium to high level operations. ... The *Orions* serve an important role. With suitable upgrading with *Harpoon* missiles they could readily take over the full maritime strike role.[82]

Labour had given every indication that they agreed with these sentiments regarding the strike role. In February 2001 the Department of the Prime Minister and Cabinet produced a report, *Review of the Options for an Air Combat Capability*, which spelt out three possible options for the future of the air combat force. These three options were:

1. Retain the air combat force at present levels;
2. Retain a reduced air combat force of 14 strike aircraft; or
3. Disband the air combat force.

The *Review* noted that, with Option 2, there would be insufficient savings realised for the rebuilding of the rest of the NZDF unless it was accompanied by major cuts in other areas.[83] With Option 3, it was anticipated that savings would be produced which, 'as well as the avoidance of further capital investment in the air combat force, would assist in the rebuilding of the NZDF, significantly reducing the need for additional funding'.[84]

Confirming Quigley's assertion that 'to cancel the F-16 contract ... is considered tantamount to disbanding the RNZAF's combat capability',[85] on 8 May 2001 Clark confirmed that the New Zealand Government had decided to disband the air combat wing.[86] The response from some quarters in Australia was stinging. The following day the *Australian* ran the headline 'NZ abandons Anzac tradition'. The article went on to note: 'New Zealand yesterday abandoned 85 years of Anzac tradition by scaling down its military power,'[87] although it added that 'John Howard refrained from criticising the move yesterday, saying "What New Zealand does with New Zealand's defence force is a matter for New Zealand."'[88] Clark commented: 'Nothing about anything we've done in Defence should have been a surprise. It was all in the manifesto, as I keep pointing out.'[89]

Some commentators were pragmatic in their response to Labour's decision. Dick Gentles, former Deputy Secretary, Policy and Planning within the Ministry of Defence said:

> The Air Combat Force had very little utility to this government. The opportunity cost was enormous, and the *Skyhawks* would never have been seriously considered for deployment. I think it was probably the

right decision—it was certainly a brave one. Mark Burton did, though, get a $1 billion commitment for defence over the next 10 years.[90]

Stewart Woodman, Professor at the Australian Defence Force Academy at the University of New South Wales, had been a significant critic of what he considered a moribund approach to defence planning outlined in SONZD 97.[91] He commented: 'What utility would they really have had for the NZDF? F-16s would look funny sitting at the end of a runway in the Solomons.'[92]

Lieutenant General Lloyd Campbell, Chief of the Air Staff, Canadian Air Force, commented: 'As a friend and ally (and also former fighter pilot) I consider this (disbandment) most unfortunate. However, I also recognise the Government has spoken and it is now time to salute and get on with life.'[93]

No. 2, No. 14 and No. 75 Squadron were officially disbanded at Ohakea on 13 December 2001.[94] The last fully airworthy A-4 *Skyhawk* flew out of Ohakea airbase on 30 July 2004, to join the rest of the mothballed fleet of *Skyhawks* at RNZAF Woodburn in Blenheim.[95]

Summary

The 1997 White Paper indicated that the defence policy that had been set out in the previous 1991 White Paper was still the most appropriate to guide policy decision-making: 'Self-Reliance in Partnership' remained the cornerstone of Defence Policy.[96] There was a reaffirmation of the balanced force approach, and the philosophy of incrementalism was reinforced:

> The Government has concluded that for the near-to-medium term New Zealand's security interests are best served within the structural framework that has evolved over the past several decades. This is an acknowledgement that our Army, Air and Naval forces have served us well, and with some shift in force configuration would continue to do so.[97]

With regards to the future of the Air Combat Force, the White Paper was unequivocal in its support. Taking account of New Zealand's role in the world and external influences it commented:

> We require an **air combat capability** (sic) to deal with surface threats and be capable of providing air support for both ground and naval forces. It must be capable of operating as part of a larger force, either in support of New Zealand naval and land forces, or as part of a combined force as a New Zealand contribution to collective defence.[98]

The 'opportunity purchase' of the 28 F-16 A/B fighters, allowed for the possibility of upgrading the air combat capability, whilst enhancing relationships with both Australia and the United States. Trade-offs also played a part as it was a way of softening the blow of not purchasing a third ANZAC frigate. A further trade-off though was to be further delays in re-equipping the New Zealand Army (and this was where bureaucratic politics came in), and the air transport capability of the RNZAF. In order to develop an enhanced air combat capability, the National Coalition was prepared to once more delay Priority One projects and set acquisition targets which Treasury clearly saw as unattainable within the funding envelope.

When the Labour-led Coalition came to power, it was on the clear basis that they would not support the F-16 purchase, and that the Government was intent on following an independent policy on defence purchases. Whilst there were many dissenting voices, there was nonetheless clear public support for Labour's position. In a parliamentary debate on the issue of the F-16s, Clark was able to note public opinion saying: 'I thought I saw last night that 68 per cent of people did not want the planes bought.'[99] When weighing up the options available for future defence expenditure, the Labour-led Government quickly chose to disband the air combat capability, redefining New Zealand's role in the world with its requirement 'for well-equipped, combat trained land forces which are also able to act as effective peacekeepers, supported by the Navy and Air Force'.[100] Labour viewed external influences and the world situation quite differently from National, with Clark echoing the sentiment expressed by Norman Kirk almost 30 years previously:

> We're quite widely respected for being an independent-minded small Western nation. We don't carry other people's agendas ... what matters to me is that when people hear New Zealand speak they know that's New Zealand speaking, not something someone else just whispered in its ear.[101]

To give substance to this outlook, the new Government committed itself to rebuilding defence force capabilities to achieve a 'modern, sustainable Defence Force that will meet the government's defence policy objectives'.[102] New Zealand was not to see F-16s in its skies.

ENDNOTES

[1] *Inquiry into Defence Beyond 2000*, Interim Report of the Foreign Affairs, Defence and Trade Committee, House of Representatives, Wellington, November 1998.

[2] Hon. Derek Quigley, *Review of the Lease of F-16 Aircraft for the Royal New Zealand Air Force*, Wellington, 6 March 2000.

[3] *Review of Defence Policy 1966*, Government Printer, Wellington, 1966, p. 16.

[4] Matthew Wright, *Kiwi Air Power*, Reed Books, Auckland, 1998, p. 157.

[5] Peter Clarke, 'Farewell to the RNZAF's Hotrod', *Pacific Wings*, February 2002, p. 23.

[6] Geoffrey Bentley and Maurice Conley, *Portrait of an Air Force*, Grantham House, Wellington, 1987, pp. 154–56.

[7] Bentley and Conley, *Portrait of an Air Force*; and *Defence Review 1983*, Government Printer, Wellington, 1983, p. 32.

[8] Martyn Gosling, 'Paddy's Axe gets a New Blade', *New Zealand Defence Quarterly*, no. 1, Winter 1993, p. 29.
[9] *Defence of New Zealand, Review of Defence Policy 1987*, Government Printer, Wellington, 1987, p. 36.
[10] Wright, *Kiwi Air Power*, p. 157.
[11] Gosling, 'Paddy's Axe gets a New Blade', p. 27.
[12] Gosling, 'Paddy's Axe gets a New Blade', p. 30.
[13] *The Shape of New Zealand's Defence, A White Paper*, Ministry of Defence, Wellington, November 1997, p. 49.
[14] *New Zealand Herald*, 12 November 1997.
[15] Max Bradford, Minister of Defence, reported in the *New Zealand Herald*, 2 December 1998.
[16] 'A Year in Review: The RNZAF in 1998', *RNZAF News Special*, December 1998, p. 11.
[17] Ian Bostock, 'NZ Air Force clinches bargain fighter deal', *Jane's Defence Weekly*, 9 December 1998, p. 3.
[18] What was not widely discussed throughout the whole F-16 debate was that the deal with Pakistan was not the only one that had fallen through. In 1994 US President Bill Clinton's Administration had offered the F-16s to Indonesia's President Suharto. In April 1994 Indonesia agreed to buy 11 of the aircraft, and in November they were offered a 'great deal' on the remaining 17 aircraft. Whilst the Clinton Administration had banned the sale of small arms to Indonesia because of the human rights abuses attributed to the regime, there was no law preventing the sale of jet fighters. In August 1996 there were riots in Jakarta and the United States put the sale on hold, but then reversed the decision. The US Department of State's announcement said: 'A regionally respected (Indonesian) armed forces, with credible defence capabilities, that trains and operates in a non-threatening manner is an important contribution to regional stability'. However, there were allegations raised that Indonesian nationals had made illegal campaign contributions to the Democratic Party before the US elections, and Indonesia cancelled the sale after queries were raised about Suharto's close financial relationship with Clinton and other senior Democratic Party members. 'Pakistani F-16 Jets Going to US Navy, USAF', available at <http://www.archive.newsmax.com/activities/articles/2002/6/12/154700.shtml>, accessed 27 October 2008.
[19] Gerald Hensley, Personal interview, 9 November 2003.
[20] Sir Wilson Whineray, *Final Report of the Air Combat Capability Policy Study*, Wellington, October 1998. Whilst the study was being undertaken, it was reported that Poland had entered the arena. 'Poland has expressed interest in leasing or buying 28 Lockheed Martin F-16 A/Bs originally intended for Pakistan. ... Sources say the Government is preparing information on the options available to Poland.' *Flight International*, 8–14 July 1998, p. 22.
[21] Whineray, *Final Report of the Air Combat Capability Policy Study*, p. ii.
[22] Whineray, *Final Report of the Air Combat Capability Policy Study*, p. v. For a complete summary of the recommendations from the Report, see Appendix 4.
[23] Max Bradford, Personal interview, 10 November 2003. In 2001 six *Skyhawks* were permanently grounded because of cracks in a structural component holding the tailfin to the fuselage. *New Zealand Herald*, 25 August 2001.
[24] Letter from Minister of Defence, Hon Max Bradford, 'Lease of F-16 Aircraft'. Attached to Cabinet paper CAB (98) 853.
[25] Letter from Minister of Defence, Hon Max Bradford, 'Lease of F-16 Aircraft', p. 5.
[26] Cabinet Paper CAB (1998) 854.
[27] *Defence 10 Year Capital Plan, Executive Summary*. Paper attached to Cabinet paper CAB (1998) 854.
[28] *Defence 10 Year Capital Plan, Executive Summary*.
[29] *Defence 10 Year Capital Plan, Executive Summary*, p. 14.
[30] *Defence 10 Year Capital Plan, Executive Summary*, p. 15.
[31] *Lease of F-16 Aircraft*. Paper attached to Cabinet paper CAB (98) 853, p. 6.
[32] Gordon Campbell, 'Pop Gun', *New Zealand Listener*, 9 January 1999, p. 18.
[33] Campbell, 'Pop Gun', p. 18.
[34] Campbell, 'Pop Gun', p. 18.
[35] *Inquiry into Defence Beyond 2000*, Interim Report of the Foreign Affairs, Defence and Trade Committee, pp. 27–28.

36 Media Release, Hon. Max Bradford, Minister of Defence, 1 December 1998.

37 Group Captain Ian Brunton, '"Pop Gun" Article incorrect and misleading', *RNZAF News*, vol. 1, February 1999, p. 5.

38 Jeffrey McCausland, *The Gulf Conflict: A Military Analysis*, Adelphi Paper no. 202, International Institute for Strategic Studies, London, 1993, p. 63, cited in Major G Hingsdon, 'How will the F-16 A/B lease impact on future NZDF operations?', Staff Course 2000, Whenuapai, p. 16.

39 Campbell, 'Pop Gun', p. 20.

40 Campbell, 'Pop Gun', p. 20.

41 Brunton, '"Pop Gun" Article incorrect and misleading', p. 4.

42 Brunton, '"Pop Gun" Article incorrect and misleading', p. 5.

43 Brunton, '"Pop Gun" Article incorrect and misleading', p. 5.

44 Derek Quigley, speech to Massey University Forum, Palmerston North, 9 September 1999, p. 6.

45 *Government Response to the Interim Report of the Foreign Affairs Defence and Trade Committee*, Wellington, September 1988, p. 17.

46 Brunton, '"Pop Gun" Article incorrect and misleading', p. 5.

47 *New Zealand Herald*, 2 December 1998.

48 Chief of Air Staff, AVM Carey Adamson, 'The F-16s and the Future', *RNZAF News*, December 1998.

49 *New Zealand Herald*, 1 December 1998.

50 'Providing our friends with challenging training' was a slogan used in an RNZAF advertisement in circulation in 2000. *Air Force News*, no. 11, December 2000.

51 Gerald Hensley, 'New Zealand's Strategic Environment', RNZAF Air Power Seminar, Wellington, 3 May 1999, p. 6.

52 Hon. Max Bradford, Minister of Defence, Media Release, 'F-16 Lease Deal Approved', 26 July 1999.

53 *Inquiry into Defence Beyond 2000*, Report of the Foreign Affairs, Defence and Trade Committee, p. 99.

54 *New Zealand Herald*, 31 August 1999.

55 *Evening Standard*, 1 September 1999.

56 Phil Goff, 'Preventing Aggression and Upholding International Law', in Rouben Azizian and Malcolm McNamara (eds), *New Zealand Foreign and Defence Policy at the End of the 20th Century: Views of Political Parties*, Centre for Strategic Studies, Wellington, 1991, p. 11.

57 Wayne Mapp, 'Dealing with the Consequence of Victory in the Cold War', in Azizian and McNamara (eds), *New Zealand Foreign and Defence Policy at the End of the 20th Century: Views of Political Parties*, p. 9.

58 *New Zealand Herald*, 14 December 1999.

59 Quigley, *Review of the Lease of the F-16 Aircraft for the Royal New Zealand Air Force*, p. 4.

60 Stephen Hoadley, 'F-16 diplomacy will test the mantle of Labour-Alliance Government', *National Business Review*, 10 December 1999.

61 John Armstrong, 'Killing F-16 deal risks allies' anger', *New Zealand Herald*, 14 December 1999.

62 Armstrong, 'Killing F-16 deal risks allies' anger'.

63 Greg Ansley, 'F-16 retreat will be seen as more New Zealand scrounging', *New Zealand Herald*, 14 December 1999.

64 Max Bradford, 'Fighters vital for our security', *New Zealand Herald*, 17 December 1999.

65 Editorial, *Press*, 15 December 1999.

66 *Press*, 18 December 1999.

67 *Evening Post*, 16 December 1999.

68 Editorial, *The Independent Business Weekly*, 22 December 1999.

69 Quigley, *Review of the Lease of the F-16 Aircraft for the Royal New Zealand Air Force*, p. 1.

70 Quigley, *Review of the Lease of the F-16 Aircraft for the Royal New Zealand Air Force*, p. 45. [my emphasis]

71 Quigley, *Review of the Lease of the F-16 Aircraft for the Royal New Zealand Air Force*, p. 17.

72 Quigley, *Review of the Lease of the F-16 Aircraft for the Royal New Zealand Air Force*, p. 17.

73 Quigley, *Review of the Lease of the F-16 Aircraft for the Royal New Zealand Air Force*, p. 52.

74 Quigley, *Review of the Lease of the F-16 Aircraft for the Royal New Zealand Air Force*, p. 47.

75 Quigley, *Review of the Lease of the F-16 Aircraft for the Royal New Zealand Air Force*, p. 55.
76 *New Zealand Herald*, 6 March 2000.
77 Rt. Hon. Helen Clark, *Prime Ministerial Statement on F-16s Decision*, 20 March 2000, p. 1.
78 Clark, *Prime Ministerial Statement on F-16s Decision*, p. 1.
79 Media Statement, Prime Minister Rt. Hon. Helen Clark, 20 March 2000. [my emphasis]
80 Wayne Mapp in fact was not the only senior National Party member to have considered disbanding the air strike wing. In 1997, Max Bradford was reported as wanting, 'to scrap our air combat forces entirely'. (Gordon Campbell, 'Clearing the Air', *New Zealand Listener*, 11 March 2000, p. 21). Gordon Campbell went on to note that, in an article in the *Dominion* on 10 June 1997, former Air Vice Marshall Ewan Jamieson was reported as saying: 'A few weeks ago, Cabinet Minister Max Bradford was reported as arguing that the air fighter/attack capability should be abandoned in favour of the purchase of one or more additional frigates. … He asserted that a *Skyhawk* replacement would be "too costly" to include in future defence plans.'
81 Quigley, *Review of the Lease of the F-16 Aircraft for the Royal New Zealand Air Force*, p. 20.
82 Wayne Mapp, 'Restructuring New Zealand's Defence Force', *Policy*, Spring 1991, pp. 27–28.
83 *Review of the Options for An Air Combat Capability*, Wellington, February 2001, p. 34.
84 *Review of the Options for An Air Combat Capability*, Wellington, February 2001, p. 34.
85 Quigley, *Review of the Lease of the F-16 Aircraft for the Royal New Zealand Air Force*, p. 46.
86 Phillip McKinnon, 'New Zealand scraps air combat role', *Jane's Defence Weekly*, 16 May 2001, p. 3.
87 Robert Ayson, Director of Graduate Studies in Strategy and Defence at The Australian National University, and formerly Adviser to the Foreign Affairs, Defence and Trade Committee in 1998, subsequently commented: 'I think the decisions on the air combat force were expected. If New Zealand had presented the Long Term Development Plan at the time of the announcement it would have brought forth a different response.' (Personal interview, 21 July 2003)
88 *Australian*, 9 May 2001.
89 Brian Edwards, *helen, Portrait of a Prime Minister*, Exisle Publishing, Auckland, 2001, p. 322.
90 Dick Gentles, Personal interview, 12 November 2003.
91 Stuart Woodman, 'Back to the Future', *New Zealand International Review*, vol. XXIII, no. 2, March/April 1998, pp. 2–5.
92 Stuart Woodman, Personal interview, 18 July 2003.
93 Lieutenant General Lloyd Campbell, 'A message from CAS, Canada', in 'Disbandment of the Air Combat Force', *Air Force News*, no. 23, January 2002, p. 24.
94 Peter Clarke, 'Farewell to the RNZAF's Hot Rod', p. 26.
95 *Manawatu Standard*, 31 July 2004.
96 *The Shape of New Zealand's Defence, A White Paper*, p. 7.
97 *The Shape of New Zealand's Defence, A White Paper*, p. 6. In its response to the *Inquiry Into Defence Beyond 2000*, the Government once more reinforced its goals and objectives, stating that it 'believes a balanced force approach enables New Zealand to deliver a realistic response to threats to our interests, and those of our regional friends and partners, and to participate in global security activities'. (*Government Response to the Report of the Foreign Affairs, Defence and Trade Committee on The Inquiry Into Defence Beyond 2000*, Wellington, 1999, p. 3.)
98 *The Shape of New Zealand's Defence, A White Paper*, p. 49. In its response to the *Inquiry Into Defence Beyond 2000*, the Government reiterated that it 'believes that an air combat capability is fundamental to demonstrate that New Zealand is serious about its own defence, and is committed to broader security.' (*Government Response to the Report of the Foreign Affairs, Defence and Trade Committee on The Inquiry Into Defence Beyond 2000*, p. 3.)
99 Rt. Hon. Helen Clark, Parliamentary debate, 21 March 2000.
100 *The Government's Defence Policy Framework*, p. 7.
101 Edwards, *helen, Portrait of a Prime Minister*, pp. 324–25.
102 *A Modern, Sustainable Defence Force Matched to New Zealand's Needs*, Government Defence Statement, The Ministry of Defence, Wellington, 8 May 2001, p. 15.

Chapter 6

'I see no submarines' — Upgrading the *Orions*

Prior to the debate over the leasing of the F-16s, the New Zealand Government had already committed itself to extending the structural life of the P-3K *Orion* aircraft which provide New Zealand's maritime air patrol capability. In the 1997 Defence White Paper, the Government acknowledged that New Zealand's *Orions* had far exceeded their planned service life, but the planning for refurbishment and/or replacement of major structural components was well underway. However, the White Paper also went on to note that:

> There are serious deficiencies in the *Orions*' sensor suite that impairs its ability to carry out both surface and sub-surface surveillance tasks. These will be addressed (Project *Sirius*) as one of the most important priorities in the rebuilding of the NZDF's capabilities.[1]

The re-winging of the *Orions*, Project *Kestrel*,[2] was intended to extend the life of the airframe for some 20 years. Project *Sirius* was intended to replace the aircraft's tactical system, in order to provide an effective maritime patrol capability, with the ability to work alongside coalition partners.

Approval in principle to pursue the project was given by the National-led Coalition Government in March 1998, with an estimated cost of NZ$236 million. Following Labour's return to power, the Minister of Defence sought direction on the future of the *Orion* Maritime Patrol Force, and whether Project *Sirius* should proceed. By this time, the costs associated with the project had more than doubled to NZ$562.1 million.[3] The Government rejected the proposal and decided not to proceed with Project *Sirius*.

This chapter explores the events that led to the initial decision to proceed with Project *Sirius*, and subsequent events that led to its cancellation. It then goes on to examine the recommendations of the *Maritime Patrol Review* of February 2001,[4] and the decisions taken by the Labour-led Government in relation to maritime air patrol three and a half years later, to proceed with Project *Guardian*.[5] Project *Guardian* is itself a comprehensive upgrade of systems for the *Orions*, which is similar in many respects to the original Project *Sirius*. The major elements which have had a bearing on the metamorphosis of Project *Sirius* under National into Project *Guardian* under Labour will be highlighted.

History and Background

In late 1944, the Government purchased for the Royal New Zealand Air Force (RNZAF) its first four *Short Sunderland* Mark III flying boats.[6] These aircraft were based at Hobsonville and were used to transport freight into the South Pacific. As part of the restructuring process following the Second World War, the RNZAF in June 1953 took delivery of 16 refurbished *Short Sunderland* flying boats for maritime reconnaissance. These were assigned to No. 5 Squadron based at Lauthala Bay, Fiji, and performed a maritime reconnaissance and anti-submarine warfare role. In the Defence White Paper, *Review of Defence Policy 1961*, it was noted that the aircraft had first entered service some 25 years previously, and were now an old design.[7] There were no suitable replacement flying boats available, and a suitable land-based aircraft was to be considered. That aircraft was to be the Lockheed P-3B *Orion*.

The Chief of Air Staff appointed in June 1962 was Air Vice Marshal Ian G. Morrison, who was to oversee the modernisation of the RNZAF. Morrison saw the three elements of the Air Force—strike capability, transport, and maritime patrol—as being of equal value, and sought improvements in aircraft in each area. He sought a replacement for the *Sunderlands* and found it in the *Orion*. Five new *Orions* were ordered in March 1964, and delivered to No. 5 Squadron at Whenuapai between September and December 1966. The cost was to be NZ£8.7 million, including support equipment. In light of the contemporary debate about Project *Sirius*, the comment on the purchase in the 1966 Defence White Paper is noteworthy:

> The *Orion* is the most modern and effective surveillance and anti-submarine aircraft available anywhere, and will put the RNZAF on a basis of full compatibility with the RAAF and the United States Navy in this important role.[8]

The *Orions* proved to be a valuable asset, and over the next decade performed their surveillance role with distinction. However, by the late 1970s it was clear that their avionics suite had fallen behind recent improvements in capability overseas, and the 1978 *Defence Review* foreshadowed a progressive upgrading of capability to enhance their compatibility with allies and to improve their effectiveness.[9]

A two-phase modernisation process, Project *Rigel*, was decided upon to provide a comprehensive systems upgrade, and in July 1980 the Boeing Company was awarded a contract for Phase One of the project. Phase One included improved data systems, modernised tactical displays, and improved surveillance and navigation equipment. A significant enhancement of radar capability and night search capability was included, with a new infra-red detection system.

The first modified aircraft was completed in November 1983, and the last in May 1984.[10] The total cost for the first phase was NZ$42 million.[11]

The 1983 *Defence Review* noted that the project was nearing completion and would provide 'a capability for surface surveillance by day or night which will be second to none'. It went on to say, though:

> The need remains to improve the aircraft's ability to detect and attack submarines and to upgrade its effectiveness in electronic warfare. It is intended to undertake a second phase of the *Orion* modernisation programme for this purpose.[12]

This was not to happen however. With a change of government, the 1987 Defence White Paper spelt out the Labour Party's priorities. There was still a recognition that maritime surveillance was important, and that aircraft were required to 'provide the means for quick reaction, and for monitoring both submarine and surface activity'. The White Paper acknowledged that improved systems had been installed in the *Orions* and noted that 'improved acoustic and electronic capabilities for both the RNZN and the RNZAF will be considered'.[13]

Tenders were called for Phase Two in 1988, but the project failed to proceed when the RNZAF was unable to get a commitment from the Government for the proposal.

Project *Kestrel*

By the early 1990s the *Orions* had been in service for a quarter of a century, and were amongst some of the most intensively used aircraft of their type in the world. The fleet now consisted of six aircraft, a further aircraft having been purchased second-hand from the Royal Australian Air Force (RAAF) in 1985, at a cost NZ$19 million. In 1993 a fatigue analysis was undertaken, which showed that the aircraft had been used to such an extent that their fatigue life index was 135 against a baseline index of 100. This was quite a remarkable figure compared with the US Navy *Orions*, most of which were retired at fatigue life indices between 60 and 80.[14]

By this stage it was clear that, in most circumstances, the most favoured replacement for an old *Orion* was a new one, and amongst the options reviewed was that of purchasing new aircraft. But, at a cost of NZ$1 billion, that was unlikely.[15] Other options then explored included the possible purchase of new airframes and then transferring engines and sensors from current aircraft, at an estimated cost of NZ$600 million; refurbishing second-hand aircraft purchased from the United States; or undertaking significant structural refurbishment of the current aircraft by replacing major structural panels.[16] Engineering studies were undertaken by Lockheed Martin, and these confirmed that it was possible to replace significant structural portions of the aircraft with a low engineering risk associated with the project. Completion of the project would extend the life of the aircraft by 20 years.[17]

Project *Kestrel* was to be a world first, and was truly an international project. Wings, horizontal stabilisers, and engine nacelles were all to be replaced. The outer-wing panels were to be manufactured in South Korea; the horizontal stabilisers were built by British Aerosystems in the United Kingdom; and the centre wing section lower skin came from Lockheed Martin in Georgia in the United States.[18] Engine nacelles were refurbished by Celsius Hawker Pacific in Australia, and the installation of components and completion of the refurbished aircraft was undertaken by Hawker Pacific in Sydney.[19]

Project *Kestrel* was, like Project *Rigel* a two-phase project. Unlike Project *Rigel*, *Kestrel* was completed on time and on budget, with a total cost of less than NZ$100 million—one tenth of the cost of new aircraft. Work had begun on the re-integration phase on the first aircraft in November 1997, and the final aircraft returned to RNZAF service on 21 August 2001. The Air Component Commander at the time, Air Commodore John Hamilton, commented:

> The concept is complex but has been built on the knowledge, innovation, skills and abilities of Air Force engineering personnel—engineering and design skills that were not readily available offshore except in the aircraft's original design office. It exemplifies what can be done by New Zealanders with the right background and opportunities.

No-one, not even Lockheed Martin, had ever re-winged a P-5B *Orion* with P-5C wings, the only ones now available new. The RNZAF project team worked with Lockheed Martin to develop the interface design and the reassembly protocol, and the project was a complete success. Air Commodore John Hamilton added:

> It has given the Air Force a significant extension in the life of the *Orion* fleet at a reasonable cost. The *Orion* is now well placed to take on upgraded sensors and equipment which will allow them to serve New Zealand's interests for another 20 years.[20]

Updating sensors and avionics equipment had never been completed under Project *Rigel*. This deficit was intended to be rectified by the implementation of Project *Sirius*.

Project *Sirius*

The 1991 *Defence Review* called for a review of maritime surveillance capability, but the results of the policy study were classified and never released publicly.[21]

Having affirmed that 'Self-Reliance in Partnership' remained central to New Zealand Defence policy, the 1997 White Paper emphasised the importance of maintaining force capabilities which would allow New Zealand to adequately monitor and protect those areas which fell under New Zealand's responsibility. The White Paper made the point that the United States 'has neither the power nor the inclination to be the sole guarantor of the region's security. It expects others to carry a proportionate share of the burden.'[22] In order to maintain its share of the burden, New Zealand needed to maintain a capability for maritime surveillance from the air, and Project *Sirius* was intended to provide that capability. The latest Defence White Paper highlighted the impaired capacity of the *Orion*'s tactical systems to undertake its maritime surveillance role, and noted that the deficiencies would be addressed by Project *Sirius*. The previous month, Cabinet had agreed with the Minister of Defence's recommendation that the *Orions* be equipped with updated sensors and communication suites, with a subsequent decision to be made regarding implementation.[23] The Government subsequently gave approval-in-principle for Project *Sirius* to proceed, at a Cabinet Meeting on 23 March 1998. This approval was seen by the RNZAF to be the culmination of over a decade's work, which had begun following the cancellation of Project *Rigel* in the late 1980s. In commenting on the approval, the Chief of Air Staff, Air Vice Marshal Carey Adamson said: 'Yesterday's decision was a major milestone for the project; however, a continuation of this hard work will be needed to bring SIRIUS to a successful conclusion.'[24] In this, he was to be proven to be correct.

The Invitation to Register (ITR), which the Ministry of Defence was to use to identify potential prime contractors, was issued on 9 October 1998. The Request for Tender was subsequently issued in February 1999, and Raytheon was chosen as the preferred prime contractor. The request for a Best and Final Offer was issued in November 1999, but by that time the Labour Party had returned to power. The Ministry was to continue working hard to try and ensure that Project *Sirius* did reach a successful conclusion; nevertheless *Sirius*, like *Rigel* before it, was not to succeed.

The Failure of Project *Sirius* and its Metamorphosis into Project *Guardian*

The Best and Final Offer price from Raytheon was indicated as being NZ$445 million,[25] and the final decision on the offer was due on 28 May 2000. A briefing for the Minister of Defence was conducted in April 2000, prior to the decision going to Cabinet the following month. In the event, Raytheon extended its offer until 25 August 2000, allowing somewhat more time for the issues involved to be considered both by the Minister of Defence, Mark Burton, and by the Government.

The potential expenditure of almost half a billion dollars once more generated significant media comment. Gordon Campbell, in an article in the *New Zealand Listener* commented:

> The F-16s were an easy call. In coming weeks, the Clark Government faces a tough and diplomatically fraught decision over Project *Sirius*, the hugely expensive upgrade of our six *Orion* maritime surveillance aircraft. Secrecy rules. For the last couple of years, the cost estimates for *Sirius* ... have been kept under wraps.[26]

The Government subsequently released the *Defence Policy Framework* in June 2000. In the Introduction to the *Framework*, it was emphasised that a new approach to defence was one of the Government's major policies when it sought election. Within the new framework it was still recognised that maintaining effective maritime surveillance capabilities of the RNZAF remained one of the greatest needs. The emphasis however, was to be 'within the New Zealand EEZ [Exclusive Economic Zone] and the EEZs of Pacific Island States'.[27] Nevertheless Cabinet, at a meeting on 12 June 2000, did allow for consideration of Project *Sirius* before completion of the *Maritime Patrol Review*:[28]

> (e) agreed that urgent acquisitions which are fully consistent with the Government's defence policy, goals and priorities may be considered prior to the completion of the reviews referred to in paragraph (c) above.[29]

By the time Project *Sirius* went to Cabinet for a decision in August 2000, the costs however were only too clear. In a paper to Cabinet dated 14 August 2000, the Minister of Defence proposed four possible options for the future of the *Orion* Maritime Patrol Force:

- Do nothing and lose the airborne maritime surveillance capability;
- Retain the capability, and accept the Raytheon Project *Sirius* offer at approximately NZ$562.10 million;
- Accept a reduced capability (without a sub-surface capability) at a cost of approximately NZ$520 million; or
- Reduce capability by equipping for civil tasks only, and invite the preparation of Terms of Reference for a new project study.[30]

The response, noted in the Cabinet Minutes of 21 August 2000, was brief and to the point: '(b), agreed not to proceed with Project *Sirius*'.[31]

The response by Opposition parties to the announcement was swift, with both ACT and National suggesting that the Labour–Alliance Coalition was dragging New Zealand into an isolationist stance. Wayne Mapp, National's defence spokesperson, suggested that the focus on re-equipping the Army was being used as a smokescreen whilst the Air Force was downgraded, 'into some kind of "freight service."'[32] The response by the Australians was equally swift, but muted, with their Minister for Defence, John Moore, saying: 'We understand the priorities assigned by the Government of New Zealand to upgrading the capabilities of its army ... we are disappointed though, by the New Zealand government's decision to cancel Project *Sirius*.'[33]

The United States was said to be highly concerned about the Cabinet decision on Project *Sirius*, having indicated previously that approval would be a sign that the Coalition Government was serious about regional security. However Phil Goff, Minister of Foreign Affairs and Trade, speaking on the eve of his departure to the United States, said he did not expect a cool response from the Americans over the decision. The Green Party, on the other hand, was very pleased, and gave strong support to the Government's decision. Wayne Mapp went so far as to suggest that the Greens controlled defence policy. He commented, 'Labour has rolled over to extreme Green isolationist views', and added, 'abandoning the upgrading of the *Orions* means we will no longer have proper surveillance of our region.'[34] However, Keith Locke was delighted to see this apparent shift away from combat capabilities. He noted that the decision would see New Zealand move away from operations such as those in the Persian Gulf with the US-led task force simply because the *Orions* would no longer have the sophisticated capability necessary to operate with US and coalition partners.[35]

Lending weight to the notion of the abandonment of a sophisticated upgrade for the *Orions*, two days later the Prime Minister commented: 'Anyone who argues $560 million for the *Orions* when there is no evidence of hostile submarines in our area would have to be barking.'[36] Weighing up trade-offs was to be part of the remit of the *Maritime Patrol Review*.[37] However, Helen Clark commented on this in an article in the *RSA Review* in October 2000, saying:

> Defence purchasing is hugely expensive, and there are severe limits on what the government can do without seriously affecting baseline expenditure on and capital provision for other top priorities like Health, Education and Infrastructure. The purchase of 105 armoured personnel carriers and 1853 radios for the Army represents a very significant increase in defence spending. It is not possible to accommodate that and other high priorities as well as invest in the proposed $562 million *Orion* upgrade.[38]

Notwithstanding the cancellation of Project *Sirius*, the Government had signalled the importance of maintaining effective aerial maritime surveillance in its *Defence Policy Framework* announced in June 2000. Defining what 'effective' meant was to be the task of a committee convened by the Department of the Prime Minister and Cabinet. At its meeting on 21 August, Cabinet had proposed the establishment of a special group, chaired by the Prime Minister, to include the Deputy Prime Minister, Minister of Finance, Minister of Defence, and Minister of Fisheries, consulting with other relevant Ministers. This group was to examine how civilian requirements for maritime patrol could be best met, and whether a military maritime patrol capability should be retained at all. They were to be assisted in this task by the Officials Committee, whose report was to be completed by February 2001.

At the time of the announcement of the cancellation of Project *Sirius*, the Chief of Air Staff, Air Vice Marshal Don Hamilton, was pragmatic in his response. In an article in *Air Force News* in September 2000, he said: 'I too share your disappointment, and we must simply now take the time to absorb the Government's direction and define the new role requirement.'[39] The definition of the new role requirement was once more to see the conventional role of the *Orions* being questioned, with stinging criticism from a number of quarters.

Having been asked to examine whether a military maritime patrol capability should be retained, the *Review* Committee, echoing somewhat the arguments that had been put forward with regards to the air strike capability, commented:

> While the *Orions* have provided military benefits in training and exercises in the 35 years that the RNZAF has operated them, the reality is that on no occasion have they been used in combat or peace keeping duties, despite a willingness and capability to use them. It is the view of the committee that New Zealand does not need to maintain a maritime patrol force that includes an anti-submarine capability. In neither the arguments we have heard in the course of our review, nor in past experience, have we found compelling evidence that such a capability is essential for national security.[40]

The *Review* Committee went on to say:

> If anti-submarine warfare is no longer a priority, it could be argued that there is less case for keeping the *Orions*, because ASW [anti-submarine warfare] is the main thing they did markedly better than the alternatives. We already own the *Orions* however, and the Air Force has accumulated considerable expertise in their use. If the government wanted to retain them for their long distance and long endurance capabilities, our assessment is that they could be upgraded to do local tasks, civilian and military, perfectly well at a modest cost per aircraft.[41]

The Government's *Defence Policy Framework* had also clearly spelt out the Government's defence policy objectives and these were:

- to defend New Zealand and to protect its people, land, territorial waters, EEZ, natural resources and critical infrastructure;
- to meet New Zealand's alliance commitments to Australia by maintaining a close defence partnership in pursuit of common security interests;

- to assist in the maintenance of security in the South Pacific and to provide assistance to New Zealand's Pacific neighbours;
- to play an appropriate role in the maintenance of security in the Asia–Pacific region, including meeting New Zealand's obligations as a member of the Five Power Defence Arrangements (FPDA); and
- to contribute to global security and peacekeeping through participation in the full range of UN and other appropriate multilateral peace support and humanitarian relief operations.[42]

However, in the somewhat benign environment of late 2000 and early 2001, the *Maritime Patrol Review*, in reviewing the need for Military Maritime Patrol Capabilities (MMPC), sought to concentrate on only the first four of the five stated Government policy objectives. The *Review* effectively dismissed any future global role for the *Orions*, with their observation that the *Orions* had never been used in combat or peacekeeping duties, and their recommendation that the maritime patrol force did not need an ASW capability.[43] When it came to anti-submarine capabilities, the Prime Minister was not convinced either: 'We would be most unlikely to spend on the anti-submarine warfare capability', she said in March, following the release of the *Review*. 'We were being asked to spend more than half a billion dollars to spot vessels which aren't there and haven't been found to be there in the entire time we've been trying to spot them.'[44]

There was a very real threat to the future of the *Orions* contained within the *Maritime Patrol Review*. The *Review* Committee noted that savings of the order of NZ$40-60 million could be made annually if the *Orions* were disposed of, though they did acknowledge this might mean buying more C-130 *Hercules* to take over the role. The committee found that, overall, a ten-fold increase in aerial patrol was necessary to fulfil civil surveillance needs, but that much of this extra effort was needed to cover mid-range contingencies, and suggested either the use of commercial services, or using RNZAF *King Air* aircraft in conjunction with pilot training. For long distance surveillance they suggested two options also:

- retain some *Orions* as the long range aircraft for SAR [search and rescue] and distant surveillance purposes; or
- utilise C-130s which have comparable capabilities (in range etc) by fitting new sensors to some or all five aircraft in the RNZAF. This could require the purchase of additional C-130 capacity, depending on whether the Government wants to increase its South Pacific operations.[45]

The following month the Minister of Defence responded to the *Review*, in a paper to the Cabinet Policy Committee, *Sustainable Capability Plan for the New Zealand Defence Force*. In this paper the Minister noted that NZ$100 million had been spent on Project *Kestrel*, providing an effective aircraft for a further 20 years, and that it made no sense to look at alternatives. Everyone though agreed that the sensors on the *Orions* needed to be replaced, but the capability that would have been offered by Project *Sirius* was not required. The Minister recommended instead: '65.7.2—A limited upgrade for the *Orions* be progressively implemented with priority given to those systems that would give them an appropriate and affordable suite of sensors to perform these tasks.'[46]

Cabinet agreed, almost. The Minutes of the meeting of 2 April 2001 record the decision as follows: '1.7.2—A limited upgrade for the *Orions*, using good quality commercial systems wherever possible be progressively implemented, with priority given to those systems that will give them an appropriate and affordable suite of sensors to perform these tasks.'[47]

The Government, however, was yet to define what 'good quality commercial systems' actually meant.

Before the recommendations to equip the *Orions* with commercial surveillance equipment could be implemented, however, international circumstances were to change. On 11 September 2001, nine months after the *Review* was published, the world we live in was to change. The destruction of the twin towers of the New York World Trade Center, and the attack on the Pentagon in Arlington, VA, was to help define a new focus for the Western alliance. The 'war on terror' was about to commence, and as US President George W. Bush said so clearly in November 2001: 'A coalition partner must do more than just express sympathy; a coalition partner must perform … all nations, if they want to fight terror, must do something.' To underscore the importance of the message, Bush added what were to become immortal words: 'Over time, it's going to be important for nations to know they will be held accountable for inactivity. You are either with us or against us in the fight against terror.'[48]

On this occasion New Zealand was with the United States, and was to make a substantial contribution to the 'war on terror'.

In May 2002 a proposal for a NZ$390 million upgrade was to have gone before Cabinet, but the Prime Minister was said to have asked officials to come back with a less expensive option saying 'officials beaver away, but the Government is not going to tolerate a reinvention of *Sirius* under another name'.[49]

During 2002, however, the Government's attitude towards the Project began to change. As the nature of the upgrade was investigated further, politicians who had originally opposed the upgrade came to see its wider utility:

> As we told them what was needed to meet the Government's requirements, although there was no requirement for an ASW upgrade, almost every other piece of equipment to be upgraded met a clearly identified need. What distinguished Project *Guardian* from *Sirius* was

the amount of consultation undertaken. So many agencies had an interest, and so many agencies wanted the upgrade. Project *Guardian* was very much tailored to a whole of government solution.[50]

Ultimately the predicted costs in the *Defence Long-Term Development Plan* published in June 2002 were set at NZ$150–220 million for the Missions Systems Upgrade, with a share of a further NZ$320 million for the Communications and Navigations Systems Upgrade, for a total of 11 *Orions* and *Hercules*.[51]

In November 2002 the Government announced its intention to send *Hercules* and *Orion* aircraft to Afghanistan and the Persian Gulf to join Operation *Enduring Freedom*.[52] The country's response to, and willingness to be involved in, the 'war on terror', as well as a growing recognition of security needs close to home, clearly reinforced the need for an airborne surveillance facility of significant ability.

That same month, with officials having continued to beaver away, the Minister of Defence put forward a proposal for approval to go to tender for the *Orions*' Mission Systems Upgrade and Communication and Navigation Systems Upgrade.[53] In this paper the Minister put forward three options for the Mission Systems Upgrade. In the attached *Defence Long-Term Development Plan Update*, the Minister noted that, because of the differences in requirements for the *Orions* and the *Hercules* Communications and Navigation Systems upgrade, the projects had been de-coupled, and significant savings could be made on the *Orion* upgrade.[54] Approval to go to tender was given at a Cabinet meeting on 11 December 2002, and the Minister said that the cost of the upgrade would probably be in excess of NZ$300 million, and that tender costs would go to Cabinet at the end of 2003.

It was in fact January 2004 when the preferred tenderer was chosen, and August 2004 when Government approval to negotiate was given. On 5 October 2004 a contract for NZ$352 million was signed for the upgrade package. In a background paper attached to the media statement announcing the signing of the *Orion* upgrade, the Labour-led Government's goals and objectives were spelt out:

> The *Orions* play an important part in the surveillance of New Zealand's Exclusive Economic Zone (EEZ) and surrounding waters, the Southern Ocean and the Ross Sea. The aircraft are also used to meet our South Pacific search and rescue obligations and assisting with EEZ surveillance. The *Orions* can also contribute to regional and global security, such as their recently completed deployment to the Arabian Sea area in support of the international campaign against terrorism.[55]

Without any change in the *Government Defence Statement*,[56] the interpretation of what was needed to meet the Government's goals and objectives had moved significantly from what had been signalled in the *Maritime Patrol Review*—an aircraft which 'could be upgraded to do local tasks, civilian and military, at a modest cost per aircraft'.[57] What the Government clearly signalled when the new upgrade contract was signed was a move to a level of sophistication and capability, albeit without an upgraded ASW capability, that had been sought under Project *Sirius*. As the Minister explained:

> The *Orions* will have a similar suite of sensors to the maritime patrol craft operated by our main security partners. They will also have a range of communication systems capable of sharing information with other forces. These capabilities will ensure that the aircraft are fully inter-operable and able to work closely with our security partners.[58]

The Minister continued:

> Maritime patrol aircraft, such as the *Orion*, have traditionally been used primarily to conduct maritime surveillance operations. It is now increasingly regarded as a multi-role aircraft. Once upgraded its ability to support both maritime and land operations will significantly enhance the NZDF's ability to achieve a range of policy objectives.[59]

Wing Commander John Lovatt, the Commanding Officer of No. 5 Squadron clarified some of the new capabilities in an article in *Air Force News*:

> Increasingly we can expect to see the P-3 providing support to new and emerging security threats, in particular transnational crime (including illegal immigration, drug trafficking, and smuggling of endangered species), the exploitation of natural resources and terrorism. ... The *Orion* will evolve from a maritime patrol aircraft into a multi-mission platform that is able to effectively conduct, coordinate and participate in both our traditional roles and evolving surveillance and reconnaissance operations, spanning maritime, littoral, and overland environments.[60]

The *Orions* in Action

Although the *Maritime Patrol Review* had emphasised that on no occasion over a 35-year period had the *Orions* been used for combat or peacekeeping duties, all that was to change given the events subsequent to the terrorist attacks of 11 September 2001. Following the Government's announcement in November 2002 that RNZAF aircraft would participate in Operation *Enduring Freedom*, the first rotation of the P-3K *Orions* left on 11 May 2003. The deployment of an *Orion* to the Persian Gulf on Operation *Troy* provided the RNZAF with another opportunity to demonstrate Kiwi ingenuity. The *Orion* required some major upgrades to allow it to work in a coalition environment. Most notable were the Link 11 communications system which was borrowed from a frigate; an FF 9000 high frequency radio; a satellite phone for transmission of digital imagery; and what was described as 'other specialist mission equipment'.[61]

Initially the deployment was to have been for a period of six months, but it was so successful that on 13 October 2003 the Government announced that the deployment would be extended by three months. Four air crew rotations and three support crew rotations were deployed throughout the nine months of the mission, providing significant experience for No. 5 Squadron in a demanding environment. Over the first five month period since initial deployment, No. 5 Squadron had flown over 600 hours and over 90 sorties, prompting the Minister of Defence, Mark Burton, to comment that the level of operational tempo had impressed Coalition partners. Indicating not only a change in the world situation but also in geographical priorities and New Zealand's role in the world, the Minister added: 'New Zealand is committed to working closely with others globally to counter the continuing threat of terrorism to international security and the extension of this deployment illustrates that commitment.'[62]

The Upgrade

The National-led Government of the late 1990s was very clear that it wanted an *Orion* that could undertake both tasks to protect New Zealand's sovereignty and surface and sub-surface tasks in a collective endeavour with other forces. In 1996 the Ministry of Defence awarded a contract for a Project Definition Study to the US firm Boeing. According to Boeing, the purpose of the study was to obtain an independent assessment of what would be needed for an *Orion* upgrade, based upon evaluation of a number of equipment and system options. This was to take into account an analysis of operational scenarios. Project *Sirius* was the outcome.

Some three years later Boeing was amongst the contenders for Project *Sirius*, when the Request for Tender was called for in March 1999. At this point the defence contractor DaimlerChrysler Aerospace (DASA) pulled out; Lockheed's proposal was unacceptable and Boeing and Raytheon were left as serious bidders. Both were said to have tendered in the NZ$650–$700 million range.[63] Raytheon had in fact offered a trimmed-down version at NZ$450 million, but (as stated in the Introduction to this chapter) the price quoted at the time the Labour Government rejected the deal was NZ$562.1 million.

Wing Commander Carl Nixon, subsequently Commanding Officer of No. 5 Squadron, was a member of the Project *Sirius* team at the time tenders were called for, and in discussing the project said: 'I am very proud that back in the late 1990s, the Air Force was part of re-defining acquisition processes to acquire capabilities by defining outputs functionally, rather than specifying equipment directly.'[64]

The Key Capabilities were spelt out in a briefing to the Minister of Defence in July 2000. The capabilities included:

- Data Management Function (DMF);
- Radar;
- Electronic Surveillance Measures (ESM);
- Electro-optics;
- Acoustics;
- Magnetic Anomaly Detection;
- Communications;
- Navigation; and
- Mission Support.[65]

No equipment was specified in the briefing, but Nicky Hager provided details that same month, although he did not quote a source for the information. Details were as follows:

- Surveillance Radar—Elta EL/-2022 (version 3);
- Signals intelligence equipment (Electronic Surveillance Measures)—Elta EL/M 8300 system;
- Infra-red electro-optical system: Super Star SAFIRE system, made by FLIR Systems Inc.;
- Anti-submarine acoustic processor: CDC UYS-970 (capable of processing data from 32 sonobuoys), made by Computing Devices Canada Ltd; and
- Magnetic Anomaly Detector (MAD): CAE ASQ-504 made by CAE Electronics Ltd, Canada.[66]

In a briefing to the Minister some three months previously in April 2000, the point was made that, without the ability to detect, track and deal with anti-surface threats, the *Orion* would only be able to make a limited contribution to a combined force. (This same paper clearly stated that Project *Sirius* was fully equivalent to Australian capabilities.) Nevertheless, with the Government's antipathy towards anti-submarine capability, by the time of the July 2000 briefing the Ministry of Defence had made provisional allowance for the removal of the acoustics equipment and magnetic anomaly detector. They offered two scenarios—(1) fitted for but not with the equipment, with a saving of some NZ$12.9 million; or (2) none of these capabilities at all, leading to a combined saving of NZ$33.16 million, or 7 per cent of the upgrade cost.

The Labour Government was adamant about the cancellation of Project *Sirius*. However, what was clear though was that much of the capability that had been sought under Project *Sirius* was inherent in Project *Guardian*. ('It's better actually', one well-placed source commented.) The successful tenderer was L-3 IS Communications Integrated Systems (L-3), the company which, trading under its previous name of Raytheon Corporation, had been chosen as preferred contractor for Project *Sirius*.[67] Project *Sirius* was to have cost NZ$562.10 million (US$236 million at the then current exchange rate of US$0.42/NZ$ or US$229 million without a sub-surface capability). Project *Guardian* was agreed to in 2004 with a contract price of NZ$352 million (US$232 million at an exchange rate of US$0.66/NZ$). The sophisticated radar, the ELTA EL/M–2022 (v)3 series, which was sought for *Sirius*, is central to the upgrade. The electro-optics system, the Wescam MX-20 infra-red camera, provides a significant capability; and central to the *Orion*'s developing role is a Ground Moving Target Indicator (GMTI). Handling the large volumes of information will be L-3's Integrated Data Handling System (IDHS). The result is 'an optimised platform that can operate over land and sea as well as providing air-to-air surveillance'.[68]

With the signing of the contract in October 2004, the Project *Guardian* upgrade began in 2005 with the installation of the electro-optics system as a first stage. The full upgrade was started on the first aircraft in 2006 at L-3's base in Texas, with system proving, testing and completion to be undertaken by 2009. The remaining five aircraft are to be modified by Safe Air Ltd in Blenheim, to be delivered by 2011.

Summary

Whilst bureaucratic politics and political influence had a part to play during the decision-making processes of both National and Labour-led Governments, trade-offs and judgement of utility and acceptable risks were increasingly significant elements for both Governments as they struggled to modernise New Zealand's defence forces. For example, shortly after Labour was elected to lead the Government in 1999, they proceeded with a number of policy reviews, the *Maritime Patrol Review* being amongst them.[69] In considering the judgement of utility and acceptable risks, the *Review* questioned the need to retain any of the *Orions*, but recommended that if they were to be retained they should use 'good quality commercial systems wherever possible'.[70] The radical change recommended to the operational capability of the P-3K *Orion* reflected what was seen at the time as an 'incredibly benign strategic environment'.[71]

However, although the domestic aspects of decision-making were important, the influencing elements of (1) external sources, (2) the world situation, (3) New Zealand's role in the world, and (4) geographical priorities (an international focus) were more significant. These elements, coupled with timing, seem to have been crucial factors in the ultimate decision to proceed with the upgrade. The world situation was to change dramatically as a result of the events of 11 September 2001 and, along with it, a change to New Zealand's role in the world. Border security and EEZ protection took on new meaning in the changed security environment. Whilst domestic concerns had a part to play, ultimately it was the international situation and timing which played the most significant roles in the decision to proceed with a sophisticated upgrading of the *Orion* aircraft.

ENDNOTES

1. *The Shape of New Zealand's Defences, a White Paper*, Ministry of Defence, Wellington, November 1997, p. 49.
2. 'What's the latest with Project Kestrel?', *RNZAF News*, July 1996, vol. II, pp. 6–7.
3. *New Zealand's Orion Maritime Patrol Force*, Office of the Minister of Defence. Paper attached to POL (OO 1993).
4. *Maritime Patrol Review*, Department of the Prime Minister and Cabinet, Wellington, February 2001.
5. Phillip McKinnon, 'New Zealand to request tenders for Orion upgrade', *Jane's Navy International*, June 2003, p. 7.
6. Matthew Wright, *Kiwi Air Power*, Reed Books, Auckland, 1998, p. 109.
7. *Review of Defence Policy 1961*, Government Printer, Wellington, p. 15.
8. *Review of Defence Policy 1966*, Government Printer, Wellington, p. 17.
9. *Defence Review 1978*, Government Printer, Wellington, 1978, p. 39.
10. Geoffrey Bentley and Maurice Conley, *Portrait of an Air Force*, Grantham House, Wellington, 1987, p. 175.
11. Gordon Campbell, 'More Sirius money', *New Zealand Listener*, 20 May 2000, p. 31.
12. *Defence Review 1983*, Government Printer, Wellington, 1983, p. 31.
13. *Defence of New Zealand, Review of Defence Policy 1987*, Government Printer, Wellington, 1987, p. 33.
14. 'What's the Latest with Project Kestrel', p. 6.
15. Martyn Gosling, 'New Wings for a Watchdog', *New Zealand Defence Quarterly*, no. 18, Spring 1997, p. 19.
16. Colin James, 'Rewinging an Old Warrior', *New Zealand Defence Quarterly*, no. 23, Summer 1998, p. 18.
17. What's the Latest with Project Kestrel', p. 6.
18. 'Contract signed for Kestrel integration', *RNZAF News*, July 1997, vol. I, p. 16.
19. 'Project Kestrel Completed', *Air Force News*, no. 19, September 2001, p. 7.
20. 'Project Kestrel Completed', pp. 7–8.
21. Gordon Campbell, 'Sirius Money', *New Zealand Listener*, 29 April 2000, p. 23.
22. *The Shape of New Zealand's Defence, a White Paper*, p. 20.
23. ERD (1997) 18, p. 3.
24. 'Go-ahead for Project SIRIUS', *RNZAF News*, April 1998, vol. I, p. 13.
25. Keith Locke, 'Project Sirius is needless keeping up with Joneses', *New Zealand Herald*, 9 May 2000.
26. Campbell, 'More Sirius money', p. 22.
27. *The Government's Defence Policy Framework*, Ministry of Defence, Wellington, June 2000, p. 8.
28. *Maritime Patrol Review*.
29. CAB (00) M 19–10, p. 1.
30. POL (OO) 1993, pp. 1–2.
31. CAB (OO) M28/9.
32. *New Zealand Herald*, 24 August 2000.
33. 'New Zealand Defence Acquisitions', Media Release MIN 231/00, Hon. John Moore, MP, Minister for Defence, 23 August 2000.
34. Wayne Mapp, Press Release, 22 August 2000.
35. *New Zealand Herald*, 22 August 2000.
36. *Evening Post*, 24 August 2000.
37. *Maritime Patrol Review*.
38. Rt. Hon. Helen Clark, 'The Government's defence priorities explained', *RSA Review*, October 2000.
39. *Air Force News*, no. 8, September 2000, p. 5.

40 *Maritime Patrol Review*, p. 23.
41 *Maritime Patrol Review*, p. 28.
42 *The Government's Defence Policy Framework*, p. 4.
43 *Maritime Patrol Review*, pp. 19–23.
44 *New Zealand Herald*, 15 March 2001.
45 *Maritime Patrol Review*, p. 37.
46 *Sustainable Capability Plan for the New Zealand Defence Force*, 25 March 2001. Paper attached to POL(01)18, p. 11.
47 CAB(01)100, p. 3.
48 CNN.com, 'Bush says it is time for action', available at <http://archives.cnn.com/2001/US/11/06/ret.bush.coalition/index.html>, accessed 28 October 2008.
49 *New Zealand Herald*, 19 May 2002.
50 Graham Fortune, Secretary of Defence, Personal interview, 14 February 2005.
51 *Defence Long-Term Development Plan*, Wellington, June 2002.
52 *Air Force News*, July 2003, p. 11.
53 *P-3 Mission Systems Upgrade and Communications and Navigation Systems Upgrade*. A paper prepared for Cabinet from Office of Minister of Defence, November 2002.
54 *Defence Long-Term Development Plan (LTDP)—Updated*, November 2002.
55 Minister of Defence, Hon. Mark Burton, *Background: Royal New Zealand Air Force P-3 Orions*, Wellington, 5 October 2004, p. 1.
56 Government Defence Statement, *A Modern, Sustainable Defence Force Matched to New Zealand's needs*, Ministry of Defence, Wellington, 2001.
57 *Maritime Patrol Review*, p. 28.
58 Burton, *Background: Royal New Zealand Air Force P-3 Orions*, p. 3.
59 Burton, *Background: Royal New Zealand Air Force P-3 Orions*, p. 1.
60 *Air Force News*, February 2005, p. 2.
61 'Orion operational upgrades', *Air Force News*, October 2003, p. 23.
62 *Air Force News*, November 2003, p. 19.
63 Campbell, 'Sirius Money', p. 24.
64 Wing Commander Carl Nixon, Personal interview, 17 October 2004.
65 Project Sirius: Briefing to the Minister of Defence, Power Point Slides, July 2000.
66 Nicky Hager, 'Project Sirius', 23 July 2000, available at <http://www.converge.org.nz/pma/siriuspj.htm>, accessed 29 October 2008.
67 *Sunday Star-Times*, 7 March 2004.
68 *Air Force News*, November 2004, pp. 20–21.
69 *Maritime Patrol Review*.
70 CAB (01) 100.
71 *New Zealand Herald*, 18 October 2002.

Chapter 7

Plotting and Sedition, or Necessary Acquisition? The LAV IIIs

At the time of the publication of the 1997 Defence White Paper, it had become apparent that the New Zealand Government was being faced with a range of decisions which it needed to take to overcome the widespread obsolescence of major items of military equipment. Whilst previous chapters have focused on some of the major needs of the Royal New Zealand Navy (RNZN) or the Royal New Zealand Air Force (RNZAF), or, as in the case of HMNZS *Charles Upham* joint service requirements, this chapter will focus on one central requirement necessary for re-equipping the Army—Light Armoured Vehicles, or LAVs.

The 1997 White Paper noted that 'immediate priorities include the replacement or upgrading of the current fleet of M113 Armoured Personnel Carriers'.[1] At a Cabinet Meeting the previous month, it had been agreed that upgrading the Army's combat capability was a priority 'to overcome current shortcomings in its ability to undertake the more likely short term tasks, particularly peacekeeping missions'.[2] The following year Cabinet approved in principle the expenditure of NZ$180 million to acquire armoured vehicles, comprising both Armoured Personnel Carriers (APCs) and Fire Support Vehicles (FSVs). The funding was to provide sufficient armoured protection for the deployment of an infantry company group, replacing the 77 M113s and eight *Scorpion* FSVs which were then being operated.

Just over a year later, the Cabinet Strategy Committee approved a major change to the operational concept of the Army, agreeing that it become a motorised infantry force. This move to motorisation of the Army was to require a significant increase in the number of armoured vehicles required, and, as an interim measure, approval was given for the expenditure of NZ$212 million, which it was estimated would provide sufficient lift for one battalion group, and for one company from the second battalion. Cabinet approved both the change in operational concept and funding at a meeting on 24 May 1999.

With the return of a Labour-led government later that year, a commitment to re-equipping the Army was reinforced. *The Government's Defence Policy Framework*, released in June 2000, noted:

> Priority will be given to the acquisition and maintenance of essential equipment. Our core requirement is for well-equipped, combat trained

land forces which are also able to act as effective peacekeepers, supported by the Navy and Air Force.[3]

Two months later at a meeting on 21 August 2000, Cabinet approved in principle the purchase of 105 Light armoured vehicles at a projected cost of NZ$611 million. This was to be a significantly controversial acquisition project decision, leading to no less than four official reviews or inquiries.[4]

This chapter briefly explores the development of the use of armoured vehicles in the New Zealand Army and then examines the events that led to National's initial decision in 1997 to proceed with acquiring new armoured vehicles. The subsequent decisions to approve the motorisation of the Army, and increase the amount of funding available shall then be reviewed, before exploring the decisions of the Labour-led Government which led to the purchase of 105 fully equipped LAV IIIs, and, finally, commenting on their introduction into service.

History and Background

New Zealand's first armoured regiment was the Divisional Cavalry Regiment, formed during the Second World War. The Regiment was despatched overseas in three echelons, the second of which was diverted to England to assist in its defence during the Battle of Britain. The Regiment operated a variety of tracked and wheeled armoured vehicles, and saw action in Greece, Crete, the Middle East, North Africa and Italy.

Following the war, for several decades the New Zealand Army operated both wheeled scout cars and armoured cars (predominately made by Daimler), as well as tanks. *Valentine* tanks were introduced in 1941 and served until 1960. *Centurions* were operated between 1950 and 1968[5], whilst the last tank operated by the Army, the M41 light tank, ten of which were introduced from 1960 on, was officially withdrawn from service in 1983.

By this time, the Army was operating two main types of armoured vehicle, the venerable M113A1 APC, and the *Scorpion* FSV. Designed in the United States in the mid-1950s, the M113 had entered New Zealand Army service in 1969, and over the next few years 77 were delivered in total. The M113 proved to be reliable for many years, and it saw service overseas in both Bosnia and East Timor. The last of the M113s were formally withdrawn from service on 19 November 2004. The *Scorpion*, which entered service in 1983, was a somewhat different proposition.

The 1978 *Defence Review* indicated that New Zealand could no longer afford main battle tanks, and that the M41s would be replaced with a 'cost effective alternative',—the *Scorpion*.[6] The first *Scorpions*, built by Alvis Limited of Coventry, were delivered to the British Army in 1972. Designated a Combat Vehicle Reconnaissance (Tracked) or CVR (T), the *Scorpion* was fitted with a

76mm gun, and a militarised 4.2 litre Jaguar petrol engine. Twenty-six *Scorpions* were delivered to the New Zealand Army from August 1982 onwards. Major General Piers Reid, former Chief of General Staff, was scathing about the vehicle: 'We bought the *Scorpion*—that was a bad decision. It was a disastrous vehicle, built for Autobahns. It fell apart in the matter of a decade.'[7] These sentiments were echoed by officials:

> The *Scorpion* light tank is currently in use as a reconnaissance and fire support vehicle. It is not well-suited to the fire support role. It has experienced recurring mechanical problems which have attracted high maintenance costs and have forced the withdrawal of all but eight of the original 26 vehicles.[8]

The *Scorpions* were finally withdrawn from active service in July 1998.

Equipping an Expeditionary Force—Lessons from Bosnia

Ever since the first contingent of New Zealand troops left for the Boer War in October 1899, New Zealand has had a tradition of developing and maintaining expeditionary forces.[9] This is no less important today than it was over a century ago. As the Chief of Defence Force highlighted in 2004, 'New Zealand's geo-strategic position and reliance upon international trade fundamentally influences the way NZDF doctrine is derived and applied. As a result NZDF doctrine focuses upon our need to develop and sustain expeditionary forces'.[10]

When 250 New Zealand troops arrived in the former Yugoslavia in September 1994, their Commanding Officer, Lieutenant Colonel Graeme Williams, described the deployment of Kiwi Company as 'the largest number of troops in one deployment that the Government has committed to active service since the Korean War of the 1950s'.[11] Unlike the 8000 horses which served the New Zealand contingent during the Boer War, the main mount for Kiwi Company was to be the M113A1 Armoured Personnel Carrier. Twenty-six M113s were despatched to Bosnia, but undertook major modifications before arrival 'in order to deploy safely to Bosnia', as a Cabinet Committee paper in March 1998 indicated. The paper did go on to acknowledge that adding further armour to the vehicle to improve crew survivability adversely affected the vehicle's mobility and performance in roles such as convoy protection. Speaking in Parliament later that year, Helen Clark was more direct with her concern: 'The Army was sent to Bosnia with armoured personnel carriers from the Vietnam War and those men were endangered.'[12] Cabinet papers the following year underscored this point:

> The deficiencies in the NZ Army's capabilities were confirmed by the Kiwi Company deployment to Bosnia. This deployment showed that the NZ Army, with its current equipment types and method of operation, would be incapable of operating effectively in anything other than a

benign environment, without imposing significant risk on the wider force within which it would work.[13]

Whilst the deployment of three contingents of troops to Bosnia was an enormous public relations success, both politically and for the NZDF, there was clearly a large amount of risk involved. Brigadier Roger Mortlock commented:

> The M113s were slow—as they were re-armoured they became very slow. The initial British brigadier gave Kiwi Company the safest area to patrol, but he was still worried that he wouldn't get to them in time if they were in real trouble.[14]

The nature of the operational area was underscored by Captain Marcus Culley of Kiwi II Company:

> With the increase in size of the company's area of responsibility as a result of the deployment of United Nations Task Force *Alpha*, the workload on soldiers has increased. … Fortunately the danger has not increased, with the Vitez pocket remaining one of the quieter places in Central Bosnia.[15]

The former Secretary of Defence, Gerald Hensley, also commented on their limits: 'In 1994 I said they were old and worn out. Deployed on a mission they were on the limits of their capability.'[16] The limits on the capability of the M113s meant that there was also a severe limit on the utility of New Zealand forces. In order to have a minimum level of acceptable protection, NZ$3.2 million had been spent on modifying the M113s before they left for Bosnia. In addition, belly armour for mine protection, and sponson armour to protect against shrapnel, was borrowed from Australia. The result of the modifications was such that, 'although the level of protection of these vehicles was improved, their mobility was severely compromised'.[17] The significant constraints this placed on Kiwi Company were emphasised in a paper arguing for the motorisation of the New Zealand Army:

> This (deficiency) has implications for the value that our traditional defence partners place on New Zealand's peacekeeping efforts. Bosnia highlighted that the Army lacks the means to be able to move and manoeuvre its forces with the necessary degree of protection and speed to ensure the survivability of the force while it completes the assigned tasks in a timely manner.[18]

In order to ensure any meaningful place for a New Zealand contribution, remedial action was clearly necessary.

From Armoured Personnel Carrier to Infantry Fighting Vehicle — The Motorisation of the New Zealand Army

With the experience of Bosnia fresh in everyone's minds, the 1997 *Defence Assessment* identified that priority should be given to upgrading the combat capability of the Army. The subsequent 1997 White Paper acknowledged that there were major deficiencies which needed to be addressed:

> The Government's first priority will be to rectify the most critical deficiencies in those capabilities where there is more likely to be a need in the short term, that is re-equipping the Army so that it can undertake the more demanding peace support operations.[19]

Here the White Paper also noted the changing nature of peace support operations. The history of peacekeeping for over 40 years had been one requiring lightly armed forces, usually deployed at the agreement of both parties to a conflict. During the 1990s that had changed, and the White Paper acknowledged this:

> Since the end of the Cold War, however, peace missions have increasingly been launched during hostilities. The consent of the warring parties has been neither complete nor continuous. These peace enforcement missions are a higher-order task than peacekeeping as they involve conventional high-intensity operations.[20]

Along with the change in the nature of peacekeeping, it was acknowledged that there had been significant advances in technology, and that the capabilities of New Zealand's security partners had continued to grow. This had resulted in a capability gap between New Zealand and its potential partners. The White Paper acknowledged: 'Because others are now better able to perform peacekeeping tasks, New Zealand's ability to offer operationally useful contributions to peacekeeping is diminishing.'[21] This had significant implications for New Zealand, a country which took pride in its contribution to peacekeeping efforts throughout the world. The White Paper went on to add: 'As the deployment of land forces on peacekeeping operations is the most likely task to be assigned to the NZDF in the short term, these upgrades are a top priority in the investment plan.'[22]

Some five months later, on 23 March 1998, Cabinet approved in principle the purchase of armoured vehicles at an estimated cost of NZ$180 million. Indicative costings were based on a new fleet of armoured vehicles composed of 69 APCs and 12 FSVs. Consideration was being given at the time to either purchasing new APCs, or upgrading the M113A1 to current M113A4 configuration, but officials made it clear that a new FSV, preferably sharing the same hull as the APC, would be required.

James Rolfe, a former Army officer, commented that the Army tried to identify its requirements during 1996 and 1997, but had problems deciding whether wheeled or tracked armoured vehicles were most appropriate.[23] Gerald Hensley, Secretary of Defence at the time, was more direct:

> In attempting to define the problem 'How do we replace the APCs?' there were two fundamental issues to be addressed: 'What sort of vehicles did we want, and how many would we need?' Each of these questions was to prove difficult to answer. Our battles with the Army were great. The basic question was do we have wheeled or tracked vehicles? The Army was riven by factions. The Armoured Corps people felt if they gave up on tracks that would be the end of the Armoured Corps—they delayed the procurement by up to a year. The answer eventually came back that in 80% of cases wheels were better than tracks.[24]

Before the end of 1998, as discussed in previous chapters, the Minister of Defence sought the opportunity to purchase F-16 strike aircraft, and a third ANZAC frigate. Supporting papers at the time indicated that 'there have been changes in project timings ... (with) an extended delivery of armoured vehicles'.[25] The paper went on to say that the extended delivery period reflected 'the availability of the likely preferred option', and noted that it was planned that the NZDF would cooperate with the Australian Defence Force (ADF) on the possible joint purchase of armoured vehicles.

The following month, in December 1998, a Project Team of two Ministry of Defence officials and four New Zealand Army personnel visited Australia to discuss the ASLAV—Australian Light Armoured Vehicle—project. Australia was in the process of deciding on orders for further ASLAVS for 1999 and, in the spirit of Closer Defence Relations, the opportunity was taken to explore whether a joint order might be desirable. The project team also visited the manufacturer of the base vehicle, the LAV II, General Motors Defense (GMD) in February 1999. (In fact, familiarisation with the ASLAV project had begun in 1996 with a visit of two officers from the Queen Alexandra's Mounted Rifles (QAMR) to the 2nd Cavalry Regiment (Reconnaissance), Royal Australian Armoured Corps.)

However, by May 1999 it was clear that the operational requirements of the two armies were different. By this stage the New Zealand Army had sought approval to change the operating concept of the Army to that of a motorised infantry. Whilst the Army had for some years based its doctrine on that of manoeuvre warfare, it was clear from the experience in Bosnia that the equipment available to the Army did not support the Army's doctrine. The change in operating concept was a significant change, which would see the whole of a battalion being capable of being transported to the battlefield in vehicles with armoured protection. Having previously sought approval to purchase approximately 69 APCs and 12 FSVs, it was 'now suggested that approximately 127 Infantry Mobility Vehicles (IMVs) and 24 FSVs would be required. This could cost up to $408 million (excluding Goods and Services Tax (GST)). The Defence Capital Plan (DCP) has funding provision of NZ$212 million (excluding GST).'[26]

Three options were therefore put to Cabinet at this point:

1. Buy all of the required vehicles in one tranche through an increase in funding.
2. Buy all of the required FSVs and sufficient IMVs to equip one full battalion, plus sufficient for one company of the second battalion. This option was said to fall within the already approved budget envelope.
3. Buy the vehicles required to fully equip two battalions in two tranches, the first purchase as in option (2), and the remainder at a later date.

The Ministry indicated that the first option was the preferred option if funding was not a constraint, but this was considered to be unrealistic. The second option, which the Government approved, was not favoured either. The Ministry was concerned that this option would have long-term training implications for the Army, as it would have battalions training for two different types of operations. It was also concerned that there would be a negative impact on the training of reinforcements, and that there would be an increased risk of being unable to maintain a sufficient force of vehicles in theatre. 'It is therefore,' the Ministry contended, 'the weakest of the three options.' The Minister's preferred choice was option three—to purchase in two tranches. In the short term the implications were the same as option two, but in the long term this option would simplify training, whilst also simplifying reinforcement and rotation problems. The Ministry's assessment was: 'This option provides a balance between risk and operational effectiveness, when considered over the longer term.'[27]

At the time of its decision, National were once more wanting to enhance relationships with Australia and the United States and were committed to using New Zealand forces in peace support roles. Whilst they had indicated support for new wheeled armoured vehicles, trade-offs were in the equation as they were also committed to Project *Sirius* and the F-16s, and remained officially committed to a third surface combatant. Max Bradford said: 'We had other equipment to replace.'[28] The Auditor-General's Report commented: 'Cabinet had considered—and rejected—an option of equipping two battalions, either in the present or in the future.'[29] Perhaps, not surprisingly, Cabinet on 24 May 1999 approved the second option.

The Cabinet paper on *Motorisation of the NZ Army* had noted: 'A review of recent technological developments together with discussions with our immediate allies on the concept of operations led to the conclusion that the characteristics of wheeled armoured vehicles would better suit New Zealand's requirements than tracked vehicles.'[30]

The paper went on to comment on the changing nature of both warlike and peace support operations, with a strengthening of weapons capability amongst protagonists in disputes. The possession of increasingly lethal weaponry and vehicles with greater levels of armour and mobility had led to New Zealand's traditional defence partners taking serious account of these developments as they re-shaped their own forces. They had therefore either already developed infantry battalions with armoured mobility, as in the case of the United States, Canada and the United Kingdom, or as in Australia's case were moving towards such a capability.[31] The importance of interoperability with allies had been stressed already in a previous paper.

The increase in the size of operational areas being assigned to infantry battalions was also stressed. This had been made possible by motorisation, and the formidable task allotted to Kiwi Company as a result was used as an illustration of the difficulties New Zealand faced with its current equipment and operational doctrine:

> A force one third the size of a battalion was assigned an area 12.5 times larger than that a complete battalion would reasonably be given, based upon traditional foot mobility. Therefore, the effective increase in the size of operations, when compared at battalion level, is a factor of 36 times.[32]

The annex attached to the paper (and a similar annex attached to the *Light Armoured Vehicle Project* paper the following year) made much of the capability of wheeled IMVs to self-deploy, and having the ability to cover ground quickly and reliably when compared to tracked APCs.

In June 1999, speaking at Trentham Army Camp, the Minister of Defence, Max Bradford, indicated that a total of 104 wheeled vehicles (not 81) would replace the M113s. These would comprise the 24 FSVs previously approved, and approximately 80 IMVs. Bradford indicated that 'the choice of wheeled over tracked vehicles had been made after careful thought. They were more reliable over long distances and could be more easily upgraded over their 25 year service life.'[33]

Assessing the Alternatives

Also in June 1999, the Acquisition Division of the Ministry of Defence had decided that an independent reviewer should examine the service specifications which had been developed for the tender documents. They engaged HVR Consulting Services (HVR) in the United Kingdom to provide an independent opinion on the validity of the specifications. An initial finding of HVR's report was that it appeared that the specifications were based on one vehicle—the LAV III. This was despite the fact that the tender documents had specifically sought a mix of FSVs and IMVs, on a ratio of 1:5. The LAV III was manufactured only as an FSV. HVR recommended that if the Ministry were to go to tender, it should change the specifications to make them more open to a wider range of vehicles. Those changes were subsequently made. However, the report considered that the specification of the LAV III 'was so far ahead of the competition that HVR recommended that the Ministry of Defence should consider direct purchase, rather than conducting a tender'.[34]

At the same time as asking HVR for their independent review, the Ministry of Defence had also issued a request for registration of interest to over 70 potential suppliers. Sixteen responses were received; those 16 respondents offered between them 17 vehicles, and HVR reviewed each of them against 10 of the key criteria that were required for the vehicle. HVR reviewed the vehicles for consideration and, apart from its consideration that the LAV III was the outstanding vehicle, found that only one other came close, 'but that it had almost reached the end of its development life'. HVR suggested that if the Ministry was determined to go to tender, it should remove the requirement for air transportability by the C-130 *Hercules*, thus allowing two, and potentially four, other vehicles to compete in the tender process. One of those other alternatives was the FOX 6x6, or FUCHS as it was known in Germany, where it was manufactured by Henschel Wehrtechnik. Early in October 1999 the New Zealand agent for the FOX, H.W. Munroe, wrote to the Ministry of Defence expressing its concern about the tender process, saying: 'A careful examination of the User Requirements shows that the LAV III vehicle is the only vehicle that meets all essential criteria. Therefore, we must ask why any other vehicle manufacturers were issued with tender documents?'[35]

Later that month the Ministry of Defence called a conference of tenderers, and at this time agreed to a system of waivers. This was to allow those tenderers whose products did not meet the essential requirements to ask for an exemption, or a series of exemptions, to allow them to proceed. When the tenders closed in December 1999 only two vehicles were in contention, the LAV III and the FOX 6x6. At least one company had decided not to bid from the outset, as it knew its product was unable to meet all the essential criteria.

Tenders had been sought for a total of either 102 or 152 vehicles, 26 FSVs and 126 IMVs. Whilst seven tenderers had been approached for possible pricing, only three responses had been received. These indicated a choice of two vehicles: the Canadian-built LAV III 8x8, and the German-built FOX 6x6. Significantly, neither the LAV III nor the FOX 6x6 complied with all of the tender requirements. However, the Ministry of Defence indicated that the areas of non-compliance on the LAV III were minor. Furthermore, because of its FSV configuration, only two thirds of the original number estimated would be required to equip both battalions. The FOX on the other hand was found to have significant shortcomings. Perhaps the most important of these was that the proposed FSV turret had never been fitted to a FOX before. At the time of assessing the tenders, it was considered that the FOX would have cost 15–20 per cent more for the total project. With the shift in exchange rates by August 2000, this expense had increased by 5–10 per cent, despite an individual vehicle cost of NZ$3.4 million for a specially upgraded FOX, as opposed to about NZ$6 million for a LAV III.[36] Preference was given to the LAV III, a recently designed third-generation vehicle fitted with a turreted weapon system and able to carry a crew of three and a section of seven troops. Whilst the LAV III was only available in turreted form, fitted with a stabilised 25mm cannon, 7.62mm machine gun, and eight smoke grenade launchers, it combined the functions of an FSV and an IMV. This allowed a reduction in the numbers of vehicles required from 152 to 105.

Controversy and Accusation — The Purchase of the LAV IIIs

When the Labour-led Government came to power, they had already declared that they would, in large part, be following the recommendations of *Defence Beyond 2000*. One of those options was 'an Army force structure based on two highly mobile light infantry battalions'.[37] After coming to power, the new Government set up a series of reviews of defence priorities. The impact of some of those reviews has been explored in earlier chapters; taking account of New Zealand's role in the world, the judgement of utility, and trade-offs, decisions were made not to proceed with the conversion of HMNZS *Charles Upham*; not to proceed with a third frigate; to cancel the lease of the F-16s, and to disband the Air Force strike wing. The light armoured vehicle project was identified as a high priority purchase. The question remained, how many to purchase?

The Secretary of Defence briefed the Minister in June 2000, and advised that the LAV III had been identified as the most suitable vehicle, and that 105 would fulfil all requirements. However, the Secretary went on to note that this number would cost significantly more than the NZ$212 million budgeted by the previous Government, and advised two options. The first of these was to buy 35 LAVs, which would fit within the previous budget envelope; the second was to buy 55 LAVs at a likely cost of NZ$337 million, with the suggestion of buying the other 50 at a later date.[38] The Auditor-General's Report indicated that the Minister felt that these options were insufficient, and the Secretary was asked to prepare a draft Cabinet paper.

In another reflection of bureaucratic politics, the Ministry of Defence produced a draft paper in July 2000, which gave three options:

1. The recommendation of the Army to purchase 105 Light armoured vehicles for delivery over a 5-year period;
2. The recommendation of the MoD (with which the NZDF concurred) to purchase 55 light armoured vehicles with an option of 50 further vehicles—the purchase decision on these latter vehicles would depend upon the outcome of the land force capability review that had been commissioned under *The Government's Defence Policy Framework*; or
3. A third option—to purchase 75 light armoured vehicles (delivered over a 3–4 year period), with the option of 30 more later.[39]

Following this the Minister asked for a briefing from the Chief of Defence Force (CDF), who asked the Army to provide one. The Chief of General Staff (CGS) provided the briefing on 1 August 2000. On 9 August the Minister met with the Secretary of Defence and the CDF, and was specific about the options he wanted to be included in the paper. Despite the Army's strong objection, the Ministry of Defence included the following paragraph in the final Cabinet paper:

> In its desired requirements the Army indicated a preference for a common body shell type for the FSV and IMV. This commonality introduces operational, logistic, training and maintenance advantages. One common vehicle type can limit flexibility, and may be initially more expensive. For instance having one battalion equipped with the LAV III and the other equipped with an upgrade[d] M113 APC or similar may be a cheaper and more versatile combination. This concept has not been tested.[40]

This statement effectively supported a fourth option, namely to 'redefine the project requirements'. The Army had pointed out that a combined fleet was outside the *Force Development Proposal* of May 1999, and the Minister of Defence had previously indicated that it would restrict the tender process to wheeled vehicles.

Three options were put to Cabinet in August 2000, with a recommendation for approval in principle of the procurement of the LAV III. Options put forward were:

1. Purchase 75, to be delivered over a 3–4 year period at a cost of NZ$472 million, with an option to purchase 30 later;
2. Purchase 55, to be delivered over a 3-year period at a cost of NZ$389 million, with an option to purchase a further 50 at a later date; or
3. Redefine the project requirements entirely.[41]

Major General Piers Reid commented: 'The ultimate question was should we buy the vehicles in tranches, or should we buy them all at once? Treasury said "Buy them all at once".'[42] In commenting on the proposal, Treasury said:

> If 105 vehicles were purchased, then Ministers would be able to deploy one three-company battalion offshore for six months, while a further similar battalion remains under training in New Zealand. Having a second battalion under training in New Zealand means that a fully trained equivalent unit can replace the Army battalion that is deployed offshore. This involves a considerable deepening of the Army's current capability. … If Ministers want the capability outlined above, it will be cheaper to purchase the 105 vehicles in one batch.[43]

Even after allowing for the GST component, Option 3, at a net cost of NZ$340 million, was over 50 per cent more costly than the NZ$212 million approved by the National Government. However, having made much of defence decision-making as an election issue, it was now time for the Labour Government to front up with the money. At a meeting on 21 August 2000, Cabinet approved in principle the purchase of 105 Light armoured vehicles for delivery over a 5-year period at a cost not to exceed NZ$611,764,613 (GST inclusive). Later that week, an Editorial in the *New Zealand Herald* commented:

> The Army of course is the big winner in the Government's decision-making. The $611 million to be spent on 105 new light armoured vehicles could reasonably be described as lavish. The Army's present M113s date back to the Vietnam War, have proved an embarrassment in Bosnia and East Timor, and clearly need replacement urgently. The Canadian-built LAV III is the Army's choice and, with its ability to fill both troop-carrying and fire-support roles, it will be a considerable morale-booster. Yet in its wildest dreams, the Army could not have guessed that its request for such a large number of vehicles would be granted.[44]

However, when the Prime Minister, Helen Clark, announced the purchase of the LAV IIIs following the Cabinet decision in August 2000, she was clear about the importance of replacing the M113s, saying:

> The equipment the Army has been putting up with just isn't good enough for the tasks it is asked to do. The deficiencies of the existing Armoured Personnel Carriers (APCs) … have been clear in recent deployments. … In Bosnia and East Timor the APCs haven't been up to the job.[45]

Following Cabinet's approval-in-principle, a contract was signed on 29 January 2001 with General Motors of Canada Ltd for 105 LAV IIIs.

The Army's 'big win' was to hit the headlines long before any of the new vehicles arrived in New Zealand. In November 2000 the Secretary of Defence, Graham Fortune, had asked the Auditor-General to undertake a review of the processes used for the acquisition of the LAVs. The Auditor-General's Report was published in August 2001. The findings of the Report were damning, and included concerns that:

- from the start, the project was poorly defined;
- the changing project definition led to a lack of clarity of the number of vehicles required;
- the approach to research of the market was deficient;
- the scope for competition was restricted;
- there was no strategic management of the project;
- in at least two instances the MoD failed to consult appropriately;
- relationships between the MoD, the NZDF and the Army were dysfunctional;
- pursuit of the project diverged considerably from Cabinet approvals in a number of respects;
- the longer the acquisition was delayed, the more expensive it became;
- there was insufficient documentation of some key decisions; and finally
- the significant capability requirements associated with the acquisition of 105 LAV IIIs were inadequately assessed before the decision was made to acquire the vehicles.[46]

The political fall-out was immediate. Earlier in the month there had been a Parliamentary debacle as questions were raised about the suitability of the LAV III for operating in areas such as East Timor. ACT MP Rodney Hide had tabled a written question asking whether an LAV III could have reached the area where Private Leonard Manning was shot in a firefight. The Minister, Mark Burton, in his reply suggested that the noise of the vehicle would have put off potential attackers. However, Hide obtained a copy of a draft response which said that using the LAV 'would not have been practicable', but that in fact an M113 had got within 30 metres of the scene of the incident. With the publication of the Auditor-General's report, Hide took the opportunity again to attack the Minister:

> The process was dysfunctional, the tender screwed, and Cabinet was sidelined. It's inconceivable that such a process would hit the jackpot and reach the right decision. Heads should role (sic). The first head on the pike should be Minister of Defence, Mark Burton's.[47]

Hide went on to call for fewer wheeled armoured personnel carriers, and an upgrade of the M113s. By contrast, the Green Party's Defence Spokesperson, Keith Locke, took a different perspective:

> Acquisition of armoured vehicles was paralysed as the Army tried to overcome resistance from defence dinosaurs who still put priority on air and naval combat. ... The report shows the Defence Force wanted to go ahead with the purchase of only 50 LAVs, presumably to free up money for the navy or air force.[48]

The week following the debacle in Parliament, Max Bradford demanded a broader investigation of 'the whole scene'. He was himself, it was reported, in an embarrassing situation as he had recommended the purchase of LAVs in 1998, 'but now he says important information was withheld from him at the time'. The same article which had commented on Bradford's wish for a broader inquiry also noted: 'Something else that is interesting is the amount of information Hide, Bradford and New Zealand First MP Ron Mark, a former Army officer, are receiving. It obviously comes from military sources.'[49]

During the same month in which the Auditor-General's Report was released, a letter (which was to become known as 'The Gordon Letter'[50]), was tabled in Parliament, a copy having been given to Bradford by Robin Johansen, who had previously been Deputy Secretary for Defence Acquisition in the Ministry of Defence.[51] The letter, which Lieutenant Colonel I.J.M. Gordon indicated was triggered by the Army's embarrassing experience with its equipment in Bosnia, was described by the Leader of the Opposition, Jenny Shipley, as 'seditious'.[52] In the letter, Gordon encouraged the Army to open a 'second front' in its war with the Defence chiefs. The *New Zealand Herald* commented:

> Over the next few days, the impression left by the Gordon letter was reinforced with leaks about private briefings and a dinner attended by the Army high command and Defence Minister Mark Burton of which the Chief of Defence Forces was unaware. … The leaking of the Gordon letter finally pushed the Government into ordering an investigation.[53]

The Auditor-General's Report had, as we have seen, commented strongly on the dysfunctional nature of the relationships between the Ministry of Defence, the NZDF and the Army. Less than three weeks after the Report was published, the Minister of Defence announced the following major review and two inquiries:

1. A review of accountabilities and structural arrangements between the Ministry of Defence and the NZDF—the Hunn report;
2. An inquiry into standards of behaviour, the leaking of documents and the inappropriate use of information and position by NZDF personnel—the White and Ansell report; and
3. An inquiry through the office of the Judge Advocate General into the propriety of a letter allegedly generated from within the Army and an e-mail allegedly generated from within the RNZN—the Carruthers report.

The first of the reports to be completed was the White and Ansell report, published on 20 December 2001. There were two aspects to the report, the first concerning standards of behaviour more generally, and the second regarding the leaking of information. The report's authors analysed 62 possible 'unauthorised disclosures', and found that 30 might be classified as 'probable leaks', that is 'the deliberate and improper covert release of official information to advance a particular agenda or embarrass'.[54] Of particular significance to this chapter was the finding of four probable leaks during August 2001, the month in which the Auditor-General's Report, with its many critical findings, was published. White and Ansell in commenting on the leaks said:

> We were not asked to identify the individuals responsible for these deliberate 'leaks' and, as we have made it plain, there is no clear evidence of culpability. We were guided in most cases by the weight of opinion in the responses to our inquiry. Nevertheless it became apparent to us that they probably came largely from factions in the Army. ... It is difficult to escape the conclusion that the 'leaks' which occurred were originally designed to advance the interests of the Army, primarily against the interests of the other Services. Subsequently the 'leaks' were designed to counter the influence of a faction in the Army by causing personal embarrassment to the CGS.[55]

Robin Johansen, former Deputy Secretary–Acquisitions commented: 'It is my view that there was a concerted effort by Army to step outside established processes to achieve goals which were not shared across the whole of the defence community.'[56]

Some months later, in February 2002, the Foreign Affairs, Defence and Trade Committee published a further report, saying that 'the Army's purchase of 105 Light armoured vehicles (LAVs) is a "sorry chapter" for major capital acquisition projects in New Zealand.'[57] This time it was the National MP Max Bradford who said the Minister should reconsider the LAV purchase: 'The world has changed and, with it, the appropriateness of the LAV purchase.'[58] There was, though, to be no change.

By May 2002 the first LAV, NZLAV001, was close to completion. Having had its gun turret fitted in California, it was shipped to Arizona for gun performance and vehicle testing.[59] In June 2002 a group of 15 Army personnel were visiting Canadian forces to learn about the Canadian experience with the LAV.[60] By January 2003 a Transition Training Team (TTT) had been set up at Waiouru to conduct training for instructors and crews; it was intended to disband the TTT after crews for both the 1st Battalion Royal New Zealand Infantry Regiment (RNZIR) and 2nd/1st Battalion had been trained.[61] The first batch of seven NZLAVs arrived in New Zealand in August 2003[62] and, just as in August 2001, the LAV once again became the focus both of media and political attention.

The Introduction into Service of the LAV IIIs

At the end of July 2003, National MP Simon Power had said: 'It has also been suggested that the Army will struggle to man the new Light Armoured Vehicles (LAV3s) that are due for delivery in September.'[63] That was to be confirmed a week later, when NZDF papers obtained under the *Official Information Act* 1982 indicated that the Army was particularly concerned about shortages of crew, mechanics and electronics technicians for the LAVs. The *New Zealand Herald* went on to note that the NZDF papers said that 'there are already shortages in these trades and the nature and complexity of the Lav (sic) will exacerbate them', though added that the Minister's Office had said that 'its latest advice is that the Army is on track to fully crew the vehicles'.[64]

Late in August 2003 a television documentary about the LAVs screened on the *Sunday* program on TV One.[65] This program challenged the purchase of the LAV IIIs yet again and reopened the 'wheels versus tracks' debate. Politics were also present again, with New Zealand First MP Ron Mark commenting that the purchase of the LAVs 'is a $1 billion bungle—I wrote to the Prime Minister personally to ask her to stop the project'.[66] Major General Jerry Mateparae, Chief of General Staff, not surprisingly said: 'It's money well spent.'[67]

The issue of 'wheels versus tracks' was raised in relation to both the utility of the LAVs and trade-offs. A soldier in East Timor was quoted as saying: 'I'm currently serving as a crew commander in East Timor. You just won't get a LAV where we go. In a country like this the M113 is ideal—keep the LAV for the desert.'[68] However, another experienced M113 commander, Captain Dougal Baker, who had been deployed to both Bosnia and East Timor, said:

> The LAV is a far superior machine. Of course there are areas you can't go through with wheels, but you can go to 95% of the places you'd go with tracks. For the rest—you can travel around the obstacle faster than a tracked vehicle can go through it.[69]

A week after the television program aired, I met with Major General Piers Reid. Concerning the politics he said: 'Ron Mark is using the vehicle to keep up his profile. Max Bradford has used it for his political survival.' As regards utility he commented: 'There's probably only 1 or 2% of an area where you can get an M113 where you can't get an LAV III.' He then added:

> You'd get the impression from Ron Mark that an M113 could go over a mine—it can't. The design of the LAV III is excellent for protection against mines. A mine will blow a wheel off, but the tub will protect the occupants.[70] The occupants will also be protected by the 25mm gun, which will deal with armoured vehicles.[71] The M113 has a 12.7mm machine gun.[72]

Rod Vaughan, the television program's commentator, said:

> Off road, the M113 has the edge. It's amphibious and light enough to be air-dropped by parachute. Ron Mark says the bulky LAV will prove to be a lemon. ... Getting to the battlefield is a real challenge. The original specifications called for transportability in a *Hercules*.[73] At 14 tonnes

it's almost twice the weight of an M113. ... The Army rejected the possibility of upgrading the M113s in Australia for a third of the price.[74]

The Minister of Defence, Mark Burton, replied: 'Upgrading the M113s would have given an 8-10 year life extension. In the end we had to make a decision, and I'm confident we made the right decision here.'[75] The first deliveries took place in August 2003, and Burton formally accepted delivery at a ceremony at Waiouru on 24 October 2003.

Teething problems

Just three months after the LAVs were officially accepted, reports of mechanical breakdowns surfaced. 'Breakdowns plague Army's new vehicles' ran a headline in the *New Zealand Herald* on 21 January 2004. The article went on to say that mechanical faults had struck the first batch of LAVs, listing faults in a heater, turbo unit, and auxiliary power unit. Two days later the manufacturers were reported as having responded that the faults were all minor and easily repaired. In July 2004 criticisms of the vehicle were levelled by National MP Simon Power, who asked if the vehicles were a 'bottomless pit' of extra costs after the Army had sought an extra NZ$6 million for spare parts. (The request was declined.) And in December 2004 it was reported that four LAVs out of the 18, which had been sent to Australia for Exercise *Predators Gallop*, had been put out of action for several days after hitting tree stumps. Air Marshal Bruce Ferguson, Chief of Defence Force, responded to the concern saying: 'Our loss of vehicles for that reason was not greater than the Australian loss of vehicles.'[76] Perhaps of more concern than the vehicles' capabilities is the ability of the Army to provide sufficient personnel to both crew and maintain the vehicles.

Addressing trade-offs, Robert Ayson, a strategic and defence studies specialist at The Australian National University, and former adviser to the Foreign Affairs, Defence and Trade Committee, raised the following questions: 'I wonder why they bought so many LAVs? I wonder about the Army's ability to sustain them? Have the Government replaced one display capability, the strike wing, with another?'[77]

Jennie Derby, Senior Advisor to the Minister of Defence, noted: 'Labour was determined to reverse the trend of National. ... Timing is everything. Labour had said in its manifesto that they would re-equip the Army. With the benefit of hindsight would they order 105 again?—yes they would.'[78] The Chief of Army, Major General Jerry Mateparae, was unequivocal in his support for the decision to buy 105 LAVs, saying that he was 'sure that the New Zealand Army needs all 105 NZLAV. Any less and we will compromise our ability to deliver and sustain a motorised light infantry battalion group'.[79]

In June 2004 the Chief of Defence Force, speaking at the Royal New Zealand Returned and Services' Association (RSA) Conference in Wellington, warned that the NZDF was undermanned, saying:

> What I'm doing right now—it's being done independently—is a review of what I think we need in resources, basically personnel, and what Government expects in outputs. There is a gap in my view right now—it's the expectations of what defence forces need to do and my capacity to meet them.[80]

In addressing the issue of utility, the following month, reporting in the NZDF *Annual Report*, the CDF said:

> There remain some risks with the project, as while the NZDF is on track to introduce the NZLAV, the development of the motorised battalion is a complex task. ... 1 RNZIR [is] expected to become operational at the end of 2005. With the current operational tempo and the challenges of recruitment and retention the NZDF faces, the delivery of a complete second battalion capability will be delayed until sufficient personnel are available to be assigned.[81]

Recruitment and retention were a concern, with an attrition rate of 16.5 per cent to 17.5 per cent over the previous two years.[82] Then, in December 2004, the CDF was reported as advising the Foreign Affairs and Trade Select Committee:

> The Army has changed its mind about motorising both the regular force infantry battalions using the LAV3s. Instead the Burnham-based 2nd/1st Battalion would provide back up for the Linton-based 1st Battalion, a unit which is kept at a higher state of readiness.[83]

Colonel Mark Wheeler in March 2005 noted that there were no factors which were limiting constraints on the timed introduction into service of the LAVs, commenting:

> Two LAV battalions was a limiting factor for operations. We have structured as a heavy motorised battalion (1/1), and a light battalion with LAV support (2/1). 49 LAVs will go to 1/1 at Linton, with a further 14 to combat support and logistics there. QAMR will have 30 at Burnham, where 2/2 has been organised into two companies and 12 will go to training establishments at Waiouru and Trentham.[84]

Wheeler was pleased that the required levels of capability for crewing the LAVs were in fact ahead of schedule, with 64 operational crews to be trained by December 2005, more than sufficient to achieve a Motorised Infantry Battalion.[85]

Whilst the first batch of vehicles were on their way, the Minister had said: 'We expect the first company group of LAV3s to be deployment ready for December 2004, with the first full battalion group of up to 51 LAV3s ready for overseas deployment by December 2005.'[86] In the event, 2 LAV Platoon and Victor Company of 1st Battalion RNZIR were ready for deployment to Australia in June 2004.[87] By this stage, 91 LAVs were in New Zealand, with 57 in service with the Army. The final batch of vehicles was delivered on schedule in November 2004,[88] though the contract price had increased to NZ$653 million.[89] In November 2005, a battalion group of 800 soldiers and 51 LAVs took part in Exercise *Silver Warrior*, demonstrating the capability of both the LAV III and 1st Battalion RNZIR and drawing forth the comment from one of the Exercise's senior observers, Lieutenant Colonel Phil McKee, that 'the NZLAV performed better than anyone's wildest expectations'.[90]

Summary

The acquisition and introduction into service of the LAV IIIs brought about one of the most contentious periods of debates about defence equipment since the hue and cry over the original ANZAC frigate decision in 1989. Important issues for both National and Labour-led Governments were the number of new armoured vehicles to buy, whether to purchase new vehicles or upgrade the existing M113s, and what the implications of these decisions would mean for other acquisitions. The whole notion of 'balanced forces' was put under the spotlight; National wished to retain the 'balanced force' concept, whilst Labour chose to emphasise the importance of well-equipped land forces. Yet though this chapter has outlined how much criticism was levelled at the Government when the decision to purchase 105 LAVs was taken, a battalion was made operationally ready within the agreed timeframe. How the LAVs perform on operational deployment will, however, remain the litmus test for this particular acquisition decision. In exploring the events surrounding the decision-making process for this particular case, it is strongly apparent that the decision to procure the LAV IIIs provided fertile ground for much political argument and debate within the New Zealand context. The purchase price was considerable, and the additional investment to ensure the ongoing operational capability of a motorised battalion continues to be significant. However bureaucratic politics, with the observation that relationships between the Ministry of Defence, the NZDF, and the Army were dysfunctional, and above all timing, with the election of a Labour-led Government, were ultimately the dominant factors as the decision-making process for the acquisition of the LAV IIIs unfolded.

ENDNOTES

[1] *The Shape of New Zealand's Defence, A White Paper*, Ministry of Defence, Wellington, November 1997, p. 9.

[2] Cabinet paper CAB (97) M40/8A, p. 2.

[3] *The Government's Defence Policy Framework*, Ministry of Defence, Wellington, June 2000, p. 7.

[4] These were:

1. *Ministry of Defence: Acquisition of Light Armoured Vehicles and Light Operational Vehicles*, Report of the Controller and Auditor-General, Wellington, August 2001, p. 20;
2. Douglas White QC and Graham Ansell, *Review of the Performance of the Defence Force in Relation to the Expected Standards of Behaviour, and in Particular the Leaking and Inappropriate Use of Information by Defence Force Personnel*, Report to the State Services Commission, Wellington, 20 December 2001;
3. C.R. Carruthers QC, *Report of Inquiry into the Propriety of a Letter Allegedly Generated from within the Army*, Wellington, 18 March 2002; and
4. D.K. Hunn, *Review of Accountability and Structural Arrangements between the Ministry of Defence and the New Zealand Defence Force*, Wellington, 30 September 2002.

[5] *Centurions in New Zealand*, available at <http://kiwisinarmour.hobbyvista.com>, accessed 27 October 2008.

[6] *Defence Review 1978*, Government Printer, Wellington, p. 35.

[7] Major General Piers Reid, Personal interview, 3 September 2003.

[8] *Armoured Vehicles*, Cabinet Paper attached to STR (98) 34.

[9] Major G.J. Clayton, *The New Zealand Army, A History from the 1840s to the 1990s*, New Zealand Army, Wellington, 1990, p. 64.

[10] *Foundations of New Zealand Military Doctrine*, New Zealand Defence Force, Wellington, 2004, p. I–3.

[11] Paul Bensemann, 'The War with no Enemy', *NZ Defence Quarterly*, Summer 1994, p. 2.

[12] Helen Clark, Parliamentary Debate, 4 November 1998.

[13] *Motorisation of the NZ Army*, Paper attached to STR (99) 87, p. 3.

[14] Brigadier Roger Mortlock, Personal interview, 25 August 2003.

[15] *Army News*, no. 113, 23 August 1995.

[16] Gerald Hensley, Personal interview, 9 November 2003.

[17] Hensley, Personal interview, 9 November 2003.

[18] *Motorisation of the NZ Army*, p. 3.

[19] *The Shape of New Zealand's Defence, A White Paper*, p. 8.

[20] *The Shape of New Zealand's Defence, A White Paper*, p. 27.

[21] *The Shape of New Zealand's Defence, A White Paper*, p. 27.

[22] *The Shape of New Zealand's Defence, A White Paper*, p. 27.

[23] James Rolfe, *The Armed Forces of New Zealand*, Allen and Unwin, St. Leonards, NSW, 1999, p. 129.

[24] Gerald Hensley, Personal interview, 9 November 2000.

[25] *Defence 10 Year Capital Plan*, paper attached to Cabinet paper CAB (98) 854.

[26] STR (99) 87, p. 1.

[27] *Motorisation of the Army*, p. 7 and p. 9.

[28] Max Bradford, Personal interview, 10 November 2003.

[29] *Ministry of Defence: Acquisition of Light Armoured Vehicles and Light Operational Vehicles*, Report of the Controller and Auditor-General, p. 32.

[30] *Motorisation of the NZ Army*, p. 2.

[31] *Motorisation of the NZ Army*, p. 2. The growing popularity of 8x8 armoured vehicles was highlighted in an article in *Jane's International Defence Review* (vol. 37, pp. 40–47, January 2004) headed 'Armies go for eight-wheelers'. It commented, 'once a rarity, eight-wheeled armoured vehicles have proliferated to such an extent that there are now more models of them in service or under development around the world than of any other type of armoured vehicle'. (p. 40.) It added 'a dramatic demonstration of [greater operational mobility] was provided by the dash of a Russian unit equipped with BTR-80, which seized control of Pristina airport ahead of NATO forces during the 1999 operations in Kosovo. As a result the

32 *Motorisation of the NZ Army*, p. 2.

33 Hon. Max Bradford, Minister of Defence, Media Release, 'Armoured Vehicle Project Underway', 2 June 1999.

34 *Ministry of Defence: Acquisition of Light Armoured Vehicles and Light Operational Vehicles*, Report of the Controller and Auditor-General, p. 25.

35 *Ministry of Defence: Acquisition of Light Armoured Vehicles and Light Operational Vehicles*, Report of the Controller and Auditor-General, p. 26.

36 Gordon Campbell, 'Over and out', *New Zealand Listener*, 26 August 2000.

37 *Inquiry into Defence Beyond 2000*, Report of the Foreign Affairs, Defence and Trade Committee, Government Printer, Wellington, 1998, p. 23.

38 *Ministry of Defence: Acquisition of Light Armoured Vehicles and Light Operational Vehicles*, Report of the Controller and Auditor-General, p. 32. (Graham Fortune clarified that, at this point, he had not made a recommendation; rather he was advising what the Government could expect for the money. Personal interview, 14 February 2005)

39 *Ministry of Defence: Acquisition of Light Armoured Vehicles and Light Operational Vehicles*, Report of the Controller and Auditor-General, p. 32. This time, the Secretary of Defence noted that this was a recommendation, and that the Government were getting separate streams of advice from the Army, the NZDF, the MoD and Treasury. (Graham Fortune, Personal interview, 14 February 2005)

40 *Light Armoured Vehicle Project: Cabinet Paper Seeking Approval in Principle to Purchase up to 105 Light Armoured Vehicles*, 10 August 2000, p. 6.

41 *Light Armoured Vehicle Project: Cabinet Paper Seeking Approval in Principle to Purchase up to 105 Light Armoured Vehicles*, p. 13.

42 Major General Piers Reid, Personal interview, 3 September 2003.

43 *Light Armoured Vehicle Project: Cabinet Paper Seeking Approval in Principle to Purchase up to 105 Light Armoured Vehicles*, p. 12.

44 *New Zealand Herald*, 25 August 2000.

45 *Army News*, no. 230, 12 September 2000.

46 *Ministry of Defence: Acquisition of Light Armoured Vehicles and Light Operational Vehicles*, Report of the Controller and Auditor-General, pp. 42–47.

47 'Report on LAV III Only The First Step', Press Release, ACT New Zealand, Wednesday 22 August 2001, available at <http://www.scoop.co.nz/mason/stories/PA0108/S00440.htm>, accessed 29 October 2008.

48 Keith Locke, 'Defence dinosaurs cause of LAV3 confusion', available at <http://www.greens.org.nz/searchdocs/PR4565.html>, accessed 24 June 2008.

49 *Hawkes Bay Today*, 20 August 2001.

50 Suggesting that Bureaucratic Politics be used to its maximum, Lieutenant Colonel I.J.M. Gordon had written a nine page briefing letter to the Deputy Chief of General Staff, Brigadier Rick Ottaway. (Influence in the Centre, Opening the Second Front, 21 March 1997. *Letter attached to the Review of the Performance of the Defence Force in Relation to Expected Standards of Behaviour, and in Particular the Leaking and Inappropriate Use of Information by Defence Force Personnel, Report to the State Services Commission*, by Douglas White QC and Graham Ansell, Wellington, 20 December 2001.) In the letter, Gordon contended that the Army had lost influence and that the Navy and Air Force had been more successful in securing funding. He suggested that 'Army appears to lack influence in the Centre and a different approach is now required to regain this influence. Army must now open a "second front" in its war with the Centre' (p. 1). Later in the letter he added, 'the vulnerability of the air strike capability needs to be exploited to the Army's advantage' (p. 4).

51 C.R. Carruthers QC, *Report of Inquiry into the Propriety of a Letter Allegedly Generated from within the Army*, Wellington, 18 March 2002, p. 4.

52 *New Zealand Herald*, 5 January 2002.

53 *New Zealand Herald*, 5 January 2002.

54 White and Ansell, *Review of the Performance of the Defence Force in Relation to the Expected Standards of Behaviour, and in Particular the Leaking and Inappropriate Use of Information by Defence Force Personnel, Report to the State Services Commission*, p. 35.

[55] White and Ansell, *Review of the Performance of the Defence Force in Relation to the Expected Standards of Behaviour, and in Particular the Leaking and Inappropriate Use of Information by Defence Force Personnel, Report to the State Services Commission*, p. 36.
[56] Robin Johansen, Personal interview 29 April 2005.
[57] *New Zealand Herald*, 20 February 2002.
[58] *New Zealand Herald*, 20 February 2002.
[59] *Army News*, no. 266, 21 May 2002.
[60] *Army News*, no. 268, 18 June 2002.
[61] *Army News*, no. 289, 17 June 2003.
[62] *Army News*, no. 294, 26 August 2003.
[63] *New Zealand Herald*, 30 July 2003.
[64] *New Zealand Herald*, 8 August 2003.
[65] *Sunday*, TV One, 24 August 2003.
[66] *Sunday*, TV One, 24 August 2003.
[67] *Sunday*, TV One, 24 August 2003.
[68] *Sunday*, TV One, 24 August 2003.
[69] Captain Dougal Baker, Personal interview, 9 March 2005.
[70] The May 2005 issue of *Army News* carried a story written by the commander of the US 1st Battalion, 24th Infantry Regiment Stryker Brigade Combat Team, in which he indicated that one *Stryker* (LAV equivalent without the 25mm turret) had been hit over a six-month period by one suicide car bomb, nine IEDs, and eight RPG direct hits as well as small arms fire. Six soldiers from the squad had been wounded, but all were still fighting in Iraq and the vehicle was never out of action for more than 48 hours. (*Army News*, no. 330, 3 May 2005)
[71] The August 2003 issue of *Army News* carried an article which gave some indication of the ability of the 25 mm cannon saying:

1. A LAV company can engage and destroy targets at well over two kilometres and along a frontage of up to four kilometres or more;
2. The co-ordinated fire from the LAVs can kill a large portion of tanks in existence today, excluding newer generation tanks; and
3. On recent UN operations in East Africa, it was assessed that neither of the former warring factions possessed any AFV that could not be destroyed by a LAV.

(*Army News*, no. 293, 12 August 2003)
If in fact Defence had gone for an M113 upgrade to M113A4 specifications, as Major-General Piers Reid indicated was the likely alternative initially, there would have been very little weight difference between the LAV III and the M113A4. The M113A4 is a recycled M113, lengthened by 34 inches, and with an additional road wheel on each side to help spread the extra 4000 kg weight over a regular M113. (Refer Global Security.Org, 'M113A3+/M113A4 Mobile Tactical Vehicle Light (MTVL)' available at <http://www.globalsecurity.org/military/systems/ground/m113a4.htm>, accessed 24 June 2008) The M113A4 Infantry Fighting Vehicle is built on the same lengthened, heavier hull as the MTVL, but carries the additional weight of a turret fitted with a 25mm chain gun. (Global Security.Org, 'M113A3+/M113A4 Infantry Fighting Vehicle Light (IFVL)', available at <http://www.globalsecurity.org/military/systems/ground/m113a4-ifvl.htm>, accessed 24 June 2008)
[72] Major General Piers Reid, Personal interview, 3 September 2003.
[73] The day after the television program, Brigadier Roger Mortlock posed the question: 'Why would you want to put one on a *Hercules* anyway? We would normally send them by sea.' (Personal interview, 25 August 2003) It was true that that had been the case in Bosnia, and mostly the case in East Timor. With the development of a multi-role vessel under Project *Protector*, New Zealand now has its own tactical lift ship, but there may still be times when you do want armoured vehicles to be air-transportable, as was the case with East Timor. The MV *Edamgracht*, a Dutch merchant vessel, left Wellington bound for Darwin on 30 September with 21 M113s on board. (*Army News*, no. 210, 12 October 1999) However four M113s left 10 days earlier for Darwin aboard RNZAF *Hercules* aircraft (*Army News*, no. 209, 28 September 1999), and were transported into theatre by RCAF C-130s. (John Crawford and Glyn Harper, *Operation East Timor: The New Zealand Defence Force in East Timor 1999-2001*, Reed Books, Auckland, 2001, p. 64–IV.) The main body of *Victor* Company arrived in Dili on 29 September 1999 (Crawford and Harper, *Operation East Timor*, p. 70) The Australians had two battalions in Dili, but the

Indonesian Army had eleven, and there were an unknown number of militia. Crawford and Harper wrote: 'Little wonder then that the arrival of an additional rifle company, complete with four armoured personnel carriers, was greatly welcomed by the Australians. ... As Major General Cosgrove acknowledged, getting *Victor* Company to East Timor so quickly was "like gold".' (Crawford and Harper, *Operation East Timor*, p. 71.)

The first successful flight of a NZLAV in a RNZAF *Hercules* took place from Ohakea on 24 April 2004. (*Army News*, no. 308, 11 May 2004)

[74] *Sunday*, TV One, 24 August 2003.
[75] *Sunday*, TV One, 24 August 2003.
[76] *New Zealand Herald*, 3 December 2004.
[77] Robert Ayson, Director of Graduate Studies in Strategy and Defence at The Australian National University, and formerly Advisor to the Foreign Affairs, Defence and Trade Committee in 1998. Personal interview, 21 July 2003.
[78] Jennie Derby, Personal interview, 14 February 2005.
[79] *Army News*, no. 330, 3 May 2005.
[80] *New Zealand Herald*, 16 June 2004. The review was the *Defence Capability and Resourcing Review* (DCARR) published in February 2005, which formed the basis for *The Defence Sustainability Initiative: Building a long-term future for the New Zealand Defence Force*, released on 2 May 2005. The *Initiative* promised an increase of NZ$4.4 billion in baseline funding over 10 years, and a further NZ$209 million of additional capital for the LTDP. Following the publication of the *Initiative*, the Chief of Army noted that the CDF had 'agreed for Army to grow by 741 people'. (*Army News*, no. 330, 3 May 2005)
[81] New Zealand Defence Force, *New Zealand Defence Force Annual Report 2003-2004*, NZDF, Wellington, 2004, p. 10.
[82] *Questions and Answers, The NZ Light Armoured Vehicle (NZ LAV)*, paper provided by the New Zealand Army on 9 March 2005.
[83] *New Zealand Herald*, 3 December 2004.
[84] Colonel Mark Wheeler, Personal interview, 9 March 2005.
[85] Wheeler, Personal interview, 9 March 2005.
[86] *New Zealand Herald*, 30 July 2003.
[87] *Army News*, no. 312, 6 July 2004.
[88] Ministry of Defence, 'Light Armoured Vehicle Acquisition Project'.
[89] Ministry of Defence, 'Light Armoured Vehicle Acquisition Project'.
[90] *Army News*, no. 346, 13 December 2005.

Chapter 8

Politics and Processes: Reflections on the Characteristics of the Decision-Making Process

By the 1980s New Zealand's defence forces were facing the prospect of block obsolescence of many major military platforms. The six case studies described and analysed in this volume provide an insight into the way defence decision-making processes have been undertaken since this time. This chapter now outlines the processes involved in defence decision-making activities, and identifies those factors which have had most impact on the development of the decision-making process in the recent New Zealand context. In so doing, the chapter answers the two questions posed at the beginning of this volume, namely: (1) What are the processes involved in New Zealand defence acquisition policy decision-making activities?; and (2) What factors are brought to bear to influence the decision-making process? In particular this chapter draws out the role personalities have played in individual cases, as well as the role of officials in providing free and frank advice to Ministers. Finally, the chapter concludes with further observations on the nature of the decision-making process, drawing particular attention to the importance of politics and timing in the process.

The Characteristics of the Decision-Making Process

Each of the influencing elements identified in the case studies has had greater or lesser significance at various points throughout the process. The contemporary situation, which includes how New Zealand sees its role in the world and the influence of external actors (particularly the United States and Australia) along with the world situation, is particularly relevant at the beginning of the process when goals and objectives are being set. The influence of external factors then consistently has an impact until a decision on choice has been made. The analysis suggests that timing is most critical both early in the process and ultimately when a decision on choice is being made. Considered judgement nonetheless is also apparent every step of the way.

Politics (including governmental politics and bureaucratic politics) and public opinion both have their place. Public opinion was most influential during the time of the first ANZAC frigate decision, and played its part during subsequent decisions about ANZAC purchases, but has continued to have an influence on other decisions at times. Bureaucratic politics has been demonstrated to often have a part to play from time to time throughout the process. It is at the time of deciding whether to choose a particular platform or upgrade when political influence and judging political side effects most strongly come to the fore.

Notwithstanding those influencing elements which have already been identified, another practice which has impacted on the decision-making process has become apparent during the case studies, namely incrementalism.

Incrementalism

Incrementalism, or the method of successive limited comparison, was identified by Charles Lindblom many years ago as the regular practice of public servants in approaching decision making.[1] Here the decision-maker identifies few alternatives, none of which are radically different from those which have gone before. In the event, it is clear that this approach has been used in every case but one under discussion in this volume. (The exception was HMNZS *Charles Upham*, and this was because the Royal New Zealand Navy (RNZN) had never operated a logistic support ship (LSS) previously.) For example, although David Lange indicated 'we are not in the frigate business', the specification of the ANZAC frigates was clearly based on the development of a modern warship, rather than an ocean patrol vessel. When the lease of the F-16s was under consideration, Derek Quigley raised questions about the role expected of new aircraft observing that:

> It seems likely that the policy requirement for an air combat force to perform the three specified roles ... arose simply because there is already a fighter attack force in being, those are the roles that the air combat force is capable of performing, and the RNZAF is keen to maintain a fighter capability.[2]

With the *Orion* upgrade, Project *Sirius* was intended to update the aircraft's systems so that it could continue with its customary role of surface and sub-surface surveillance. When that project was cancelled, it took careful and sustained work to convince Cabinet of the utility of an upgrade under Project *Guardian* which was similar in so many respects to Project *Sirius*. Further, whilst the 105 LAVs were to allow the introduction of a new concept, that of a motorised infantry, they were nevertheless replacing a previous total of 103 APCs and fire support vehicles.

Whether the incremental method has sufficient dynamism to allow organisations to conceptualise decisions that are sufficiently innovative for a rapidly changing environment has been open to question. It might be argued that incrementalism has been successfully challenged by the intervention of the Department of the Prime Minister and Cabinet with the *Maritime Patrol Review* and the introduction of new capabilities to be made possible by the completion of seven new vessels under Project *Protector*, but in the case of those capabilities under review in this study incrementalism has remained a powerful feature.

The role of individuals

In this section further reflection is offered on the roles individuals have played, and this is most clearly illustrated in the first four of the case studies. In the case of the ANZAC frigates it was Geoffrey Palmer who ultimately had to weigh up the relative importance of external interests, public opinion and politics and political side effects. He had a clear picture of how he and senior colleagues Russell Marshall and Bob Tizard saw New Zealand's role in the world, and he was determined that the frigate purchase would proceed. His recent appointment as Prime Minister was used to advantage to lever influence with Cabinet and Caucus colleagues to ensure the acquisition went ahead in the face of what had previously been strong opposition.

The Prime Minister of the day was to play an important role in developments concerning the purchase and plans for conversion of HMNZS *Charles Upham*. The 1997 *Review of acquisition and proposed conversion* had noted that, as early as 1993, the Prime Minister's Department had indicated that the project to acquire an MSS should not be pursued with any vigour. Warren Cooper, at the time Minister of Defence, made it clear that Jim Bolger was not at all enthusiastic about the proposal to buy and convert the *Charles Upham*. Once the ship had been purchased, Jim Bolger then sent David Jack from the Department of the Prime Minister and Cabinet to warn officials in Defence that conversion work on the *Charles Upham* 'would not happen'. When Winston Peters became Treasurer following the 1996 election, he was just as determined that money would not be spent on the ship, and it never was.

Peters again loomed large in the debate over the second frigate decision. He had made it known at the time of the election that his Party was against purchasing further frigates. As Treasurer and Deputy Prime Minister, he declared his opposition once more when the matter was under discussion in October 1997. The day after this assertion, Bolger announced that no decision on further frigate purchases would be taken before the next election.

Just two months later, in December 1997, Bolger himself was ousted from his position as Prime Minister and replaced by Jenny Shipley, with Paul East being replaced as Minister of Defence by Max Bradford. Bradford was determined to see the decision-making process for the ANZAC frigates rekindled. Knowing that a new-build ANZAC was going to be unacceptable to his colleagues in Government, Bradford worked hard with the Australians to ensure the prospect of a second-hand ANZAC being made available, which the Australians would themselves replace with a new vessel. Opposition to the purchase came from both within and outside the Party. Bill English, who was to become Leader of the Opposition, led a group who were against the purchase of the frigates apparently because they were 'poll driven'.[3] The ACT Party, United Future and a number of independent MPs were also against the purchase, yet their support for the Government was critical to ensure its survival. In the end, the need for political survival overcame any perceived need for a third ANZAC and the decision not to proceed with the purchase was made.

There were essentially three people who were central to the decisions surrounding the lease of the F-16s. The first of these was Secretary of Defence Gerald Hensley, who was the first to be approached (by American Deputy Secretary Kurt Campbell) about a possible lease deal. The second was Max Bradford, who championed the lease and saw the debate through a difficult time in Cabinet to an apparently successful conclusion. Helen Clark was the third actor, voicing determined opposition to the lease as leader of the Labour Party prior to the election, and demonstrating just as much determined opposition as Prime Minister after the election in 1999. Whilst Bradford suggested that Major General Maurice Dodson, Chief of General Staff, played a significant role in arguing that the lease of the F-16s would starve the New Zealand Army of funds, it would seem that Clark and her Cabinet colleagues had already been attracted by the recommendations of the Quigley Report. In March 2000 the decision not to proceed with the lease was made.

The roles played by individuals in the final two case studies are somewhat less clear. Clark was adamantly against a sophisticated upgrading of the *Orions*, and for a time the future of the P-3s was clearly in doubt. In the end however a sophisticated upgrade was agreed to. Whilst Graham Fortune spelt out that the utility of the upgraded aircraft to meet the combined needs for the military and for civilian agencies was a convincing factor, it still remains unclear just what constellation of events occurred during 2002 to bring about such a change in attitude.

Much was made of the attempts by Army to influence the Government over the LAV decision. Charges were made in the White and Ansell report that 'leaks' from the Army had been used to advance the Army's interests over those of other Services. Yet again it was clear that the Labour-led Government was determined from the outset to ensure that the Army did receive significant support for new equipment. Opportunities remain to explore at some future point the personal influence of Helen Clark as Prime Minister and Mark Burton as Minister of Defence on this particular acquisition.

The role of officials

In these final reflections, I want to comment on the role of officials in the decision-making process. The insistence, persistence and foresight of officials in providing robust advice to Ministers have been essential in ensuring that New Zealand retains a credible Defence Force. When first undertaking research for this book, I suspected that I might find a bureaucracy riven with factions, endeavouring to control the decision-making process in classic 'Mandarin' fashion. Whilst there has been clear evidence that at times there *have* been factions and divisions between the three Service branches, and those Service branches and the Ministry of Defence, nevertheless it remains apparent that officials have endeavoured to work with rigour over time to provide the best judgement and advice possible to assist politicians in determining the most appropriate decisions for the cases under review. Three out of six of the case studies which have been analysed, the ANZAC frigates, the upgrade of the P-3 *Orions* and the LAV III, have been or are in the process of successful implementation. In each case, officials have worked to ensure that they provided the Government of the day with the most appropriate advice upon which to base decisions despite that advice not always proving popular.

Perhaps not surprisingly, homeostasis is sought when major decisions are being considered. No single individual or organisation wants to face massive change, and incrementalism has been attractive within Defence as it helps ensure that those changes which do take place are not too dramatic. Whilst this may have limited innovative thinking at times (and prompted the involvement of the Department of the Prime Minister and Cabinet), nevertheless incrementalism has also had demonstrated success. For example, the availability of two ANZAC frigates has provided a capability which the Government has been able to use to advantage to pursue New Zealand's policy goals. Whilst David Lange said that no one could tell him how the frigates would be used, the deployments to the Persian Gulf in support of Operation *Enduring Freedom* clearly underscore the frigates' utility. The other asset which the Government has deployed to the Persian Gulf has been the P-3K *Orion*, yet another platform which drew criticism because of its high cost and lack of previous operational deployment. Whilst the deployment required the Royal New Zealand Air Force to borrow equipment from the Royal New Zealand Navy to enable its aircraft to operate in a coalition environment, nonetheless it was possible, and the aircraft and their crews performed with distinction. Officials are charged with providing the Minister of the day with free and frank advice. In the case of the ANZAC frigates, insistence on them having upgraded facilities initially, and more sophisticated equipment than some politicians might have been comfortable with, has helped ensure that they remain a credible and viable platform in today's operating environment. Had the Naval Combat Force been abandoned and replaced only with patrol boats, successive governments would have had severely limited options available to them to help implement policy. Had there been less persistence on the part of officials to ensure a credible upgrade of the *Orions*, once again policy options would have been severely curtailed. One has only to review the marginal utility of the M113s in Bosnia to see the danger of forces becoming irrelevant if forced to operate with outdated or inadequate equipment.

Conclusion

In reviewing each of the case studies, as indicated above, it is clear that there are a myriad of factors influencing the decision-making process at any given time. How New Zealand views the world; external sources of influence, particularly the pressures brought to bear by the United States and Australia; public opinion; and bureaucratic politics—all these factors have played a significant part. Most recently, international developments regionally and globally have been of great importance. However, in each case study I have been particularly struck by the clear importance of both politics and timing in the decision-making process. The change in the voting system to Mixed Member Proportional (MMP) representation had its own impact. Whilst the politics of a given situation can be subject to manipulation by individuals involved in the process, there is somewhat less possibility for controlling timing. The juxtaposition of events and correlation of forces surrounding a process may be less subject to individual control, but a skilled leader will recognise when the time is right for a particular course of action, as Geoffrey Palmer did during the ANZAC frigate decision process. As Palmer said:

'Timing in politics is everything'

In each of the cases under review in this book, that has clearly been the case.

ENDNOTES

[1] Charles E. Lindblom, 'The Science of Muddling Through', *Public Administration Review*, vol. 19, 1959, pp. 79–88.

[2] *Inquiry into Defence Beyond 2000*, Interim Report of the Foreign Affairs, Defence and Trade Committee, House of Representatives, Wellington, November 1998, p. 96.

[3] Max Bradford, Personal interview, 10 November 2003.

Appendix 1: Sole, Prime and Shared Responsibilities

Secretary of Defence Force High-Level Sole, Prime and Shared Responsibilities

Sole	Prime	Shared
Formulating advice on defence and international defence relations policy and strategies at the governmental level	Developing security scenarios and planning guidelines from defence policy and strategy	Conducting analyses of the strategic environment
Purchase advice on NZDF outputs policy effects	Preparing business cases for acquisition proposals	Analysing and setting military capability requirements
Equipment purchasing	Evaluating Defence organisation outputs and contributions to national security outcomes	Defining a joint future capability vision
MoD resource management		Drafting long-term development and medium-term output plans for the Defence organisation
Evaluation of and accounting for MoD outputs		

Chief of Defence Force High-Level Sole, Prime and Shared Responsibilities

Sole	Prime	Shared
Commanding the NZDF	Formulating international defence relations strategies and outputs at the military level	Conducting analyses of the strategic environment
Commissioning new equipment into service	Analysing military capability gaps, testing options and refining solutions	Analysing and setting military capability requirements
Supporting, supplying and maintaining NZDF capabilities	Advice on military responses to security crises	Defining a joint future capability vision
Conducting military operations		Drafting long-term development and medium-term output plans for the Defence organisation
NZDF Resources management		
Evaluation of and accounting for NZDF outputs		

(*Source*: Cabinet Policy Committee Cabinet Paper: 'Improving Joint Effectiveness in Defence', March 2003, p. 7, available at <http://www.defence.govt.nz/ pdfs/archive-publications/cabpr-ijed.pdf> accessed 12 March 2009)

Appendix 2: ANZAC Ship Baseline Characteristics

Major Characteristics

The ship shall exhibit the following major characteristics:

- a range of 6000 nautical miles at 18 knots with no fuel remaining;
- a minimum endurance for logistic supplies of 30 days;
- a propulsion system consisting of two cruise diesel engines and a gas turbine capable of a maximum speed of at least 27 knots and capable of continuous slow speed operation down to 5 knots in calm seas;
- sea keeping qualities that will enable weapon, crew, sensor, replenishment and helicopter operations in sea state 5;
- the ability to operate and hangar the *Seahawk* helicopter, and to maintain a medium sized (up to 10,000kg) helicopter including a simple helicopter securing and traversing system;
- reduced magnetic, acoustic, radar and infra red signature levels; and
- damage control measures to combat flood, fire, smoke and shock.

Fitted Equipment

The following equipment shall be fitted on board:

- a 76mm gun with magazine capacity for a minimum of 600 rounds of ammunition, with an option for a 127mm gun in lieu of the 76mm;
- an austere point defence missile system (PDMS) with an 8 cell vertical launch system (VLS);
- a target indication/fire control system shared between the gun and the PDMS;
- a two-dimensional air surveillance radar with integral Identification Friend or Foe (IFF);
- an electronic support measures (ESM) system providing a surveillance and anti-ship missile warning capability over the frequency range 0.1 to 18 GHZ and a communication intercept/DF system covering the frequency range of 1 to 500 MHz;
- a chaff dispensing system;
- a hull mounted sonar;
- a torpedo decoy system;
- a modern, modular and proven command and control system compatible with the above equipment, and capable of modification as necessary to accommodate any or all of the equipment in 1.3 and 1.4; and
- a communications transmission, reception and message handling system, for which the MF/HF communications sub-system shall be broadband.

Provision for Fitting of Equipment
1.3 Fit for But Not With (FFBNW)

- a towed array of the 2031 type or a derivative thereof; and
- a ship launched torpedo system compatible with Mk 46 and *Stingray* torpedoes.

Allowance for Fitting of Equipment

Space and Weight (S&W) allowance shall be made for the later fitting of the following equipment:

- a Close in Weapon System (CIWS);
- an electronic countermeasures (ECM) system covering the frequency range 7.5 to 18 GHz;
- an anti-ship missile defence (ASMD) decoy; and
- anti-ship capable missiles in canister configuration.

Appendix 3: User Requirement

Defence's evaluation and subsequent purchase of *Mercandian Queen II* was based on the document 'MILITARY SEALIFT SHIP (MSS): USER REQUIREMENT Version as at 6 Dec 92', which is summarised below.

Primary Purpose

The fundamental requirement is for ship to be able to transport a range of Ready Reaction Force stores, vehicles and equipment, plus up to 150 troops, and autonomously unload alongside an unimproved wharf.

General Requirements

Roll on/roll off type vessel, of not less than 5000 DWT, with a quarter or stern slewing ramp:

- To be maintained in Lloyds class and to statutory requirements including firefighting and lifesaving (65 crew) for a cargo RoRo vessel
- To comply with passenger RoRo ship intact and damaged stability requirements
- Size of vessel not to exceed Calliope Dock capacity
- Speed not less than 15 knots, range of at least 6000 miles, and autonomous endurance of at least 40 days (65 crew)
- Ship's hull, main machinery, and vital systems to have life expectancy of at least 25 years, based on 4850 hrs pa at sea and 2100 hrs pa in harbour
- Ability to manoeuvre unaided and loiter offshore
- Vessel motions such that ship is capable of operating in Sea State 5, with restricted flying operations in Sea State 4
- Main machinery to UMS standard, with adequate emergency electrical generators for specified equipment

Cargo

- At least 1000 lane metres for vehicles plus space for 30 TEU (10 refrigerated) of general stores and 10 TEU of explosives
- Ability to autonomously embark and disembark the above dry cargo, and noting that cargo may be stored on the flight deck
- Vehicle decks to have adequate strength for 20 t axle loads, 5 m deck height, and vehicle lifts of 40 t capacity to all decks
- Specified capacities and transfer facilities for dieso, avcat, water and lubricants
- Petrol to be carried in containers or tankers
- Quarter or stern slewing ramp for a access to unimproved wharf with working load of 60 t

- Storerooms as specified for dry and refrigerated foods and stores and spares for general ship use
- Three 15 t per day reverse osmosis fresh water plants
- Light jackstay rigs for underway replenishment, and ability to replenish liquids to a vessel berthed alongside

Accommodation

- Accommodation for 65 naval crew to normal standards, plus reduced standard accommodation (and military lifesaving gear etc) for 150 additional persons
- Two sewage treatment plants, sized for peak load but either to be able to handle normal crew of 65
- Single galley sized for peak load (215 persons) plus separate messes
- Laundry facilities for 65 persons on self help basis
- Two berth sick bay and supporting first aid equipment
- Offices and workshops as specified
- Air conditioning (tropical standard) for work and accommodation spaces plus heating and ventilation for hangar and vehicle decks
- Specified restrictions on hazardous materials and products

Aviation and Boats

- Facilities to operate and hangar two medium helicopters, with main and emergency landing spots
- Ability to land a *Chinook*, with a suitable Vertrep point
- Facilities to carry and operate one RNZN rigid-hulled inflatable boat (RHIB)
- A crane with 25 t capacity at 7 m for aircraft recovery

Military Items

- Pintles for 4 machine guns and small arms magazine
- Provision for 4 SRBOC (decoy) launchers and supporting ESM facilities
- Normal navigation and command facilities, with some facilities for training and provision for a briefing room
- Naval communications and signalling equipment as specified with associated aerials and office space, plus internal communications and closed-circuit television (CCTV)

Appendix 4: Recommendations of the Final Report of the Air Combat Capability Study — October 1998

Recommendations

This study recommends that the Secretary of Defence:

- **note** that this study has confirmed the White Paper requirement for New Zealand to retain an air combat capability.
- **note** that an air combat capability has high utility in contributing to New Zealand's defence strategy of self-reliance in partnership, including low level security challenges to New Zealand sovereignty, our security relationship with Australia, and supporting regional and global security.
- **note** that the study has confirmed the three operational roles of Close Air Support, Air Interdiction and Maritime Strike, as the best match with New Zealand's security requirements.
- **agree** that the capability of the A-AK *Skyhawk* with the upgrades identified in the White Paper, while broadly satisfactory, has a number of operational and policy limitations which will increase as the *Skyhawk* approaches the end of its life.
- **agree** that other broad capability options such as Surface-to-Surface missiles, Long-range Artillery, Fighter-Bomber Aircraft, and Surface Combatants are not suitable for meeting New Zealand's air combat capability requirements, and should not be considered further.
- **agree** that New Zealand should not consider further an Attack Helicopter or Light Attack Aircraft as a replacement for the A-4K *Skyhawk*. We should also not consider the P-3K *Orion* as the sole maritime strike capability.
- **agree** that the operational performance and policy value of a current production fourth generation multi-role fighter aircraft such as an F-16C/D makes it the only capability option for meeting air combat capability requirements over the longer term.
- **note** that an initial production fourth generation multi-role aircraft, such as an F-16A/B, with suitable upgrades, offers opportunities for New Zealand's replacement of the A-4K.
- **note** that the indicative through-life cost of a current production fourth generation multi-role fighter used for the purposes of this study was that of a new F-16C/D at NZ$1.8B.
- **note** that consideration should be given to acquisition strategies that introduce the capability at a lower cost, such as leasing or procuring suitable second-hand aircraft.

Bibliography

Cabinet Papers

CAB (92) M 16/20

CAB (94) M19/37

CAB (94) M 46/16

CAB (97) M40/8A

CAB (98) 853

CAB (98) 854

CAB (98) M10, 5B (2)

CAB (98) M10/5B (4)

CAB (98) M 45/25

CAB (99) M13/2B

CAB (00) M 19/10

CAB (00) M 28/7

CAB (00) M28/9

CAB Min (01) 10/10

CAB (01) 100

Replacement Frigate Project, Office of the Minister of Defence, Paper attached to CAB (98) 852

Defence 10 Year Capital Plan, Executive Summary, Paper attached to CAB (98) 854

Defence 10 Year Capital Plan, Office of the Minister of Defence, Paper attached to CAB (98) 854

'Rebuilding New Zealand's Defence Capabilities', Paper attached to CAB (98) 855

ERD (97) 18

Defence Assessment Paper, Office of the Minister of Defence, Wellington, 17 September 1997. Paper attached to ERD (97) 18

New Zealand's Orion Maritime Patrol Force, Office of the Minister of Defence, Paper attached to POL (00 1993)

Sustainable Capability Plan for the New Zealand Defence Force, 25 March 2001, Paper attached to POL (01)18

STR (98) 32

STR (98) 34

STR (99) 87

STR (99) 88

STR (99) M12/6

Armoured Vehicles, Paper attached to STR (98)34

Motorisation of the NZ Army, Paper attached to STR (99) 87

Defence Planning: Defence Capital Purchases, Paper (1) attached to STR (99) 88

Defence Planning: Defence Capital Purchases, Paper (2) attached to STR (99) 88

Interviews

Dr Robert Ayson, The Australian National University, (former Adviser to the Foreign Affairs, Defence and Trade Committee for the *Inquiry into Defence Beyond 2000*), 21 July 2003

Captain Dougal Baker, NZ Army, 9 March 2005

Peter Beveridge, former sea captain, 21 September 2001

Rt. Hon. Jim Bolger, former Prime Minister, 15 December 2005

Hon. Max Bradford, former Minister of Defence, 10 November 2003

Hon. Warren Cooper, former Minister of Defence, interviewed by telephone, 1 May 2005

Peter Cozens, Executive Director, Centre for Strategic Studies, Victoria University of Wellington, 27 August 2003

Jennie Darby, Senior Advisor, for Minister of Defence, Mark Burton, 14 February 2005

Dr Kate Dewes, Foundation for Peace Studies, 21 February 2004

Graham Fortune, Secretary of Defence, 14 February 2004

Dick Gentles, former Deputy Secretary of Defence-Policy and Planning, 12 November 2003

Wing Commander Keith Graham, Commanding Officer, 5 Squadron RNZAF, 14 May 1998

Allan Hawke, Australian High Commissioner to New Zealand, 15 October 2003

Associate Professor John Henderson, University of Canterbury, (former Head of the Prime Minister's Department), 21 August 2003

Gerald Hensley, former Secretary of Defence, 9 November 2003

Robin Johansen, former Deputy Secretary of Defence-Acquisitions, 29 April 2005

Commander Ian Logan RNZN, HMNZS *Charles Upham*, 14 July 1996

Rear Admiral Peter McHaffie, former CNS, 11 November 2004

Brigadier Roger Mortlock (retd.), 25 August 2003

Wing Commander Carl Nixon, former Commanding Officer, 5 Squadron RNZAF, 16 October 2004

Rt. Hon. Sir Geoffrey Palmer, former Prime Minister, interviewed by telephone, 2 May 2005

Major General Piers Reid CBE, former Chief of General Staff, 3 September 2003

Colonel Kevin Riordan, NZ Army, 21 August 2003

Brigadier Graeme Talbot (retd.), 27 August 2003

Admiral Sir Somerford Teagle, former CDF, 20 September 2003

Rear Admiral Jack Welch, former CNS, interviewed by telephone 31 May 2005

Colonel Mark Wheeler, NZ Army, 9 March 2005

Andrew Wierzbicki, Director, Policy and Planning, Ministry of Defence, 14 February 2005

Professor Stewart Woodman, University of New South Wales, 18 July 2003

Personal Correspondence

Rear Admiral David Campbell, RAN (retd.), 15 September 2003

Admiral Michael W. Hudson, AC RAN (retd.), 15 May 2004

Simon Murdoch, Secretary of Foreign Affairs, 20 October 2003

Derek Quigley, QSO, 23 April 2007

Further Correspondence

I was fortunate to have access to significant amounts of business correspondence regarding the frigates through the Christchurch office of the Foundation for Peace Studies Aotearoa-New Zealand and, as follows, through archival material at the University of Auckland:

Letter from Ian Bradley to John Matthews, 22 August 1989

Letter from P. Glente to Bob Tizard, 5 April 1989

Letter from P. Glente to Gerald Hensley, 10 March 1989

Letter from David Lange, Prime Minister, to J.B. Matthews, 6 June 1989

Letter from John Matthews to David Lange, Prime Minister, 18 July 1989

Letter from Robert James Tizard, Minister of Defence, to J.B. Matthews, 30 May 1989

Memorandum from Harry Duynhoven to All Cabinet Members, 20 August 1989

Open letter from John Matthews to the Government of New Zealand, 20 August 1989

Official Published Material

Backgrounder to the frigate purchase, RNZN, Wellington, (Undated)

Burton, Hon. Mark, Minister of Defence, *Background: Royal New Zealand Air Force P-3 Orions*, Wellington, 5 October 2004

Carruthers, C.R. QC, *Report of Inquiry into the Propriety of a Letter Allegedly Generated from within the Army*, Wellington, 18 March 2002

Defence Beyond 2000, Wellington, September 1998

Defence Capability and Resourcing Review (DCARR), Wellington, February 2005

Defence Long-Term Development Plan (LTDP), November 2002

Defence Long-Term Development Plan, Update, November 2004

Defence of New Zealand, Review of Defence Policy 1987, Government Printer, Wellington, 1987

Defence Review 1978, Government Printer, Wellington, 1978

Defence Review 1983, Government Printer, Wellington, 1983

Foundations of New Zealand Military Doctrine, NZDF, Wellington, 2004

Government Defence Statement: A Modern, Sustainable Defence Force Matched to New Zealand's Needs, Ministry of Defence, Wellington, 2001

Government Response to the Interim Report of the Foreign Affairs, Defence and Trade Committee on Defence Beyond 2000, Wellington, September 1998

HMNZS Charles Upham, Report on Concerns Raised by the Foreign Affairs, Defence and Trade Committee, Office of the Controller and Auditor-General, Wellington, 24 September 1998

HMNZS Charles Upham: Review of acquisition and proposed conversion, NZDF Report No. 210, 14 April 1997

Hunn, Don K., *Review of Accountabilities and Structural Arrangements between the Ministry of Defence and the New Zealand Defence Force*, Wellington, 30 September 2002

Maritime Patrol Review, Department of the Prime Minister and Cabinet, Wellington, February 2001

Memorandum of Understanding between the Government of Australia and the Government of New Zealand Concerning the Collaboration in Acquisition of New Surface Combatants, 6 March 1987

Ministry of Defence: Acquisition of Light Armoured Vehicles and Light Operational Vehicles, Report of the Controller and Auditor-General, Wellington, August 2001

Ministry of Foreign Affairs and Trade, *New Zealand's Foreign and Security Policy Challenges*, Wellington, May 2000

New Zealand Defence Force, *Force Development Processes, Defence Planning System*, First Edition, Wellington, 23 November 1994

New Zealand Defence Force, *Report of the New Zealand Defence Force for the year ended 30 June 2004*, NZDF, Wellington, 2004

New Zealand Defence Forces Capability Reviews, Phase One-Land Forces and Sealift, Ministry of Defence, Wellington, November 2000

New Zealand Foreign Affairs, Defence and Trade Committee, *Inquiry into Defence Beyond 2000, Interim Report of the Foreign Affairs, Defence and Trade Committee*, Forty-Fifth Parliament, November 1998, Government Printer, Wellington, 1998

New Zealand Foreign Affairs, Defence and Trade Committee, *Inquiry into Defence Beyond 2000, Report of the Foreign Affairs, Defence and Trade Committee*, Forty-Fifth Parliament, August 1999, Government Printer, Wellington, 1999

New Zealand in the Security Council: 1993-94, Information Bulletin No. 52, Ministry of Foreign Affairs and Trade, Wellington, March 1995

Official Information Pertaining to the Military Sealift Project HMNZS Charles Upham, Ministry of Defence, Wellington, November 1998

Project Protector, Invitation to Register, Ministry of Defence, Wellington, 26 July 2002

P-3 Mission Systems Upgrade and Communications and Navigation Systems Upgrade. A paper prepared for Cabinet from Office of Minister of Defence, November 2002

Questions and Answers, The NZ Light Armoured Vehicle (NZLAV), Paper provided by New Zealand Army, Wellington, 9 March 2005

Quigley, Hon. Derek, *Review of the Lease of F-16 Aircraft for the Royal New Zealand Air Force*, Wellington, 6 March 2000

Report of the Audit Office, The Quality and Reliability of Defence Equipment: The Army, Office of the Controller and Auditor-General, Wellington, 31 August 1990

Report of the Controller and Auditor-General, *Ministry of Defence: Acquisition of Light Armoured Vehicles and Light Operational Vehicles*, Wellington, August 2001

Report of the Controller and Auditor-General, *Ministry of Defence and New Zealand Defence Force: Further report on the acquisition and introduction into service of Light Armoured Vehicles*, Wellington, December 2004

Review of Defence Air and Sea Transport, Report of Review Team, Volume 1, 1991

Review of Defence Policy 1961, Government Printer, Wellington, 1961

Review of Defence Policy 1966, Government Printer, Wellington, 1966

Review of Defence Policy 1972, Government Printer, Wellington, 1972

RNZN Replacement Surface Combat Ships, Report of the Defence Review Officials Committee, Wellington, 18 November 1986

Royal New Zealand Navy 2000, Naval Public Relations, Wellington, 2000

Royal New Zealand Navy Annual Review 2000-2001, Wellington, 2001

Royal New Zealand Navy Annual Review 2002-2003, Wellington, 2003

Statement of Intent of the New Zealand Defence Force (NZDF) Te Ope Kaatu o Aotearoa, for the year ending 30 June 2005, HQNZDF, Wellington, 3 May 2004

Strategic Assessment 2000, External Assessments Bureau, Department of the Prime Minister and Cabinet, Wellington, 24 March 2000

Sustainable Defence Plan, Department of the Prime Minister and Cabinet, Wellington, 21 December 2000

The Defence of New Zealand 1991, A Policy Paper, GP Print Ltd, Wellington, 1991

The Defence Question: a discussion paper, Government Printer Ltd, Wellington, 1985

The Defence Sustainability Initiative: Building a long-term future for the New Zealand Defence Force, Ministry of Defence, Wellington, 2 May 2005

The Government's Defence Policy Framework, Ministry of Defence, Wellington, June 2000

The Shape of New Zealand's Defence: A White Paper, Ministry of Defence, Wellington, November 1997

Tizard, The Rt. Hon. Robert James, Minister of Defence, *The Naval Question*, Ministry of Defence, Wellington, December 1988

UMR Insight Limited, *Ministry of Defence Quantitative Summary*, Wellington, April 1995

Whineray, Sir Wilson, *Final Report of the Air Combat Capability Policy Study*, Wellington, October 1998

White, Douglas QC and Graham Ansell, *Review of the Performance of the Defence Force in Relation to the Expected Standards of Behaviour, and in Particular the Leaking and Inappropriate Use of Information by Defence Force Personnel, Report to the State Services Commission*, Wellington, 20 December 2001

Speeches, Parliamentary Debates, Presentations and Press Releases

Hon. Max Bradford, Parliamentary General Debate, 5 November 1998

Hon. Max Bradford, Minister of Defence, Media Release, 'The Government's Decisions on the New Zealand Defence Force Re-Equipment Plan', 1 December 1998

Hon. Max Bradford, Minister of Defence, Media Release, 'Armoured Vehicle Project Underway', 2 June 1999

Hon. Max Bradford, Minister of Defence, Media Release, 'F-16 Lease Deal Approved', 26 July 1999

Hon. Mark Burton, Media Release, 'Minister releases Defence briefing papers', 13 January 2000

Hon. Mark Burton, Minister of Defence, Media Statement, 'Rebuilding the capability of the New Zealand Defence Force', 23 August 2000

Minister of Defence, The Rt. Hon. Robert James Tizard, Address to Tawa Rotary Club, 1 November 1988

Office of the Minister of Defence, Press release, Wellington, 18 September 1987

Office of the Minister of Defence, Press Release, Wellington, 31 July 1989

Office of the Prime Minister, Press Statement, Wellington, 7 September 1989

Rt. Hon. Helen Clark, 'Labour's Approach to Foreign Affairs and Defence Policy', Address to the Dunedin Branch of the New Zealand Institute of Foreign Affairs, 9 August 1996

Rt. Hon. Helen Clark, Leader of the Opposition, Media Statement, 'Labour: Bradford must come out of bunker on frigate issue', 28 October 1998

Rt. Hon. Helen Clark, Leader of the Opposition, Media Statement, 'Labour: Henare party on collision course with National over frigate purchase', 28 October 1998

Rt. Hon. Helen Clark, Leader of the Opposition, Media Statement, 'Labour calls on Government to declare its intention on third frigate', 28 October 1998

Rt. Hon. Helen Clark, Leader of the Opposition, Parliamentary General Debate, 4 November 1998

Rt. Hon. Helen Clark, Leader of the Opposition, Parliamentary General Debate, 5 November 1998

Rt. Hon. Helen Clark, Media Statement, 'Labour: Bradford confirms political motives underpinning defence wish-list', 5 November 1998

Rt. Hon. Helen Clark, Media Statement, 'PM Announces Terms of Reference for F-16 Inquiry', 21 December 1999

Rt. Hon. Helen Clark, *Prime Ministerial Statement on F-16s Decision*, 20 March 2000

Rt. Hon. Helen Clark, Media Statement, 'Decision on F-16s', 20 March 2000

Rt. Hon. Helen Clark, Parliamentary debate, 21 March 2000

Rt. Hon. David Lange, Prime Minister's Press Statement, 15 July 1987

Wayne Mapp, Press Release, 22 August 2000

Hon. John Moore, MP, Minister for Defence, Media Release MIN 231/00, 'New Zealand Defence Acquisitions', 23 August 2000

Rt. Hon. Geoffrey Palmer, Post-Caucus Press Conference, Wellington, 7 September 1989

Newspapers

Dominion (1986–92)

Evening Post (1979–99)

Evening Standard (1999)

Hawkes Bay Today (2001)

Manawatu Standard (2004)

National Business Review (1983–99)

New Zealand Herald (1988–2004)

Sunday Star (1988)

Sunday Star-Times (1997–2004)

The Independent Business Weekly (1999)

The Nelson Mail (1999)

The Press (1989–2000)

Weekend Herald (2001)

Television Program

'Army vehicle raises concern', *Sunday*, TV One, 24 August 2003

Periodicals

Air Force News/RNZAF News (1996–2004)

Army News (1995–2004)

Navy Today (1996–2004)

Bensemann, Paul, 'The War with no Enemy', *NZ Defence Quarterly*, Summer 1994

Bonsignore, Ezio, 'The ANZAC Programme: Frigates for "Down Under"', *Military Technology*, vol. 13, no. 3

Bostock, Ian, 'NZ Air Force clinches bargain fighter deal', *Jane's Defence Weekly*, 9 December 1998

Campbell, Gordon, 'Clearing the Air', *New Zealand Listener*, 11 March 2000

———, 'More Sirius money', *New Zealand Listener*, 20 May 2000

———, 'Pop Gun', *New Zealand Listener*, 9 January 1999

———, 'Sirius Money', *New Zealand Listener*, 29 April 2000

———, 'The Frigates of Oz', *New Zealand Listener*, 21 November 1987

Clark, Rt. Hon. Helen, 'The Government's defence priorities explained', *RSA Review*, October 2000

Clarke, Peter, 'Farewell to the RNZAF's Hotrod', *Pacific Wings*, February 2002

Cooper, Warren, Interview, *Australian Defence Magazine*, vol. 2, no. 7, September 1994

Defense & Foreign Affairs Weekly, Volume XV, Number 32

Dicker, R.J.L., 'Renewing the Australian surface fleet', *International Defence Review*, vol. 20, no. 7, July 1987

Fry, Alexander, Editorial, *New Zealand Listener*, 3 November 1988

Gosling, Martyn, 'Paddy's Axe gets a New Blade', *New Zealand Defence Quarterly*, no. 1, Winter 1993

Grazebrook, A.W., 'ANZAC frigates sale diverging courses', *Jane's Navy International*, vol. 101, no. 9, November 1996

Hackwell, Kevin, 'The Case for Corvettes', *New Zealand International Review*, vol. XIV, no. 2, 1989

James, Colin, 'Rewinging an Old Warrior', *New Zealand Defence Quarterly*, no. 23, Summer 1998

———, 'When Peacekeeping Turns to War', *New Zealand Defence Quarterly*, no. 1, Winter 1993

Lindblom, Charles E., 'The Science of Muddling Through', *Public Administration Review*, vol. 19, 1959

Mapp, Wayne, 'Restructuring New Zealand's Defence Force', *Policy*, Spring 1991

McKinnon, Phillip, 'New Zealand reviews defence structure', *Jane's Defence Weekly*, 26 September 2001

———, 'New Zealand scraps air combat role', *Jane's Defence Weekly*, 16 May 2001

———, 'New Zealand to request tenders for Orion upgrade', *Jane's Navy International*, June 2003

———, 'RNZAF air power threatened by termination of F-16 lease plan', *Jane's Defence Weekly*, 29 March 2000

McLean, Denis, and Desmond Ball, *The ANZAC Ships*, SDSC Working Paper no. 184, Strategic and Defence Studies Centre, The Australian National University, Canberra, June 1989

McLennan, Commander Gerry, 'ANZAC ships vulnerable', *Asia Defence Reporter*, vol. 17, no. 5, November 1990

Naval Forces, vol. XIV, no. IV, 1993

New Zealand International Review, vol. XIV, nos. 1 & 2, 1989

Nichol, G.T., Letter to the *New Zealand Listener*, 6 October 2001

Ogorkiewicz, R.M., 'Armies go for eight-wheelers', *Jane's International Defence Review*, vol. 37, January 2004

Raines, John T., 'ASMC Visits…Defence Acquisition University', *Armed Forces Comptroller*, vol. 48, no. 4

Wright, Matthew, 'Sealift for Soldiers', *New Zealand Defence Quarterly*, no. 8, Autumn 1995

Young, P. Lewis, 'The Progress of the Australian and New Zealand Navies "ANZAC" Frigate Project', *Asia Defence Journal*, vol. 18, no. 11, November 1992

Books

Alliance Party, *The Biggest Lemon Ever To Leave Auckland*, Alliance Party, Wellington, July 1998

———, *The Defence of New Zealand in the Twenty First Century*, Alliance Party, Wellington, 1997

———, *The Scandal of The Charles Upham*, Alliance Party, Wellington, 1997

Allison, Graham T., *Essence of Decision*, Little, Brown and Company, Boston, 1971

Allison, Graham T. and Philip Zelikow, *Essence of Decision*, Second Edition, Longman, NY, 1999

Baugh, William H., *United States Foreign Policy Making*, Harcourt College Publishers, Fort Worth, 2000

Bentley, Geoffrey and Maurice Conley, *Portrait of an Air Force*, Grantham House, Wellington, 1987

Blunden, Margaret, 'British Defence Decision Making', in Margaret Blunden and Owen Greene (eds), *Science and Mythology in the Making of Defence Policy*, Brasseys Defence Publishers, London, 1989

Bolger, Jim, *A View From The Top*, Viking, Auckland, 1998

Bolman, Lee G. and Terrence E. Deal, *Reframing Organisations: Artistry, Choice, and Leadership*, Jossey-Bass, San Francisco, 1997

Boston, Jonathan et al, *Reshaping the State: New Zealand's Bureaucratic Revolution*, Oxford University Press, Auckland, 1991

Breen, Bob, *Giving Peace a Chance, Operation Lagoon, Bougainville 1994: A Case Study of Military Action and Diplomacy*, Strategic and Defence Studies Centre, The Australian National University, Canberra, 2001

Burgess, Michael, *Fighting Vehicles of the New Zealand Army*, Burgess Media Services, Wellington, 1980

Burnett, Alan, *The A-NZ-US Triangle*, Strategic and Defence Studies Centre, The Australian National University, Canberra, 1988

Burnham, Peter, Karin Gilland, Wyn Grant and Zig Layton-Henry, *Research Methods in Politics*, Palgrave Macmillan, Basingstoke, Hampshire, 2004

Burton, Mark, Opening Address in *Defence Policy After East Timor*, NZIIA, Wellington, 17 February 2000

Clark, Helen, 'New Zealand's Non-Nuclear Initiative', in Ranginui Walker and William Sutherland (eds), *The Pacific, Peace, Security & the Nuclear Issue*, The United Nations University, Tokyo, 1988

Clayton, Major G.J., *The New Zealand Army, A History from the 1840's to the 1990's*, New Zealand Army, Wellington, 1990

Cornell, Alexander H., *The Decision-Maker's Handbook*, Prentice-Hall, Englewood Cliffs, NJ, 1980

Crawford, John, *In the Field for Peace: New Zealand's contribution to international peace-support operations: 1950-1995*, New Zealand Defence Force, Wellington, 1996

Crawford, John and Glyn Harper, *Operation East Timor: The New Zealand Defence Force in East Timor 1999-2001*, Reed Books, Auckland, 2001

Davies, David, *The Case Against the New Zealand Frigate*, David Davies, Karori, 1988

Dewes, Kate and Robert Green, *Aotearoa/New Zealand at the World Court*, The Raven Press, Christchurch, 1999

Dibb, Paul, *Review of Australia's Defence Capabilities*, Australian Government Publishing Service, Canberra, 1986

Downs, Anthony, *Inside Bureaucracy*, Little, Brown and Company, Boston, 1966

———, *Inside Bureaucracy*, (Re-issue), Waveland Press, Prospect Heights, IL, 1994

Dull, James, *The Politics of American Foreign Policy*, Prentice-Hall, Englewood Cliffs, NJ, 1985

Edwards, Brian, *helen, Portrait of a Prime Minister*, Exisle Publishing, Auckland, 2001

Farrell, Theo, *Weapons without a Cause: The Politics of Weapons Acquisition in the United States*, Macmillan, Basingstoke, Hamphire, 1997

Farrell, Theo and Terry Terriff (eds), *The Sources of Military Change: Culture, Politics, Technology*, Lynne Rienner, Boulder, CO, 2002

———, 'The Sources of Military Change', in Farrell, Theo and Terry Terriff (eds), *The Sources of Military Change: Culture, Politics, Technology*, Lynne Rienner, Boulder, CO, 2002

George, Alexander L., 'Analysis and Judgement in Policymaking', in Stanley A. Renshon and Deborah Welch Larson (eds), *Good Judgement in Foreign Policy*, Rowman & Littlefield, Lanham, MD, 2003

Gilbert, Martin, *A History of the Twentieth Century, Volume Two: 1933-1951*, Harper Collins, London, 1998

Goff, Phil, 'Preventing Aggression and Upholding International Law', in Rouben Azizian and Malcolm McNamara (eds), *New Zealand Foreign and Defence Policy at the End of the 20th Century: Views of Political Parties*, Centre for Strategic Studies, Wellington, October 1999

Gore, Chris, Kate Murray and Bill Richardson, *Strategic Decision-Making*, Cassell, London, 1992

Hager, Nicky, *The case against new frigates*, Peace Movement Aotearoa, Wellington, August 1988

Halperin, Morton H., *Bureaucratic Politics and Foreign Policy*, Brookings Institution, Washington DC, 1974

Hickson, David J. et al, *Top Decisions*, Jossey-Bass, San Francisco, 1986

Hoadley, Steve, *The New Zealand Foreign Affairs Handbook*, Second Edition, Oxford University Press, Auckland, 1992

Jennings, David and Stuart Wattam, *Decision Making—An Integrated Approach*, Pitman Publishing, London, 1994

'Just Defence', *Submission to the Defence Committee of Enquiry*, Just Defence, Wellington, February 1986

Kennaway, Richard and John Henderson, *Beyond New Zealand II*, Foreign Policy into the 1990s, Longman Paul, Auckland, 1991

Labour's Foreign Affairs and Defence Policy: An Independent Foreign Policy, New Zealand Labour Party, Wellington, August 1996

Lange, David, *my life*, Viking, Auckland, 2005

———, *Nuclear Free–The New Zealand Way*, Penguin Books, Auckland, 1990

Levine, Stephen, Paul Spoonley & Peter Aimer, *Waging Peace Towards 2000*, Foundation for Peace Studies, Aotearoa-New Zealand, Auckland, 1995

Luand, E., *A History of the United Nations*, St Martins Press, NY, 1982

Manheim, Jarol B. and Richard C. Rich, *Empirical Political Analysis—Research Methods in Political Science*, Longman, White Plains, NY, 1995

Mapp, Wayne, 'Dealing with the Consequence of Victory in the Cold War', in Rouben Azizian and Malcolm McNamara (eds) *New Zealand Foreign and Defence Policy at the End of the 20th Century: Views of Political Parties*, Centre for Strategic Studies, Wellington, 1999

McDougall, R.J., *New Zealand Naval Vessels*, GP Books, Wellington, 1989

McGibbon, Ian, 'Forward Defence: The Southeast Asian Commitment', in Malcolm McKinnon (ed.), *New Zealand in World Affairs, Volume II 1957-1972*, NZIIA, Wellington, 1991

———, 'The Defence of New Zealand 1945 - 1957', in *New Zealand in World Affairs, Volume 1, 1945-1957*, NZIIA, Wellington, 1991

McIntosh, Sir Alister, 'The origins of the Department of External Affairs and the formulation of an independent foreign policy' in *New Zealand in World Affairs: Volume I, 1945-1957*, NZIIA, Wellington, 1991

McIntyre, W.D., 'Peter Fraser's Commonwealth: New Zealand and the Origins of the New Commonwealth in the 1940s', in *New Zealand in World Affairs, Volume 1, 1945-1957*, NZIIA, Wellington, 1991

———, *New Zealand Prepares for War*, University of Canterbury Press, Christchurch, 1998

McKinnon, Malcolm A., 'From ANZUS to SEATO', in *New Zealand in World Affairs, Volume 1, 1945-1957*, NZIIA, Wellington, 1991

———, *Independence and Foreign Policy, New Zealand in the World since 1935*, Auckland University Press, Auckland, 1993

——— (ed.), *New Zealand in World Affairs Volume II 1957-1972*, NZIIA, Wellington, 1991

McNabb, David E., *Research Methods for Political Science—Quantitative and Qualitative Methods*, M.E. Sharpe, Armonk, NY, 2004

Miles, Robert, *Scuttling the Army, The Charles Upham Scandal*, Black Diamond Press, Timaru, 1998

Monroe, Alan D., *Essentials of Political Research*, Westview Press, Boulder, CO, 2000

Pacific Institute of Resource Management, *The Anzac Frigate Debate*, Pacific Institute of Resource Management, Wellington, February 1989

Peace and Justice Forum, An Alternative Defence Policy, Wellington Labour Regional Council, Wellington, March 1985

Quigley, Hon. D.F., *New Zealand Defence, Resource Management Review 1988*, Strategos Consulting Limited, Wellington, 1988

Rabel, Roberto, 'Vietnam and Collapse of the Foreign Policy Consensus', in Malcolm McKinnon (ed.), *New Zealand in World Affairs Volume II 1957-1972*, NZIIA, Wellington, 1991

Reid, Piers, 'The Lessons of East Timor', in *Defence Policy after East Timor*, NZIIA, Wellington, 17 February 2000

Renshon, Stanley A. and Deborah Welch Larson (eds), *Good Judgement in Foreign Policy*, Rowman & Littlefield, Lanham, MD, 2003

Rolfe, James, *The Armed Forces of New Zealand*, Allen and Unwin, St. Leonards, NSW, 1999.

Rolfe, James, *Defending New Zealand; A Study of Structures, Processes and Relationships*, Institute of Policy Studies, Wellington, 1993

Rosenau, James, 'Pre-Theories and Theories of Foreign Policy', in R. Barry Farrell, ed., *Approaches to Comparative and International Politics*, Northwestern University Press, Evanston, IL, 1966

Shipley, Jenny, 'Opening Remarks', in Margaret Clark (ed.), *Holyoake's Lieutenants*, Dunmore Press, Palmerston North, 2003

Singh, Ravinder Pal (ed.), *Arms Procurement Decision Making, Volume I: China, India, Japan, South Korea and Thailand*, Oxford University Press, Oxford, 1998

———, *Arms Procurement Decision Making, Volume II: Chile, Greece, Malaysia, Poland, South Africa and Taiwan*, Oxford University Press, Oxford, 2000

Sorensen, Theodore C., *Decision-Making in the White House: The Olive Branch or the Arrows*, Columbia University Press, NY, 1963

Terriff, Terry and Theo Farrell, 'Military Change in the New Millennium', in Theo Farrell and Terry Terriff (eds), *The Sources of Military Change: Culture, Politics, Technology*, Lynne Rienner, Boulder, CO, 2002

Theodoulou, Stella Z. and Matthew A. Cahn, *Public Policy—The Essential Readings*, Prentice Hall, Englewood Cliffs, 1995

Vignaux, G. Anthony, *The Navy Critical Mass Argument*, Victoria University of Wellington, Wellington, July 1997

Williams, Steve W., *Making Better Business Decisions*, Sage, Thousand Oaks, 2002

Wood, F.L.W., 'New Zealand Foreign Policy 1945-1951', in *New Zealand in World Affairs, Volume 1 1945-1957*, NZIIA, Wellington, 1991

Woolner, Derek, *From Light Patrol Frigate to Meko 200 ANZ*, The Parliament of the Commonwealth of Australia, Canberra, August 1989

Wright, Matthew, *Blue Water Kiwis*, Reed Books, Auckland, 2003

———, *Kiwi Air Power*, Reed Books, Auckland, 1998

Electronic Sources

'ANZAC Frigate (FFH)', available at
<http://www.tss.qld.edu.au/services/navy/oto.htm>, accessed 17 April 2004

Boeing Maritime Patrol Mission System, available at
<http://www.boeing.com/defence-space/infoelect.mapatrol/index.html>, accessed 27 November 2004

Max Bradford, 'Deals tough after Orion withdrawal', *The National Party News*, available at
<http://www.maxbradford.co.nz/national_news/DEFENCE/2002-01-28_defence_brad>, accessed 27 November 2004

Hon. Mark Burton, Minister of Defence, *Questions and Answers on the LAVs*, available at
<http://www.executive.govt.nz/ministers/burton/defence-rebuilding/lav.htm> accessed 22 January 2002

Hon. Mark Burton, Minister of Defence, Media Statement, 'Contract for army vehicles signed', available at
<http://www.beehive.govt.nz/PrintDocument.cfm?DocumentID=9534>, accessed 14 December 2008

Hon. Mark Burton, Minister of Defence, Media Release, 'Surplus aircraft sold', available at <http://www.beehive.govt.nz/Print/PrintDocument.aspx?DocumentID=4155>, accessed 16 September 2005

Centurions in New Zealand, available at <http:kiwis in armour.hobbyvista.com/cent.htm>, accessed 27 October 2008

CNN.com, 'Bush says it is time for action', available at <http;//archives.cnn.com/2001/US/11/06/ret.bush.coalition/index.html>, accessed 28 October 2008

General Dynamics Land Systems, LAVIII, available at <http://www.gdls.com.programs.lav3_apl.html>, accessed 30 December 2004

Global Security.Org, *M113A3+/M113A4 Mobile Tactical Vehicle Light (MTVL)*, available at <http://www.globalsecurity.org/military/systems/ground/m113a4.htm>, accessed 24 June 2008

Global Security.Org, *M113A3+/M113A4 Infantry Fighting Vehicle Light (IFVL)*, available at <http://www.globalsecurity.org/military/systems/ground/m113a4-ifvl.htm>, accessed 24 June 2008

Global Security.Org, *M113 specifications*, available at <http://www.globalsecurity.org/military/systems/ground/m113-specs.htm>, accessed 30 December 2004

'HMAS Arunta', available at <http://www.navy.gov.au/HMAS_Arunta>, accessed 28 October 2008

Nicky Hager, 'Project Sirius', 23 July 2000, available at <http://www.converge.org.nz/pma/siriuspj.htm>, accessed 29 October 2008

'Labour—a sensible defence policy', available at <http://www.scoop.co.nz/mason/stories/PA9911/SOO167.htm>, accessed 20 September 2003

'Labour Support for Peacekeeping', available at <http://www.Labour.org.nz/infocentre1/Policies/foreignaffairspol.html>, accessed 14 November 1999

'Labour Would Ditch F-16s', available at <http://www.xtra.co.nz/homepa...tion+99%3EElection+News%3A56532,00.html>, accessed 8 November 1999

Keith Locke, 'Defence dinosaurs cause of LAV3 confusion', available at <http://www.greens.org.nz/searchdocs/PR4565.html>, accessed 24 June 2008

Hon. John Moore, MP, Minister for Defence, Media Release, available at <http://www.defence.gov.au/2000/ACFDA8.doc>, accessed 2 October 2004

Masters in Defence Acquisition Management, available at <http://www.rmcs.cranfield.ac.ik/ddmsa/postgraduateCourses/445825>, accessed 13 January 2006

Ministry of Defence, 'Light Armoured Vehicle Acquisition Project', available at <http://www.defence.govt.nz/Industry/light-aem-vehicle.shtml>, accessed 16 December 2004

Ministry of Defence, Organisational Structure of the Ministry, available at <http://www.defence.govt.nz/reports-publications/election-brief-2005/roles-org-mod.html>, accessed 12 March 2009

Ministry of Defence, 'The Ministry; about the Ministry and its roles', available at <http://www.defence.govt.nz/ministry.shtml>, accessed 29 March 2005

Ministry of Defence website, available at <http://www.defence.govt.nz/about-us/divisions/acquisition.html>, accessed 4 November 2008

National Geographic News, 15 May 2003, available at <http://news.nationalgeographic.com/news/2003/05/0515_030515_fishdecline.html>, accessed 12 December 2008

'New Zealand Divisional Cavalry Regiment', in *History of the 3rd New Zealand Tank Squadron*, available at <http://kiwis in armour.hobbyvista.com/divcav.htm>, accessed 26 December 2004

'New Zealand government introduces drastic austerity measures', available at <http://www.wsws.org/news/1998/nov1998/nz-n03.shtml>, accessed 17 April 2004

'Pakistani F-16 Jets Going to US Navy, USAF', available at <http://www.archive.newsmax.com/activities/articles/2002/6/12/154700.shtml>, accessed 27 October 2008

'Program Acquisition Costs by Weapon System', available at <http://www.dod.mil/comptroller/defbudget/fy2006/fy2006_weabook.pdf>, accessed 13 January 2006

Queen Alexandra's Squadron 1980-90s, available at <http://kiwis in armour.hobbyvista.com/qasdn.htm>, accessed 26 December 2004

'Report on LAV III Only The First Step', Press Release, ACT New Zealand, Wednesday 22 August 2001, available at <http://www.scoop.co.nz/mason/stories/PA0108/S00440.htm>, accessed 29 October 2008

'Sealift Ship Charles Upham', available at <http://www.defence.govt.nz/scripts/press/index.asp?page=34>, accessed 23 January 2002

Statute of Westminster, available at <http://www.answers.co./topic/statute-of-westminster-1931>, accessed 5 March 2005

'United States Department of Defense', available at <http://www.absoluteastronomy.com/encyclopedia/u/un/united_states_department_of_defense>, accessed 12 January 2006

Theses and Dissertations

Bruni, John-Silvano Christopher, 'Reasons for choice: Understanding the direction of Australian weapons procurement since 1963', University of New South Wales, Ph.D. Dissertation, ProQuest document ID: 730589781, 2000

Elwin, Richard James, *Project Falcon, The Procurement of the Aermacchi Jet Trainers*, unpublished, MA dissertation, University of Auckland, 1996

Jones, Richard Rhys, 'The Influences on New Zealand Defence Policy from 1984 till 2000', Unpublished thesis, La Trobe University, September 2001

Keys, Stephen, 'The ANZAC Ship Project in New Zealand', unpublished MA thesis, University of Auckland, 1990

McCue, Joseph, 'The Impact of Decision-Making Theory on the Department of Defense's Acquisition Process for the Procurement of Major Weapons Systems', The University of Alabama, Ph.D. Dissertation, Ann Arbor, MI: ProQuest, UMI Number 3092369, 2003

Unpublished Material

Forrest, Squadron Leader A.J., 'The ANZAC Frigate Decision—The Rationale of David Lange', Staff Course, RNZAF, October 1993

Hensley, Gerald, 'New Zealand's Strategic Environment', RNZAF Air Power Seminar, Wellington, 3 May 1999

Hingsdon, Major G., 'How will the F-16 A/B lease impact on future NZDF operations?', Staff Course, Whenuapai, 2000

Jennings, Peter, 'Australia, New Zealand and the ANZAC frigate project', seminar paper presented to the New Zealand Political Studies Association, Dunedin, May 1990

Meyer, Squadron Leader S., 'Four Frigates...A Navy Or Two Frigates...A Littoral Blue', Staff Course, RNZAF, 1996

Policy Committee on Foreign Affairs and Security of the New Zealand Labour Party, *Opportunity for New Vision*, Response to Conditional Proposal on ANZAC frigates submitted to Policy Committee by Prime Minister Geoffrey Palmer, Defence Minister Bob Tizard and Foreign Minister Russell Marshall. Unpublished typescript, 5 September 1989, University of Auckland archival material

'Policy Linkages', Power Point briefing to the Minister of Defence, April 2000

'Project Sirius: Briefing to the Minister of Defence', Power Point Slides, July 2000

Quigley, Derek, speech to Massey University Forum, Palmerston North, 9 September 1999

Index

Adamson, Carey 92, 96, 113
Afghanistan 119
Africa 8, 128, 148n71
aircraft:
  Beechcraft *King Air* aircraft 117
  Boeing B-727 aircraft 81
  de Havilland: *Vampire* 5; *Venom* 5
  English Electric *Canberra* bombers 5–7, 89
  General Dynamics F-111 89
  helicopters 30, 40–41, 53, 56, 61–63, 93, 159, 162–63:
    Kaman SH-2G *Super Seasprite* helicopter 46–47
    Sikorsky SH-60 *Seahawk* helicopter 159
  Lockheed/Lockheed Martin:
  C-130 *Hercules* (including the C-130J) 81, 94, 100, 117, 119, 135, 142, 148n73
  F-16 (including the F-16 A/B, F-16A-15OCU, F-16B-15OCU, F-16C and F-16 C/D) 13–14, 21n73, 72, 84, 88n31, 89–105, 106n18, 106n20, 109, 114, 132–33, 136, 152, 154, 163
  P-3 *Orion* (including the P-3B, P-3K and P-5B) 14, 18, 61, 72, 81, 93, 100, 103, 109–24, 152, 154–55, 163: *Orion* Upgrade: *see* projects: Project *Sirius*
  McDonnell Douglas (merged with Boeing in 1997):
    A-4, A-4K and TA-4K *Skyhawk* 14, 81, 89–91, 93–96, 101, 103–104, 106n23, 108n80, 163: A-4G and TA-4G trainers 90
    F-4E *Phantom* 89
    Harrier 91
    Mid-Life Upgrade (MLU) 95–96
  Northrop F-5E *Tiger* 89
  Short Brothers *Short Sunderland* Mark III flying boats 110
  (*see also* capabilities: air capability (RNZAF))

alliances 4–5, 116, 118; *see also* treaties: Pacific Security (ANZUS) Treaty
Anderson, Neil D. 23
Anglo-Malaysian Defence Agreement 8
Anglo-New Zealand-Australia-Malaya (ANZAM) 5–6
Ansell, Graham 140–41, 154
Ansley, Greg 83, 99
Antarctica 53
  Ross Dependency 47
  Ross Sea 119
Armstrong, John 98
ASEAN Regional Forum 92
Asia-Pacific Economic Cooperation (APEC) 11, 13
Audit Office 58, 65
  Audit Office Report/Review: Audit Review Team 70; Auditor-General's Report 133, 136, 138–41; Office of the Controller and Auditor-General (1998 Report from) 70
  (*see also* White Papers and Reviews: 1998 *HMNZS Charles Upham: Report on Concerns Raised by the Foreign Affairs, Defence and Trade Committee*)
Australia 4, 6–8, 10, 26–29, 31, 35, 37–39, 42, 46, 48, 54, 57–59, 84, 96, 112, 132, 143, 145, 151
  Canberra, ACT 83, 99
  Australian National University 37, 99, 108n87, 143
  Canberra conference (January 1944) 2
  Canberra Pact 2–3
  University of New South Wales (@ ADFA) 104
  Darwin, NT 57, 67, 148n73
  Newcastle, NSW 31
  Melbourne, Vic 46, 79
  Sydney, NSW 55, 112
  Launceston, Tas: Merchant Navy Training School 69
  Williamstown, Vic 31
Australia–New Zealand Agreement 2–3
Australia–New Zealand Secretariat 2
Australian Defence Force (ADF) 55, 57, 132

Australian Department of Defence 30–31, 84, 99
   and proposals to Joint Project Management Team 30–31
Australian Government 2–3, 5, 9–11, 27–30, 33–34, 36, 38–40, 42, 44–45, 48, 56–58, 60, 79, 83–85, 98–99, 115, 153, 156
   External Relations and Defence Committee 70
   Public Service 16
Australian military 2, 5, 13, 26, 39, 42, 44, 55, 91, 103, 122, 130, 132, 134, 148n73
   Australian Army: 1st Australian Task Force 7; 2nd Cavalry Regiment (Reconnaissance), Royal Australian Armoured Corps 132
   Royal Australian Air Force (RAAF) 91, 110–11
   Royal Australian Navy (RAN) 29–30, 38, 45–46, 57–59, 73n14, 83, 88n24, 90
Ayson, Robert 108n87, 143

Bagnall, Sylvia 28
Baker, Dougal 142
Ball, Desmond 37, 99
Batten, Reverend Ann 85–86
Beaglehole, John C. 3
Beazley, Kim 27–28, 37–39
blue-water capability 26–29, 31, 38, 71, 78, 87
Bolger, Jim 11, 68, 71, 79, 153
Bosnia 12–13, 15, 71, 86, 128–32, 134, 138, 140, 142, 148n73, 155
Bougainville 60, 65, 71
Bradford, Max 83–84, 86, 88n31, 93–94, 97, 99, 108n80, 133–34, 140–42, 153–54
Bradley, Ian 40–41
Braybrooke, Geoff 66, 98
Britain: *see* United Kingdom
Brunton, Ian 95–96
Burton, Mark 16, 104, 113, 121, 139–40, 143, 154

Bush, George H.W. 11
Bush, George W. 118

Campbell, David 37, 45, 58–59
Campbell, Gordon 94–95, 108n80, 114
Campbell, Kurt 92, 154
Campbell, Lloyd 104
Canada 30, 50n30, 134, 142
   Newfoundland 4
   Royal Canadian Air Force 104, 148n73
   (*see also* vehicles: Light Armoured Vehicle: LAVIII)
capabilities 12, 14, 17–18, 24, 30, 39–40, 53–54, 59, 66, 83, 94, 99–100, 105, 106n18, 109, 131, 134, 149n80, 157–58
   air capability (RNZAF) 90–97, 99, 101–105, 108n80, 108n98, 109–118, 120–23, 147n50, 152, 163
   combat capability (NZ Army) 24, 81, 115, 127, 129–31, 134, 137–39, 143–45
   maritime capability (RNZN) 26–27, 31–36, 38–40, 46–47, 53–55, 57–58, 61–62, 64, 66–67, 70, 72, 109, 113–17, 120, 122–23, 152, 155, 159
Capability Management Framework (2004) 18; *see also* New Zealand Ministry of Defence (MoD): defence planning and plans (for its precursor Defence Planning System)
Carruthers, C.R.: Carruthers Report 140
China 3, 9
Churchill, Winston 3
Clark, Helen 42, 78, 85–86, 96–98, 101–103, 105, 114–15, 129, 138, 154
Clark, Margaret: *Holyoake's Lieutenants* 85
Clinton, William (Bill) Jefferson 11, 13, 106n18
Closer Defence Relations (CDR) 57–59, 72, 132
Closer Economic Relations (CER): *see* economics: Closer Economic Relations

coalitions 3, 109, 115, 118, 120–21, 155
   Coalition Task Forces 7, 48, 115, 130
Cold War 12, 131
Collaborative Project Management
   Arrangements 31
Collier, Gary 63–64
communications 27, 69, 81, 100, 113,
   119–20, 122, 159, 162
   Communications and Navigations
      System Upgrade 119
   L-3 IS Communications Integrated
      Systems 122–23
   Link 11 communications system 120
   radar 45, 47, 95, 110, 122–23, 159
   radio 95, 115, 120–21
   satellite telephone 121
communism 5–6
companies 44, 68, 135
   A&P Appledore (Aberdeen) Ltd 51n67
   Alvis Limited 128
   Australian Marine Engineering Corp
      (Amecon) 31–32, 42–43
   Australian Warship Systems 31
   Blohm and Voss 31–32
   BMT Defence Services Limited 56, 66
   BMT Defence Services report (1993)
      56, 63
   Boeing Company 110, 121
   British Aerosystems 112
   CAE Electronics Ltd, Canada 122
   Computing Devices Canada Ltd 122
   Daimler 128
   DaimlerChrysler Aerospace 121
   FLIR Systems Inc 122
   General Motors Defense 132
   General Motors of Canada Ltd 138
   Celsius Hawker Pacific 112
    Hawker Pacific 112
   Henschel Wehrtechnik 135
   HVR Consulting Services (HVR) 134–35
   Kaman Aerospace 46–47
   L-3 IS Communications Integrated
      Systems (company) 122–23
   Lear Siegler 91
   Lockheed Martin 106n20, 110–12, 121
   Raytheon 113–14, 121–23

   Royal Schelde 31
   Rugg and Co. 56
   Safe Air Ltd 123
   Strategos Consulting 16 (*see also*
      White Papers and Reviews: 1988
      *New Zealand Defence, Resource
      Management Review*)
   Svendborg Shipyard 41
   Technic Group 40
   Tenix Corporation 85–86
   Whangarei Engineering and
      Construction Co 33
   Whangarei Engineering Company 40
   Yarrows Shipbuilding 31
Cooper, Warren 57, 61, 68, 77, 153
Cosgrove, Peter 149n73
Cozens, Peter 69, 71
Culley, Marcus 130
Curtin, John 2
Cyprus 5

Davies, David 32
decision-making processes 1, 14–15, 17–19, 29, 41–43, 48–49, 72, 79–80, 87, 104, 123, 138, 145, 151–56
Delamere, Tuariki 79
Denmark:
   Danish currency 61
   Danish vessels 40–41, 80
   Royal Danish Navy 41
Derby, Jennie 143
Dodson, Maurice 154
Doidge, Frederick Widdowson (F.W.) 4–5
Domett, Doug 38
Duynhoven, Harry 40–42, 80
Dyson, Ruth 35, 43

East, Paul 79, 81, 83–84, 153
East Timor 13, 15, 47, 60, 66–67, 71, 98, 128, 138–39, 142, 145, 148n73
economics 16–17, 24–25, 27–28, 33, 41, 54–56, 60, 64–65, 79, 85, 94, 106n18, 122, 129
   affordability 18, 23, 39, 58, 73n14, 84, 97, 101–102, 118, 128
   budgets 24, 65, 78–79, 87, 94, 98, 112, 133, 136

187

Closer Economic Relations (CER) 85
costs 23–25, 27–31, 33–35, 39–40, 43–44, 46–47, 49, 51n67, 53, 55–59, 61–62, 64–65, 67, 73n14, 80, 84, 89–91, 93, 96–97, 99, 101, 108n80, 109–112, 114, 116–17, 119–20, 122–23, 128–29, 131, 133, 136–38, 143, 145, 155, 163
Exclusive Economic Zone (EEZ) 32, 40, 114, 116, 119, 123
expenditure 15, 33–34, 61, 69–70, 78–79, 94–95, 102, 105, 114–15, 127
funding 14, 18, 40, 60, 65, 69–71, 81, 86, 94, 99–103, 105, 127–28, 133, 147n50, 149n80, 154
Goods and Services Tax (GST) 96, 133, 138
Gross Domestic Product (GDP) 79
investment 18, 97, 101, 103, 115, 131, 145
savings 93–94, 101, 103, 117, 119
trade-offs 28, 44, 59, 61, 69, 86, 94, 104–105, 115, 123, 133, 136, 142–43
elections 8, 10–12, 25, 44, 60, 66, 69, 72, 77–79, 82, 86–87, 96–98, 106n18, 114, 138, 145, 153–54
Mixed Member Proportional voting system 69, 77–79, 87, 156
English, Bill 153
equipment 1, 4, 12–13, 15, 17, 26, 32–33, 35, 40, 42, 46–47, 53–55, 60, 62–64, 66–67, 69–70, 72, 82, 86, 90, 93, 95, 98, 100, 102, 105, 110, 112–14, 118, 121–22, 127–34, 136–38, 140, 143, 145, 146n31, 154–55, 157–62
electro-optics system 122–23
engines 46, 60–61, 63, 93, 111–12, 129, 159
infra-red detection system 110, 122–23
Ground Moving Target Indicator 123
Integrated Data Handling System 123
sensors 15, 24, 30, 81, 109, 111–13, 117–18, 120, 159

European Economic Community 8
Evans, Gareth 39
Evatt, Herbert Vere (H.V.) 2

facilities 9, 53–54, 62–63, 67, 155, 161–62
Ferguson, Bruce 143
Fiji 2, 63, 110
fisheries protection 25, 32, 47, 50n30
Five Power Defence Arrangements (FPDA) 8, 20n35, 96, 117
force structure 24–25, 54, 80–81, 136
'balanced forces', concept of 87, 104, 108n97, 145
Force Development Proposal (1999) 137
forces 1–2, 4–8, 12–14, 23–28, 32, 35, 39, 42, 53, 61, 64, 71, 79, 81–83, 85, 87, 90–91, 94–97, 99–105, 106n18, 108n80, 108n87, 108n97, 109–10, 113–17, 120–23, 127–34, 136–37, 139, 141, 144–45, 146n31, 147n50, 151–52, 154–56, 161
air combat force 81, 91, 94–98, 101–104, 108n80, 108n87, 152
Commonwealth forces 5, 7
naval combat force 24, 81–83, 87, 155
Forrest, A.J. 48
Fortune, Graham 138, 147n38, 154
Foundation for Peace Studies Aotearoa-New Zealand 77–78
France 6, 30, 67
French defeat in Indochina 6
French nuclear testing 9
Fraser, Peter 2, 4
'Frigate Debate', the 30–32, 46–48
Fry, Alexander 34

Garrett III, Lawrence 45
Gentles, Dick 59, 68, 103
Germany 1, 30, 135
Glente, Peter 41
Goff, Phil 97, 115
Gordon, I.J.M 140, 147n50
Gore, Ian 91
Graham, Douglas 96
Greece 128
Green Party 115, 139

Hackwell, Kevin 36, 51n67
Hamilton, Don 116
Hamilton, John 112
Hardie, Kelvin 40
Hawke, Bob 48
Henderson, John 27, 39, 43
Hensley, Gerald 41, 59, 92, 96, 130, 132, 154
Heylen poll 33
Hide, Rodney 139–40
Hoadley, Stephen 98
Hoare, Samuel 1
Holland: *see* Netherlands
Holland, Sidney 5
Howard, John 79, 103
Hudson, Michael 26, 38
Hunn, Don K.: Hunn Report (2002) 16, 140

Imperial Conference (1937) 1
Indonesia 7, 13, 106n18
    Indonesian Army 149n73
    Jakarta 106n18
International Court of Justice 9
Invitation to Register (ITR) 113
Iraq 60, 148n70
Italy 128

Jack, David 153
Jamieson, Ewan 108n80
Japan 2, 5
Johansen, Robin 68, 71, 140–41
Johnson, Lyndon Baines 7
Jordan, William (Bill) 3
Just Defence 25, 28, 36, 40; *see also* New Zealand Government: Defence Committee of Inquiry (1985)

Kidd, Doug 25
Kirk, Norman 8–9
Knox, David 32
Korean Peninsula 4; *see also* South Korea
Kosovo 146n31

Lambie, Alastair 51n67
Lange, David 10, 26–27, 36, 39, 41–43, 47–48, 152, 155

Laugesen, Ruth 79
League of Nations 3
legislation 11, 26
    Fisheries Act (1976) 32
    Official Information Act (1982) 141–42
    Statute of Westminster (1931) 3–4
Lindblom, Charles 153
Locke, Keith 115, 139
Logan, Ian A. 63
Lovatt, John 120

maintenance 7, 30, 46, 81, 87, 96, 117, 127–29, 137
Malayan Emergency 5–6
Malaysia 96
    and 'Confrontation' with Indonesia 6–7
    Kuala Lumpur 92
    Royal Malaysian Air Force 91
Manning, Leonard 139
Mapp, Wayne 97, 102–103, 108n80, 114–15
    article titled 'Restructuring New Zealand's Defence Force' by 102–103
Mark, Ron 140, 142–43
Marshall, Russell 43, 153
Mateparae, Jerry 142–43
Matthews, John 40–41
McIntosh, Alister 2–4
McKee, Phil 145
McLean, Denis 26, 37
media 27, 31, 33–34, 39–40, 47, 114, 119, 141
    [Christchurch] *Press* 99
    Dominion newspaper 26, 108n80
    Evening Post newspaper 26, 33, 39
    Independent Business Weekly 99
    Frontline television program 33
    New Zealand Herald newspaper 39, 43, 64, 77, 79, 82–83, 91, 98–99, 138, 140, 142–43
    Sunday television program 142
    (*see also* publications)
Memorandum of Understanding 29–31, 36
Metal Workers Union 44

Middle East 2, 47–48, 95, 115, 119–20, 128, 155
Miles, Robert 25, 40, 71
Military Maritime Patrol Capabilities (MMPC) 116–17
Moore, John 115
Moore, Mike 44
Morris, Deborah 86
Morrison, Ian G. 110
Mortlock, Roger 65, 130, 148n73
Muldoon, Robert 9–10
Munroe, H.W. 135
Myers, Ransom 50n30

Nash, Walter 2, 9
Neilson, Murray 91
Netherlands 30–31
New Caledonia 2
New Zealand:
    and National Service 8
    Auckland 46–48, 54–55, 63–64, 89
     University of Auckland 98
    Blenheim 104, 123
    Chatham Islands 54
    Cook Strait 54
    Napier 63
    New Plymouth 40–41, 80
    Lyttleton 55, 63
    Timaru 71
    Wanganui 41
    Wellington 7, 25, 36, 60, 144, 148n73
     Victoria University 71
New Zealand Defence Force (NZDF) 13, 15–18, 28, 53–60, 62, 64–65, 70–71, 79, 94, 97, 99–104, 109, 120, 129–32, 137, 139–41, 144–45, 147n39, 154, 157–58
    Chief of Defence Force (CDF) 15–18, 129, 137, 140, 143–44, 149n80, 158
    Chief of General Staff (CGS) 71, 129, 137, 141–42, 154
    Executive Capability Board 18
    New Zealand Army 1, 7–8, 13, 15, 37–38, 47, 53–54, 62–63, 66, 71–72, 81, 86–87, 94, 98, 100, 104–105, 114–15, 127–34, 136–45, 147n39, 147n50, 149n80, 154: battalions 6–7, 13, 53, 67, 81, 127, 132–34, 136–38, 141, 143–45; 161 Battery, Royal New Zealand Artillery 7; Army Training Teams 8; Burnham Army base 144; Kiwi Company 12, 129–30, 134; Linton Army base 144; New Zealand Expeditionary Force 2; Queen Alexandra's Mounted Rifles (QAMR) 132, 144; Royal New Zealand Infantry Regiment (RNZIR) 7, 141, 144–45; Special Air Service (SAS) 5–7; Trentham Army Camp 134, 144; Waiouru Army Base 141, 143–44
    New Zealand Defence Staff 45, 56: Chief of Defence Staff (CDS) 16
    NZDF Annual Report for the year ending 30 June 2004 144
    recruitment of 144
    Royal New Zealand Air Force (RNZAF) 7, 14, 89–93, 95–97, 100–101, 103, 105, 110–11, 114–17, 120–21, 127–28, 136, 139, 147n50, 148n73, 152, 155: No. 2 Squadron 89–90, 104; No. 5 Squadron 110, 120–21; No. 14 Squadron 5–6, 89, 104; No. 40 Squadron 8; No. 41 Squadron 6; No. 75 Squadron 89–91, 104; RNZAF airbase at Ohakea 104, 149n73; RNZAF Woodburn, Blenheim 104; strike air combat wing 89
    Royal New Zealand Navy (RNZN) 1, 4, 7, 23–33, 35, 37, 40–41, 43, 45–47, 49, 50n31, 55, 57–58, 61, 64–65, 69, 71–72, 79–80, 83, 85, 87, 100, 111, 127, 140, 152, 155, 162: Corps of Naval Constructors 71; Naval Combat Force 24, 81–83, 87, 155; Naval Force Development 63; Navy International Program Office 45
New Zealand Defence, Resource Management Review (1988): see White Papers and Reviews: 1988 *New Zealand Defence, Resource Management Review* 'Quigley Report')

New Zealand Department of the Prime Minister and Cabinet 60–68, 103, 115, 152–53, 155

New Zealand Cabinet (and its decisions, papers and various policy and strategy committees/sub-committees) 4, 7, 10, 15, 36, 39, 41–42, 48, 56–58, 60–61, 63–64, 66–68, 70, 79–84, 86–87, 93, 98, 102–103, 113–15, 117–19, 127–29, 131, 133–34, 136–39, 152–55

New Zealand Foreign Affairs and Defence Select Committee 44, 65

New Zealand Foreign Affairs and Trade Select Committee 144

New Zealand Foreign Affairs, Defence and Trade Committee 65, 83, 97–98, 108n87, 141, 143

Inquiry Into Defence Beyond 2000 (1998) (Interim Report) 83–84, 89, 94–95, 97–98, 108n97, 108n98

New Zealand Foreign Affairs Select Committee 28

New Zealand Government 1, 7–9, 12–13, 16–18, 23–29, 31–33, 35–36, 41–43, 49, 57–58, 64–66, 68, 70, 77–79, 82–83, 85–87, 89–91, 95–96, 98–105, 108n97, 108n98, 109–111, 113–23, 127, 129, 131, 133, 138, 140, 143, 145, 147n38, 147n39, 154–55

Coalition Governments 13, 77–80, 83, 85–87, 89, 98, 102, 105, 109, 114–15

Defence Committee of Inquiry (1985) 25: 'Just Defence' submission to 25

Government's Defence Policy Framework, The (June 2000) 7, 13, 66, 114–16, 127, 137

Labour Governments 3, 8–9, 11, 13–16, 25–28, 32–34, 36, 44, 66, 72, 89–90, 94, 97–98, 103, 105, 109, 113–15, 119, 121–23, 127–28, 136, 138, 143, 145, 154

National Governments 4, 11–12, 14–15, 66, 69, 77, 79, 85–87, 89, 97, 109, 121, 123, 128, 133, 138, 143, 145

New Zealand Caucus 39–40, 43, 48, 66, 79, 88n31, 153

*New Zealand's Foreign and Security Policy Challenges (*2000) 66

New Zealand Ministry of Agriculture and Fisheries 32

New Zealand Ministry of Defence (MoD) 15–17, 23, 33, 57–58, 65, 70, 79, 92, 103, 113, 121–22, 132, 134–37, 139–40, 145, 147n39, 155, 157

Acquisition Division 15, 134

Defence Council 16

defence planning and plans 1, 4–5, 7, 13–14, 17–19, 23, 25–27, 31, 35, 40, 46, 64, 68–70, 79, 90–91, 94, 102, 104, 108n80, 108n87, 109, 131–32, 153, 157–58: Defence Consolidated Resource Plan (DCRP) 56, 61, 70; *Defence Long-Term Development Plan* (LTDP) and its *Update* 18, 119, 149n80; Defence Planning System (DPS) 17–18 (*see also* capabilities: *Capability Management Framework*); Defence Policy and Planning Unit 19; Defence 10 Year Capital Plan (DCP) 66, 93–94, 133; *Indicative Defence Resource Plan* 17; *National Real Estate Consolidation Strategy* (1998) 101; *Sustainable Capability Plan for the New Zealand Defence Force* (2001) 117–18; Sustainable Defence Plan 67

Government Defence Statement (2001) 68, 119–20

Integrated Capability Management Committee 18

Minister of Defence 15–16, 24, 28, 31, 35–36, 40–41, 56, 59–61, 63, 65, 68, 77, 79–84, 91, 93, 96–97, 109, 113–15, 117, 119, 121–22, 132, 134, 137, 139–40, 143, 153–54 (*see also* Bradford; Burton; Cooper; East; O'Flynn; Thomson; Tizard)

organisational structure (diagram) of 17

New Zealand Ministry of Foreign Affairs and Trade (formerly New Zealand Ministry of External Relations and Trade) 36, 70, 115
  (see also New Zealand Foreign Affairs and Defence Select Committee; New Zealand Foreign Affairs and Trade Select Committee; New Zealand Foreign Affairs, Defence and Trade Committee; and New Zealand Foreign Affairs Select Committee)
New Zealand political parties:
  ACT New Zealand 83, 85, 88n31, 98, 114, 139, 153
  Alliance Party 59–60, 64, 70, 114:
    The Biggest Lemon Ever To Leave Auckland 58, 65; *Scandal of The Charles Upham, The* 64–65, 70, 73n14
  New Zealand First 69, 79, 82, 140, 142
  New Zealand Labour Party 9–11, 31, 33, 35–36, 41–43, 66, 78, 85, 98, 111, 113, 154
  New Zealand National Party 4, 9, 69, 72, 97, 105, 108n80, 114, 141, 143
New Zealand Prime Minister's Department 27 (on 1 January 1990 split in two as (1) the New Zealand Department of the Prime Minister; and (2) the Prime Minister's Private Office)
New Zealand Treasury 33, 44, 60–61, 65, 67, 70, 82, 84, 87, 94, 97, 105, 137–38, 147n39
  The Navy Critical Mass Argument 82
Niue 63
Nixon, Carl 121
North Atlantic Treaty Organization (NATO) 35, 146n31
nuclear:
  French nuclear testing in the Pacific 9
  New Zealand's nuclear-free policy 9–11, 26, 28, 48–49, 91
  (see also treaties: South Pacific Nuclear-Free Zone Treaty; and weapons: nuclear weapons)

O'Brien, Terence 36
O'Flynn, Frank 36, 91
Operations and Exercises 7, 12–13, 20n35, 24, 35, 47–48, 53–54, 56–57, 60–63, 91, 101, 103, 115–17, 120–21, 130–34, 144–45, 146n31, 148n71, 155, 158
  Exercise *Predators Gallop* 143
  Exercise *Silver Warrior* 145
  Exercise *Tropic Dust* 63
  humanitarian relief operations 117
  International Force East Timor (INTERFET) 47
  Maritime Interdiction Operations (MIO) 47
  Operation *Enduring Freedom* 47, 119–20, 155
  Operation *Troy* 120
Ottaway, Rick 147n50
Ottesen, Niels 41

Pacific Institute of Resource Management 36
Pakistan 6, 92, 106n18, 106n20
Palmer, Geoffrey 42–43, 48–49, 77, 153, 156
Peace and Justice Forum 25
  An Alternative Defence Policy (1985) 25
Peace Movement Aotearoa 32–34
peacekeeping 4, 12–13, 54, 61, 97, 101, 105, 116–17, 120, 127–28, 130–31
People's Republic of China: see China
Peters, Winston 69, 82–83, 153; see also New Zealand political parties: New Zealand First
Philippines 6
Poland 1, 56, 106n20
Power, Simon 141, 143
Prebble, Richard 9
Press: see media
projects 11, 18, 23, 25, 27–28, 30–34, 37–39, 41, 43–45, 48, 49n8, 60–62, 64, 66, 68–70, 79, 94, 100–102, 105, 128, 132, 136–37, 139, 141–42, 144, 153

Project *Guardian* 15, 109, 113, 118–19, 122–23, 152
Project *Kestrel* 15, 81, 109, 111–12, 117–18
Project *Protector* 148n73, 152
Project *Rigel* 15, 110, 112–13
Project *Sirius* 13–15, 81, 100, 109–10, 112–16, 118–23, 133, 152
publications:
   Air Force News 116, 120
   American Defense & Foreign Affairs Weekly 42
   Army News 148n70, 148n71, 148n73
   Asia Defence Journal 44
   Australian Defence Magazine 77
   International Defence Review 27
   Jane's Defence Weekly 16
   Jane's International Defence Review 146n31
   Nature magazine 50n30
   Navy Today 64
   New Zealand Defence Quarterly 61–62
   New Zealand International Review 40
   New Zealand Listener 34, 71–72, 95, 114
   RNZAF News 92, 96
   RSA Review [journal of the RSA] 115
   (*see also* media)

Quigley, Derek 16, 83, 88n31, 89, 95, 98–103, 152
   Review of the *Inquiry into Defence Beyond 2000* Report (2000) 89, 97–98 (*see also* New Zealand Foreign Affairs, Defence and Trade Committee: *Inquiry Into Defence Beyond 2000* (1998) (Interim Report))
   (*see also* Strategos Consulting; New Zealand political parties: ACT New Zealand; White Papers and Reviews: 1988 *New Zealand Defence, Resource Management Review* ('Quigley Report'))

Rarotonga 62
Ray, Robert 57–58
Ready Reaction Force (RRF) 53–55, 62, 161
reconnaissance 100, 110, 120, 128–29, 132
Reid, Piers 71, 129, 137, 142, 148n71
relationships 8–9, 157–58
   NZ-Australia relations 2, 10–11, 23, 26–30, 34–40, 48, 57–58, 81–82, 87, 94, 96–98, 102, 104, 116, 132–33, 151, 153, 163
   NZ MoD-NZDF-Army relations 139–40, 145
   NZ-UK relations 5, 8
   NZ-US relations 2, 4, 9–11, 23, 26, 45, 91, 94, 97–99, 104, 133
reliability 13, 46, 63, 72, 93, 128–29, 134, 143
Returned and Services' Association (RSA) (formerly the Returned Services' Association) 36, 115, 144
risk 27, 41, 61, 64, 67, 85, 98, 111–12, 123, 130, 133, 144
Rolfe, James (Jim) 17–18, 132
Roosevelt, Franklin Delano 3
Rowling, Bill 9–10
Russia 146n31; *see also* Soviet Union

Savage, Michael 1
security 3, 13, 25, 66, 102, 104, 108n98, 116, 119–20, 123, 157–58, 163
   collective security 3–8, 12–13, 18, 26–27, 35, 39, 53, 96, 98–99, 101, 108n97, 113, 115–17, 119–21, 131, 163
'Self-Reliance in Partnership', concept of 11, 87, 104, 112, 163
Seward, John 79
Shipley, Jenny 85–86, 140, 153
Singapore 2, 5, 8, 53, 96
   Republic of Singapore Air Force 91
Solomon Islands 2, 47, 104
Somer's Committee on Nuclear Propulsion 11
South East Asia Treaty Organisation (SEATO) 4, 6–7
South Korea 112; *see also* Korean Peninsula
South Pacific region 2, 6–7, 9, 28–29, 37,

193

53–56, 62, 78, 110, 117, 119
South Vietnam 7; *see also* wars: Vietnam War
Southeast Asia 7, 53
Soviet Union 3; *see also* Russia
Spain 56, 65, 71
Suharto 106n18
surveillance 27, 81, 97, 109–15, 117–20, 122–23, 152
   Electronic Surveillance Measures (ESM) 122, 159, 162

Tasman Sea 46
Teagle, Somerford 23, 49n8, 55, 69, 71
terrorism 5, 53, 120–21
   11 September 2001 terrorist attacks 118, 120, 123
   'war on terror' 118–19
Thailand 6
   Royal Thai Air Force 91
Thomson, David 24
threats 53, 95, 104, 108n97, 120, 122
Tizard, Robert James (Bob) 28, 40–43, 153
   and presentation to Tawa Rotary Club 33–34
Tonga 63
training 2, 7–8, 16–17, 23, 26, 33, 69, 90, 93–94, 105, 106n18, 107n50, 116–17, 127–28, 133, 137–38, 141, 144, 162
treaties 2, 5–6
   ANZAC Ship Treaty 82–83
   Manila Treaty (the South East Asia Collective Defence Treaty) (1954) 6
   Pacific Security (ANZUS) Treaty (1951) 4–10, 23, 25, 33, 35, 37, 45, 48–49, 49n13
   South Pacific Nuclear-Free Zone Treaty (1985) 9

United Future 153
United Kingdom 1–6, 8, 15, 30, 40, 56, 69, 84, 112, 128, 134
   Royal Air Force (RAF) 1, 6
      British 22nd SAS Regiment 6–7
   Royal Fleet Auxiliary (RFA) 57, 69
   Royal Navy (RN) 1–2, 7, 32, 40

United Nations 3–6, 9, 11–13, 53, 61, 64, 117, 130, 148n71
United States 1–11, 14, 23, 26, 42, 45–46, 79–80, 84, 89, 91–92, 94–95, 97–99, 101–102, 104, 106n18, 111–13, 115, 118, 121, 128, 133–34, 147n31, 148n70, 151, 154, 156
   Arizona 92, 141
   California 141
   Department of State 106n18
   New York, NY 11, 118
   Pearl Harbor, Honolulu, HI 89–90
   Seattle, WA 11
   US Air Force 92
   US Army 146n31, 148n70
   US Congress 91
   US Marine Corps 90
   US Navy 47, 90, 110–11
   Washington, DC 3, 45, 96
Upham, Charles 61

Vaughan, Rod 142–43
vehicles 54–55, 67, 72, 81, 94, 100, 127–39, 142, 145, 146n31, 148n73, 161–62
   Armoured Personnel Carrier (APC) 13, 127, 131–34, 138, 152
   BTR-80 146n31
   M113 APC (including M113A1 and M113A4) 128–31, 134, 137–39, 142–43, 145, 148n71, 148n73, 155
   Fire Support Vehicle (FSV) (including *Scorpion* FSV) 127–29, 131, 133–37, 152
   FOX 6*6 (or FUCHS) vehicle 135–36
   Infantry Mobility Vehicle (IMV) 133–37
   Light Armoured Vehicle (LAV) 13, 127–28, 132, 134, 136–45, 148n71, 149n73, 152, 154
   Australian Light Armoured Vehicle (ASLAV) 132
   LAV III 15–16, 21n73, 127–28, 135–39, 141–42, 145, 148n71, 155: *Stryker* 147n31, 148n70
   tanks 128
   Centurion tank 128

Valentine tank 128
vessels 1, 10–11, 13–14, 23–43, 45–47, 49, 51n67, 53–72, 73n9, 73n14, 78–82, 84–86, 88n24, 90–91, 117, 148n73, 152–53, 159–62
    ANZAC frigates 1, 11, 14, 31–34, 36–49, 77–87, 88n24, 89, 94, 97, 105, 132, 145, 151–56, 159–60: HMAS *Anzac* 45; HMAS *Arunta* 88n24; HMNZS *Te Kaha* 45–47; HMNZS *Te Mana* 46–48, 79
    (*see also* treaties: ANZAC Ship Treaty)
    Australian tanker *Supply* 9
    chartering of 54, 61, 65, 67–68
    frigate classes (*see also* all named frigates under vessels):
        City-class frigate 30
        Duke-class (UK Type 23) frigate 84
        Leander-class frigate 23–24, 30, 33, 40, 46, 77, 80: HMNZS *Canterbury* 9, 23, 68, 85–86, 100; HMNZS *Waikato* 23, 46; HMNZS *Southland* (formerly HMS *Dido*) 24, 46; HMNZS *Wellington* (formerly HMS *Bacchante*) 24
        Maestrale-class frigate 30
        Perry-class frigate 10
        Ulsan-class frigate 30
        US FFG-7 (guided missile frigate) class 31, 80, 84
    HMAS *Tobruk* (landing ship heavy) 57–60, 71
    HMNZS *Charles Upham* (heavy lift ship) 13–14, 21n73, 54–55, 59–72, 73n14, 96, 100, 127, 136, 152–53: *Official Information Pertaining to the Military Sealift Project HMNZS Charles Upham* (1998) 65
    HMNZS *Endeavour* 69
    HMNZS *Otago* 9, 23–24
    HMNZS *Taranaki* 23
    HMNZS *Union Rotorua* 54–56, 59, 73n9
    Logistic Support Ship (LSS) 13, 47, 53, 55, 60, 72, 152
    Meko 200P 30, 31–32, 42
    Mercandian 56–57, 68: *Mercandian 1500* vessel 54–55; *Mercandian Queen II* 60, 161; *The Spirit of Freedom* (Mercandian 610) 55
    Multi-Role Vessel 72, 148n73
    MV *Edamgracht* (Dutch merchant vessel) 148n73
    Nordkapp 'coast guard frigate' 30
    Offshore Patrol Vessel (OPV) 25–26, 30, 33, 36, 152, 155
        Castle-class 25, 28, 33, 40, 51n67: HMS *Dumbarton Castle* 40; HMS *Leeds Castle* 40
        Lake-class 32, 40, 50n31: HMNZS *Hawera* 50n31; HMNZS *Pukaki* 50n31; HMNZS *Rotoiti* 50n31, 55; HMNZS *Taupo* 50n31
    Skeandu 30
    VT (Vosper Thornycroft) Mk19 30
    Yarrow OPV 30
    refit of 24, 58–61, 80
    Replacement Combat Ship 29
    sealift vessels, capability and project 53–54, 56–58, 60–62, 64–68, 70, 153, 161
    submarines 25, 49n8, 109, 111, 115; *see also* warfare: submarine warfare
    USS *Buchanan* (destroyer) 10
    USS *Okinawa* (amphibious assault ship) 89
Vietnam 9; *see also* wars: Vietnam War
Vignaux, G. Anthony 82

Ware, Peter 62
warfare:
    electronic warfare 111
    manoeuvre warfare 132
    submarine warfare 27, 91
    anti-submarine warfare (ASW) 14, 24, 33, 38, 110–11, 116–17, 122
Waring, Marilyn 9
wars:
    1991 Gulf War 95
    Boer War 129
    Falklands War 40

First World War 2–3
Korean War 6, 12, 129
Second World War 1–5, 12, 16, 110, 128
Vietnam War 6–8, 90, 129, 138
weapons: 24, 30, 44, 46, 51n67, 91, 95, 100, 134, 159
   anti-ship missile 33, 160: *Harpoon* missile 103; *Maverick* missile 47, 91
   Army Anti-Armour Weapon 100
   Army Direct Fire Support weapon 100
   cannon 136, 148n71
   grenade and grenade launcher 136, 148n70
   gun 27, 44, 46: machine gun 136, 142, 162; rifle 7, 27, 81, 132, 149n73
   Improvised Explosive Device (IED) 148n70
   Mk 11 depth charge 47
   Mk 41 vertical launch system 45
   nuclear weapons 9–11, 92
   torpedo 47, 159–60
   weapon system 33, 40, 46, 90, 136, 160: *Phalanx* weapon support system 46
Webb, Clifton 6
Welch, Jack 71
Western Samoa 63
Wheeler, Mark 144
Whineray, Wilson 92–93
White, Douglas (see White Papers and Reviews: *Review of the Performance of the Defence Force in Relation to the Expected Standards of Behaviour*)
White Papers and Reviews:
   1961 *Review of Defence Policy* 6–7, 110
   1966 *Review of Defence Policy* 89, 110
   1978 *Defence Review* 23, 31, 53, 72, 90, 110, 128
   1983 *Defence Review* 24, 31, 90, 111
   1986 *Defence Review* 25
   1987 *Defence of New Zealand, Review of Defence Policy* 11, 26, 28–29, 32–33, 36, 38, 48, 53, 66, 72, 91
   1988 *New Zealand Defence, Resource Management Review* ('Quigley Report') (1988) 16, 34–35, 83, 89, 97–98, 154
   1991 *Defence Review* 87, 117
   1991 Defence White Paper (*Defence of New Zealand 1991, A Policy Paper*) 11, 52–53, 62, 83, 104
   1991 *Review of Defence Funding* 101
   1997 *Defence Assessment* 80–81, 83–84, 91, 94, 100, 131
   1997 *Defence Review* 64, 56, 87
   1997 Defence White Paper, *The Shape of New Zealand's Defence* 12, 83, 87, 91, 104, 108n97, 108n98, 112–13, 127, 131
   1997 *HMNZS Charles Upham: Review of acquisition and proposed conversion* 55–56, 60, 62, 64, 68, 70, 153
   1998 *HMNZS Charles Upham: Report on Concerns Raised by the Foreign Affairs, Defence and Trade Committee* 60, 64–65, 69–70
   Air and Sea Transport Review 62: Air and Sea Transport Review team 54–62
   Maritime Patrol Review (2001) 109, 114–15, 117, 120, 123, 152
   Review Committee 29–30, 116–17
   Review of the Options for an Air Combat Capability 103
   Review of the Performance of the Defence Force in Relation to the Expected Standards of Behaviour ('White and Ansell' Report) 140–41, 154
   Sealift Review (2000) 67
Williams, Graeme 12, 129
Wilson, K.F. (Fred) 65
Woodman, Stewart 104
Worm, Boris 50n30

Yugoslavia 12; *see also* Bosnia

www.ingramcontent.com/pod-product-compliance
Lightning Source LLC
Chambersburg PA
CBHW060946170426
43197CB00031B/2982